D1598608

A FAITHFUL WITNESS: JOHN WESLEY'S HOMILETICAL THEOLOGY

KENNETH J. COLLINS

Wesley Heritage Press
Wilmore, Kentucky 40390

Library of Congress Cataloging-in-Publication Data
Collins, Kenneth J.
    A Faithful Witness: John Wesley's homiletical theology / Kenneth J. Collins.
        p.   cm.
    Includes bibliographical references and index.
    ISBN 0-915143-04-6
    1. Wesley, John, 1703-1791.   2. Preaching—History—18th century.
I. Title.
BX8495.W5C753   1993
230'.7'092—dc20   93-19294
                                                                        CIP

Wesley Heritage Press
Box 7
Wilmore, Kentucky 40390

Wesley Heritage Press, a ministry of the Francis Asbury Society, publishes
scholarly books pertaining to the heritage of the world-wide Wesleyan Movement.

DEDICATION

To the memory of Rev. Arthur Albrecht who
introduced me to the remarkable world of
Methodism.

Kenneth J. Collins, Ph.D., Drew University, is Associate Professor of Philosophy and Religion at Methodist College in Fayetteville, North Carolina. An ordained elder in the Free Methodist Church, Dr. Collins' scholarly interests include Wesley Studies, American Methodism, and the history of Spirituality. He has published articles in *Quarterly Review, Methodist History, Christian Scholar's Review, Asbury Theological Journal*, and the *Wesleyan Theological Journal*. Beyond his scholarly pursuits, Collins leads workshops on spiritual growth and maturation, and holds seminars on Wesley's sermons.

Kenneth J. Collins was married to Marilyn Krisnowich in 1976; they are the parents of two children, Brooke Erin and Lauren Anne.

CONTENTS

FOREWORD

Occasionally a book comes along that I wish I could have written. *A Faithful Witness* is one of them. The chief reason is my debt to John Wesley. While I was still a teenager, shortly after my conversion, I was introduced to Wesley's writings. A passionate interest developed that has kept me returning for their pleasures ever since.

Wesley's sermons became the focal point of my interest. Their clarity of argument, convicting content, and biblical soundness all conspired to bring me back to them periodically. In my judgment they are Wesley at his most excellent. They are also sermonic literature at its biblical and theological best. I have always longed for an opportunity to engage in an extended theological study of Wesley's sermons. Now I find that this has been done, and done well. Kenneth Collins has worked his way through this rich literature and now gives us the benefit of his very considerable labors. I am profoundly grateful.

Three things about Collins' book are especially striking. *First*, he writes well. Collins subjects the message of Methodism's father to rigorous analysis; the result is logical and clear at every point. One never has to wonder what Collins is saying. *Second*, he writes objectively. There is little of Kenneth Collins inserted in the text to color Wesley. I find no evidence of any pleading for support of private concerns. *Finally*, Collins organizes his material extraordinarily well. Employing the structure of the Apostle's Creed as an analytical and expository device, he offers chapters on God, Christ, the Holy Spirit, the church, humankind, salvation, and eschatology. An added chapter introduces Wesley's views on personal and social ethics, concerns not so clearly reflected in the Creed. These three things, clarity, objectivity and organization contribute to the usefulness of Collins' book and make it an especially appropriate text for classroom use.

Kenneth Collins is a careful scholar. His citations from Wesley seem especially apt and varied. He draws from the full corpus of the sermons, published and unpublished. Furthermore, though his primary interest is Wesley's sermons, Collins demonstrates a broader knowledge of Wesley by judicious quotation from the letters and other writings.

For one who has read Wesley on and off across the decades, it was a delight to again read familiar passages; to rediscover choice tidbits long forgotten and to find other choice bits never before seen. As I read this manuscript I had the feeling that I was getting an authentic presentation of how Mr. Wesley thought and spoke on the full range of theological issues under discussion.

Two convictions deepened as I considered the potential importance of this timely book. One is related to my longstanding belief that Harald Lindström's *Wesley and Sanctification* should be rewritten. In my years of classroom experience I have found Lindström's treatment of the *ordo salutis* the best available. However, for the contemporary reader a considerable percentage of Lindström's material, such as that on William Law, is much more a distraction than a help. By incorporating the fruits of contemporary scholarship, Collins has provided an even better study than I had in mind. A second conviction has to do with the unique place of John Wesley in the history of Christian thought. Wesley, it will be recalled, drew heavily upon the literature of the eastern church fathers to nourish the 18th century revival in England. I believe that the *via media* of Cranmer and Anglicanism, with its special expression in Wesley, will have a unique role in the dialogue between the East and West that now seems inescapable. If I am right, Collins' book could play a strategic role in fostering a better understanding of the treasury of divine truth; an understanding that may, in turn, lead to a more complete experience of the possibilities of grace.

Dennis F. Kinlaw
Wilmore, Kentucky

INTRODUCTION

Though in the twentieth century the sermon is seldom used as a form of literature to communicate theological truths, this was not the case in the eighteenth century. John Wesley, for example, one of the leaders of the Evangelical Revival which swept the British Isles more than two hundred years ago, produced more than one hundred and fifty sermon manuscripts, the overwhelming majority of which he saw fit to publish. However, Wesley, throughout his lengthy career, preached on many texts and topics not included in this corpus, a fact which suggests perhaps a difference in form — oral as opposed to written — if not in content. Commenting on this distinction, Albert Outler writes: "He [Wesley] saw an important difference between the principal aims of an oral and a written sermon: the former is chiefly for *proclamation* and invitation; the latter is chiefly for *nurture* and reflection."[1] Similarly, Richard Heitzenrater expressed this difference in terms of a kerygmatic intent as opposed to a didactic one.[2] Wesley's purpose in his published sermons, in other words, was to instruct the Methodists (and all others who were interested) in *the substance* of what he was preaching during the revival. Accordingly, both of these scholars contend that while there is clearly a difference in form between Wesley's oral and published sermons, there is really little difference in content.

Two other clues to Wesley's design in choosing the sermon as a literary form to communicate important theological truths can be found in his *Preface* to the *Sermons on Several Occasions* (SOSO). First of all, this *Preface* reveals that the Oxford don desired to speak plainly and convincingly to as many people as possible. His vision, in other words, was inclusive not exclusive. Indeed, his intended audience was not the learned, nor the sophisticated, but the common man and woman. "But in truth I at present designed nothing less, the Methodist leader writes, "for I now write (as I generally speak) *ad populum* — to the bulk of mankind."[3]

---

1. Albert C. Outler, ed., *The Works of John Wesley*, Vols. 1-4. *The Sermons* (Nashville: Abingdon Press, 1984), 1:14. Bracketed material is mine.
    2. Richard P. Heitzenrater, *Mirror and Memory* (Nashville, Tennessee: Kingswood Books, 1989), p. 175.
    3. Outler, *Sermons*, 1:103.

Second, the *Preface* also demonstrates that soteriology (the doctrine of salvation) was at the very heart of the entire enterprise of the published sermons, and this emphasis gives the various theological discussions within these pieces a distinctive and memorable hue. The one thing desirable to know, Wesley observes, "is the way to heaven."[1] Moreover, in this same *Preface* Wesley employs the image of an arrow in flight very effectively to convey his meaning. He writes:

> **I have thought, I am a creature of a day, passing through life as an arrow through the air. I am a spirit come from God, and returning to God: ... I want to know one thing — the way to heaven; how to land safe on that happy shore. God Himself has condescended to teach the way; for this very end He came from heaven. He hath written it down in a book. O give me that book! At any price, give me the book of God! I have it: here is knowledge enough for me.**[2]

Put another way, the sermons are, for the most part, instances of practical theology, concerned with the day to day problems of entering into and living the Christian life.

Nevertheless, although soteriology is, after all, a dominant motif in most of Wesley's published sermons and although it helps, for example, to explain the bulk of the material in the *Sermons on Several Occasions* volumes I - IV (the fifty-three "standard" sermons), the doctrine of salvation, by itself, is apparently unable to account for the diversity of *content* that emerges in the remaining ninety-eight sermons. This consideration, therefore, raises the important question of precisely what interpretive structure is best able to gather up the many kinds of doctrinal discussions present in the *entire* sermon corpus. Again, though an appeal to Wesley's *ordo salutis* is a useful hermeneutical device with respect to the fifty-three standard sermons (which I, myself, have used in the past), it will hardly work in this larger context.[3]

This problem of an appropriate interpretive structure can be further illustrated by an appeal to the following diagram of Wesley's sermons:

John Wesley's 151 Sermons

Description	As Listed in Outler's Edition
1. SOSO (Vols. I-IV)	1-53
2. SOSO (Vols. V-VIII)	54-108

1. Ibid., 1:105.
2. Ibid., 1:104-05.
3. To force a soteriological framework on the entire sermon corpus unnecessarily gives the work a decidedly anthropocentric flavor. However, in many of Wesley's sermons, especially his later pieces, God, the Father, (His personhood, attributes, and activity) the Son, and the Holy Spirit are very much at the center of things.

In category # 2 above, for example, Wesley includes such pieces as *God's Approbation of His Works*, *The Wisdom of God's Counsels*, and *On Divine Providence*, which treat the doctrine of God; *The End of Christ's Coming*, which explores Christology; *Of the Church*, *The Duty of Constant Communion*, and *On Attending the Church Service* (ecclesiology); *On the Fall of Man*, and *God's Love to Fallen Man* (anthropology); and *The General Deliverance*, *Of Hell*, *On Eternity*, and *Dives and Lazarus* (eschatology), among others. In a similar fashion, the Methodist leader examines a number of divergent subjects in his miscellaneous and manuscript sermons and in those late pieces which were prepared for publication in *The Arminian Magazine*. The latter group, for instance, contains *What is Man?*, *On the Omnipresence of God*, *The Unity of the Divine Being*, and *On Knowing Christ After the Flesh*, to name a few. Beyond this, it must also be borne in mind that even *within* many of Wesley's explicitly soteriological sermons like *The Witness of the Spirit, Discourse I* and *The Witness of the Spirit, Discourse II* (which appear in category # 1 above), other, broader theological themes are, in fact, considered.

In light of the preceding considerations, this present work employs the *Apostles' Creed* as an interpretive framework which will not only embrace the vital motif of soteriology, but which will also include the assorted doctrinal discussions present in Wesley's 151 sermons. To be sure, the *Apostles' Creed* expresses the testimony, the faithful witness, of the early church with respect to the doctrine of God, Christology, the doctrine of the Holy Spirit, ecclesiology, anthropology, soteriology, and eschatology. And this same faithful witness was maintained by Wesley in his published sermons as he affirmed in the midst of opposition, especially from the Deists: the providence of God in continually caring for His creation, the Virgin Birth, the miraculous resurrection of Jesus Christ, His second coming, as well as the promise and hope of life everlasting.[1] Indeed, when Wesley himself considered this Creed in his sermon *The Case of Reason Impartially Considered*, he noted that it is a beautiful summary of the oracles of God, the foundation of true religion,[2] a judgment which is remarkably consonant with the Methodist leader's earlier stated purpose in the *Preface* to his sermons.

---

1. Although Wesley was never content with the mere subscription to orthodoxy and, therefore, urged the Methodists, on several occasions, to cultivate inward religion, a religion of the heart, he was nevertheless highly orthodox in his own teaching as his sermons quite clearly demonstrate.
2. Outler, *Sermons*, 2:524.

Moreover, not only is this present work attentive to the structure of the *Apostles' Creed* as a useful interpretive device, but it also follows the specific sequence of doctrines within this Creed. Thus, the chapter on the church immediately follows the one on the Holy Spirit and not the doctrine of salvation as in most systematic theologies. Undoubtedly, other interpretive frameworks and sequencing could have been employed in a study of this kind. The present approach, therefore, is heuristic, not definitive; creative, not dogmatic. It attempts, in other words, to take the didactic function of the published sermons quite seriously by communicating nothing less than the rich doctrinal material of Wesley's complete sermon corpus in a way that is clear, coherent, and, most important of all, as comprehensive as possible.[1]

There is one final note to be made concerning style. This present work departs from conventional usage in one important aspect: it italicizes the names of sermons in the text, instead of placing them within quotation marks. This approach is taken so that the reader can quickly identify which sermons are covered in any given section.

---

1. Although the sermons are, indeed, the focus of this study, other relevant materials like Wesley's letters, journals, new testament notes, and his theological essays are, in fact, consulted.

CHAPTER ONE

THE DOCTRINE OF GOD
"I believe in God the Father Almighty, maker of heaven and earth."

Judging from the major work on the theology of John Wesley produced in recent times, Colin Williams' *John Wesley's Theology Today*, one can only conclude that Wesley did not consider the doctrine of God in any depth. Williams' work, for instance, essentially limits its discussion to soteriology (the doctrine of salvation), with chapters on prevenient grace, original sin, repentance and justification, the atonement, the new birth and assurance, repentance in believers, and Christian perfection. And though this book does, after all, include chapters on eschatology and the church, it unfortunately lacks one on the vital subject of God (and Christology as well).

On the other hand, Wesley's sermons, especially those produced after 1770 (which by the way have received scant attention from scholars) paint a much different picture. Beyond the prominent moral and spiritual tone of these sermons — which we've come to expect from Wesley — many of these pieces demonstrate the full range of the Methodist leader's interests in a way that his other writings do not. For instance, such "speculative" or "systematic" subjects as the doctrine of God, Christology, the doctrine of the Holy Spirit, the nature of the church, and the last judgment, just to name a few, all receive considerable attention. And though Wesley never wrote a systematic theology, he did treat the major doctrines which constitute such a work. Like Luther, Wesley crafted "occasional" pieces, treatises and sermons dictated more by the immediate spiritual needs of his people than by a tight and orderly system.

The present concern, of course, is the doctrine of God, and Wesley approached this important subject in two key ways: first, he wrote homilies directly pertaining to this issue such as *On Divine Providence, On Predestination, God's Approbation of His Works, The Wisdom of God's Counsels, The Unity of the Divine Being, and On the Omnipresence of God*; second, he interspersed comments about the nature and being of God in a host of sermons which covered several different topics. Both sources, then, form Wesley's mature doctrine of God; both, therefore, must—and will — be consulted.

I. The Essential Attributes of God

According to Albert Outler, Wesley's sermon, *On Eternity*, marks his "deepest plunge into speculative theology up to this point in his career [1786]." [1] Indeed, this is one of Wesley's more philosophical pieces, for he explores the question of God against the backdrop of both time and eternity. But in order to help his readers, to assist them in this extraordinary and at-times difficult area, Wesley not only clearly defines his terms, but also develops this sermon in a logical and easy-to-follow way. Thus, this Anglican priest, first of all, asks his readers, "what is eternity?" [2] and he immediately observes that this question must be divided into two parts: namely, *a parte ante* (eternity which is past) and *a parte post* (eternity which is to come). [3] " It is God alone," Wesley notes, "who inhabiteth eternity in both these senses. The great Creator alone (not any of his creatures) is 'from everlasting to everlasting.'" [4]

However, this last statement — that only God is from everlasting to everlasting — does not exclude the notion that human beings and angels may also be eternal, properly understood. To illustrate, Wesley appeals to and utilizes the distinction between "duration without beginning" and "duration without end" just cited above. [5] The former pertains to God alone, but the latter, remarkably enough, characterizes some of His creatures as well. Wesley elaborates:

> This [duration without end] is not an incommunicable attribute of the great Creator; but he has been graciously pleased to make innumerable multitudes of his creatures partakers of it. He has imparted this not only to angels, and archangels, and all the companies of heaven, ... but also to the inhabitants of the earth who dwell in houses of clay. [6]

In light of the preceding, it appears that eternity conceived as "duration without beginning" is especially descriptive of God, since it is a characteristic shared by no other being. In fact, Wesley uses this unique trait as a standard or norm to judge other philosophical questions such as "is matter eternal?" "Not indeed *a parte ante*," he reasons, "as some senseless philosophers, both ancient and modern, have dreamed. Not that anything had existed from eternity; seeing if so it must be God." [7] In other words, for Wesley, the past eternity of any being or thing, other than the Holy One of Israel, necessarily results in a plurality of gods and therefore in the elimination of monotheism. Simply put, there cannot be "two Gods or two Eternals." [8]

1. Albert C Outler, ed., *The Works of John Wesley*, 34 vols. *Sermons II* (Nashville: Abingdon Press, 1984), 2:358. (On Eternity) Bracketed material is mine.

2. Ibid.

3. Ibid., 2:358-59. See also Outler's note, number 1, for the sources for Wesley's distinction of *aeternitas a parte ante* and *aeternitas a parte post*.

4. Ibid., 2:359.

5. Ibid., 2:361.

6. Ibid. Bracketed material is mine.

7. Ibid.

8. Ibid., 2:362. Many early Greek philosophers maintained that matter was not created and therefore eternal, especially Parmenides and the later Atomists such as Democritus and Leucippus. Cf. Frederick Copleston, *A History of Philosophy* Vol 1. *Greece and Rome* (Garden City, New York: Image Books, 1985), p. 47-53, and 72 ff.

Closely associated with the eternity of God is another significant attribute, namely, omnipresence. In a sermon produced in the year of his brother Charles' death (1788), John Wesley considers the infinite magnitude of the Supreme Being, but in this instance not in terms of time; but in terms of space. And the text of *On the Omnipresence of God*, a suitable vehicle for this endeavor, is none other than Jeremiah 23:24 which reads: "Do not I fill heaven and earth? saith the Lord." (KJV) Accordingly, "there is no point of space," Wesley contends, "whether within or without the bounds of creation, where God is not."[1] Again, since "God acts everywhere,"[2] God is everywhere; the one implies the other.

But what is especially noteworthy about *On the Omnipresence of God* is its clear demonstration of Wesley's ever-present intention to improve the moral and spiritual stature of his readers. Many other treatments of God's omnipresence, both ancient and modern, are content with mere theory, abstractions, and speculation, as if this subject has little or no bearing upon everyday life. Notice, however, how Wesley draws out the practical implications of the Divine omnipresence in his following comments:

> **Yea, suppose one of your mortal fellow-servants, suppose only a holy man stood by you, would not you be extremely cautious how you conducted yourself, both in word and action? How much more cautious ought you to be when you know that not a holy man, not an angel of God, but God himself, the Holy One 'that inhabiteth eternity', is inspecting your heart, your tongue, your hand every moment! And that he himself will surely bring you into judgment for all you think, and speak, and act under the sun!**[3]

Just as Wesley understood the omnipresence of God as being closely "allied to the eternity of God,"[4] as noted earlier, so too did he consider the omniscience (literally all-knowing) of the Deity as "a clear and necessary consequence of his omnipresence."[5] For example, in his sermon, *The Unity of the Divine Being*, produced in 1789, the Oxford Methodist argues in this way: "If he [God] is pres-

1. Outler, *Sermons*, 4:42. (On the Omnipresence of God) In order to support his notion of the ubiquity of God, Wesley cites an ancient author who maintained that "All things are full of God," *Iovis omnis plena* (pg. 44). Outler attributes this Latin phrase to Virgil (70-19 B.C.), which is accurate since it appears in this Roman poet's *Eclogues*. However, the original source of this phrase is much earlier. Here, as in many other cases, the Romans borrowed from the Greeks, and in this particular case from Thales, the father of Western philosophy (624-547 B.C.). See the fragments of Thales' work contained in J. Burnet, trans., *Early Greek Philosophy* (London: Black, 1920), pp. 136-139.

2. Ibid.

3. Ibid., p. 46. For other references to the omnipresence of God Cf. Outler, *Sermons*, 2:569 (The Imperfection of Human Knowledge) and 3:9 (Of Good Angels).

4. Ibid., 4:61. (The Unity of the Divine Being) One of the remarkable things about this homily is that Wesley, once again, refuses to consider the attributes of God in a purely abstract way, for he is ever underscoring the moral and spiritual implications of these theological truths. Indeed, one of his principal interests in this piece is to distinguish a moralistic religion from the true worship of God, a religion of humanity from the religion of the Spirit. And at one point he even expostulates: "But how great is the number of those who, allowing religion to consist of two branches, our duty to God and our duty to our neighbour, entirely forget the first part, and put the second part for the whole, for the entire duty of man." Cf. Ibid., 4: 68-69.

5. Ibid., 4:62.

ent in every part of the universe, he cannot but know whatever is, or is done there."[1] Moreover, in another sermon, *On Divine Providence*, written three years earlier, Wesley once again draws the same relation between omnipresence and omniscience. "The omnipresent God sees and knows all the properties of all the beings that he hath made. He knows all the connections, dependencies, and relations, and all the ways wherein one of them can affect another."[2] Put another way, the infinity (and transcendence) of God in terms of space issues in and supports the idea of Divine omniscience. Because God is everywhere, He knows all that occurs anywhere.

However, and not surprisingly, the doctrine of the omniscience of God is not only sustained by a consideration of space, but it is also supported by a consideration of eternity, by an examination of the temporal aspects entailed. Since "all time, or rather all eternity (for time is only that small fragment of eternity ...) [is] present to him at once,"[3] then the Lord God knows all things, nothing is beyond His grasp. On a more philosophical level, Wesley maintains that all time, whether past or future, is present to God as "one eternal now."[4] And quite naturally, the same implications apply: the God who perceives all in a moment, in an eternal now, also knows all. This means, of course, that God, unlike His creatures, is transcendent and is not limited by either space or time.

And finally, this one-time Oxford fellow explores the omnipotence (all powerfulness) of God, the last essential attribute, in terms of the Divine omnipresence. In his homily *On the Omnipresence of God*, for instance, Wesley argues: "Therefore to deny the omnipresence of God implies likewise the denial of his omnipotence. To set bounds to the one is undoubtedly to set bounds to the other also."[5] And in *The Unity of the Divine Being* he adds: "And he is omnipotent as well as omnipresent: there can be no more bounds to his power than his presence. He hath a mighty arm; strong is his hand, and high is his right hand."[6]

But in order to appreciate fully Wesley's conception of Divine omnipotence, it is necessary to call to mind the way the eighteenth century viewed the relation between body (matter) on the one hand, and mind (spirit) on the other. Earlier, in the seventeenth-century, for instance, Galileo Galilei (1564-1642) had utilized the notion of matter in motion as his basic paradigm to explain all reality. Rene Descartes (1596-1650), aware of this shift in world-view, sought to appreciate Galileo's latest findings while at the same time he attempted to preserve the many insights of religion. In other words, Descartes" distinction of body/mind can be interpreted, at least on one level, as an apologetical attempt to maintain the *values* of religion in a world of burgeoning *facts*. If minds and bodies are different things, the Frenchman reasoned, then the findings of one cannot contradict those of the other.

1. Ibid. Bracketed material is mine.
2. Ibid., 2:539. (On Divine Providence)
3. Ibid., 2:417. (On Predestination) Bracketed material is mine.
4. Ibid., 2:420.
5. Ibid., 4:44. (On the Omnipresence of God)
6. Ibid., 4:62. (The Unity of the Divine Being)

One of the results of this Cartesian division is that matter is deemed utterly inert, lacking self-power. Again, according to Descartes, God created the material world, put a quantity of motion in it, but then quietly withdrew. Although Wesley rejected this last idea of Divine withdrawal — which by the way basically results in Deism — he, for the most part, followed the French philosopher's earlier premises as they were mediated to him by his own eighteenth century. Reflecting this influence concerning God's omnipotence, Wesley writes:

> **The name of God is God himself ... it means, therefore, together with his existence, all his attributes or perfections — his eternity ... his omnipotence; — who is indeed the only agent in the material world, all matter being essentially dull and inactive, and moving only as it is moved by the finger of God. And he is the spring of action in every creature, visible and invisible, which could neither act nor exist without the continued influx and agency of his almighty power;[1]**

The Methodist leader's last line just cited — "the continued influx and agency of his almighty power" — is revealing and distinguishes his position, in one very important respect, from that of Descartes. For Wesley at least, the omnipotence of the Creator is conceived in such a manner that the creation is not only dependent on God's power at the very beginning, but is continually so. God is transcendent, to be sure, but He is also deeply involved with the world. Here, therefore, a wind-it-up-and-watch-it-run Deism is rejected in favor of the continuous and potent activity of God. Moreover, without this sustaining motion of the Supreme Being, the world itself, and all therein, would collapse into sheer nothing. Descartes had placed God in the heavens; Wesley brought Him back to earth.

By way of summary, then, Wesley's conception of the essential[2] attributes of God may be diagramed as follows:

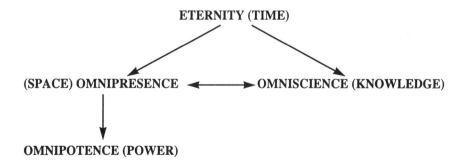

1. Ibid., 1:580-581. (Upon Our Lord's Sermon on the Mount, Discourse the Sixth)
2. The phrase "essential attributes" is Wesley's own and is found in his sermon, *The Imperfection of Human Knowledge.* Cf. Outler, *Sermons,* 2:569. The phrase "relational attributes," however, is mine; it is a heuristic device which will be used to explore Wesley's views in the material which will follow.

Note that Wesley's language, which displays the essential attributes of God, is characterized by words and phrases that point to and highlight the relationships and interconnections between the attributes — such phrases as: "the omnipresence of God *implies* ... his omnipotence,"[1] "*Nearly allied* to the eternity of God is his omnipresence,"[2] and "The omniscience of God is a clear and *necessary consequence* of his omnipresence."[3] Such phrases, no doubt, reveal the role which reason plays in this context; this instrument, therefore, is not without its use in matters pertaining to the knowledge of God. But it must be stressed that here reason is not conceived by Wesley as an autonomous and independent faculty, but instead as the product of Divine, illuminating, prevenient grace. Thus, in his commentary of *Romans* 1:19-20, a good window on this topic, Wesley asserts:

> 'For what is to be known of God' — Those great principles which are indispensably necessary to be known, 'is manifest in them; for God hath showed it to them' — By the light which enlightens every man that cometh into the world [that is, by prevenient grace].[4]

Reason, therefore, can perceive, dimly perhaps, the "great principles," the general attributes of God. Consequently, rational people of all cultures and every locale can at least understand the ideas that there is a God, and that He is eternal, omnipresent, omniscient, and omnipotent. Moreover, like Wesley, rational men and women can also explore the intelligible connections between these characteristics, the implicatory relations that the Oxonian was so fond of unraveling. Clearly, such knowledge of God is abstract, impersonal, and it does not necessarily imply redemption, but the point is that it is knowledge nevertheless.

II. The Relational Attributes of God

A. Creator
The relational attributes of God, in distinction from the essential, describe in a focused way God's connection to humanity; that is, they depict the nature and being of God as revealed to and in terms of human beings. Here, in other words, the immanence rather than the transcendence of God is stressed. And the Divine characteristics or titles which Wesley employs and which can be listed under this heading of relational attributes are two: namely, God is both a Creator and a Governor. In his sermon, *What is Man?*, for instance, Wesley remarks that the subject of Psalm 8, "celebrates the glorious wisdom and love of God as the Cre-

---

1. Ibid., 4:44. Emphasis is mine. (On the Omnipresence of God) For a modern, Wesleyan treatment of the attributes of God which highlights the eternity, personhood, and creativity of the Supreme Being Cf. Albert Truesdale, "Theism" in *A Contemporary Wesleyan Theology*, ed. Charles Carter (Grand Rapids, Michigan: Francis Asbury Press, 1983) 1:107-48.

2. Outler, *Sermons*, 4:61. Emphasis is mine. (The Unity of the Divine Being)

3. Ibid., 4:62. Emphasis is mine.

4. John Wesley, *Explanatory Notes Upon the New Testament* (Salem, Ohio: Schmul Publishers), p. 363. Bracketed material is mine. For a detailed account of Wesley's doctrine of prevenient grace and its impact on his theology, Cf. Charles Allen Rogers, "The Concept of Prevenient Grace in the Theology of John Wesley" (Ph.D. dissertation, Duke University, 1967), p. 196.

ator and Governor of all things."[1] Elsewhere, in his *New Creation*, he writes: "Thus saith the Creator and Governor of the universe, 'Behold, I make all things new:' all which are included in that expression of the Apostle, 'a new heaven and a new earth.'"[2]

Concerning the first attribute, that of Creator, it should be pointed out that God does not take on this role by any necessity or compulsion. In other words, the Most High may or may not choose to create, according to His own sovereign, free, will. Wesley expounds:

> **As a Creator, he has acted, in all things, according to his own sovereign will. Justice has not, cannot have, any place here; for nothing is due to what has no being. Here, therefore, he may, in the most absolute sense, do what he will with his own. Accordingly, he created the heavens and the earth, and all things that are therein, in every conceivable respect, 'according to his own good pleasure.'[3]**

However, the implication of Wesley's thinking here, as Cannon correctly indicates, is that once God chooses to create, He in some respect limits Himself. "Once God performed the creative act and called things into existence," Cannon writes, "he obligated himself to respect the creation which he had made..."[4] This means, of course, that, for Wesley, the idea that God is a Creator must be allowed to reflect back upon the attribute of omnipotence discussed earlier. God is all-powerful, to be sure, but because the Divine Being has chosen to create, omnipotence must now be understood against the backdrop of the creation itself—a point that theologians have tried to express more technically in their distinction between *potentia absoluta* and *potentia ordinata*.

Since Wesley maintained that there cannot be "two Gods or two eternals,"[5] as noted earlier, it is not surprising to learn that he also maintained that God created *ex nihilo*, that is, out of nothing.[6] Since only God is eternal *a parte ante* and matter is not, then the latter must be created. But even assuming the uniqueness of the Divine eternity, Wesley actually had two options available to him to explain the "how" of creation. In other words, creation *ex nihilo* is not the inevitable conclusion given Wesley's premises. He could have, for example, affirmed that God created the world out of His own being—a view which would not contradict the sole eternity of God. However, the Methodist leader apparently rejected this last view, most probably due to its pantheistic tendencies.

Nevertheless, Wesley's doctrine of creation, for all its sophistication, does indeed contain some primitive elements, even by eighteenth century standards.

---

1. Outler, *Sermons*, 3:455.
2. Ibid., 2:502.
3. Thomas Jackson, ed., *The Works of John Wesley*, 14 vols. (Grand Rapids, Michigan: Baker Book House, 1978), 10:361.
4. William R. Cannon, *The Theology of John Wesley* (Nashville: Abingdon Press, 1946), p. 172.
5. Outler, *Sermons*, 2:362. (On Eternity)
6. For references to the doctrine of creation *ex nihilo* in Wesley's sermons Cf. Outler, *Sermons*, 2:537 (On Divine Providence); 3:91 (Spiritual Worship); 2:409 (On the Fall of Man).

Thus, this Oxford fellow taught that God first of all created the four elements: earth, water, air, and fire, out of which the rest of creation was fashioned. "In the beginning God created the matter of the heavens and the earth," Wesley writes, "He first created the four elements out of which the whole universe was composed: earth, water, air, and fire, all mingled together in one common mass."[1] Ultimately, this notion of four elements or roots which make up everything goes back as far as the fifth century B.C. when the Greek philosopher Empedocles first put forth the theory.[2] A crucial difference, however, between the views of Empedocles and Wesley is that the former postulated the forces of love and hate, (affinity and antipathy) as those which organize the elements into a diversity of forms; for Wesley, it was God Himself who plays this role.

On a more favorable note, Wesley's doctrine of creation manifests a degree of elegance and subtlety when he considers the basic order established in the world at the beginning. To convey his understanding here, he appeals to the Platonic image of "a golden chain" let down from heaven—a chain which displays the gradual, as opposed to the abrupt, ascent of beings from the lowest to the highest.[3] In his sermon *Of Evil Angels*, he explains:

> **Accordingly there is one chain of beings, from the lowest to the highest point, from an unorganized particle of earth or water to Michael the archangel. And the scale of creatures does not advance *per saltum*, by leaps, but by smooth and gentle degrees; although it is true, these are frequently imperceptible to our imperfect faculties.**[4]

Again, in this same sermon, Wesley gives us some indication of the specific order, the hierarchy, which creation demonstrates, especially when he writes: "... rising one above another, first, inorganical earth, then minerals and vegetables in their several orders; afterwards insects, reptiles, fishes, birds, beasts, men, and angels."[5] However, whether this ascent of beings is scientifically accurate or not, even by his own eighteenth century standards, does not appear to be Wesley's major concern. Instead, he seems to appeal to the chain of being to demonstrate, in however limited a way, two very important points: first, that human beings are creatures rooted in a created order, subject to all its limitations; second, that human beings are in some sense capable of transcending that order through Divine grace. In other words, the blend of continuity and discontinuity

---

1. Ibid., 2:388 (God's Approbation of His Works) Concerning Wesley's sources for his doctrine of creation, Cannon argues: "Wesley shows his familiarity with the thought of Thomas Burnett in his *Sacred Theory of the Earth*, John Ray in his *Wisdom of God in Creation*, and William Derham in his Physico-Theology, or a *Demonstration of the Being and Attributes of God from His Works of Creation*. Cf. Cannon, *Theology*, p. 167. Moreover, Outler argues that since Wesley claimed that the foundations of the world were laid more than six thousand years ago, this indicates dependence on Archbishop Ussher's date for the creation (4004 B.C.). Cf. Outler, *Sermons*, 3:8, note # 15.

2. For more on Empedocles, especially his doctrine of the four roots, Cf. W.T. Jones, *A History of Western Philosophy: The Classical Mind* (New York: Harcourt, Brace, and World, Inc., 1969), p. 25-28.

3. Outler, *Sermons*, 2:397. (God's Approbation of His Works)

4. Ibid., 3:16. (Of Evil Angels)

5. Ibid.

characterizes the relation of human beings to nature *and* to the animal kingdom as well.

In what way then are human beings unique, distinct from the rest of animal creation? Wesley's own enlightened age answered this question — as did many of the ancient Greeks — basically in terms of reason. Simply put, humans are rational beings; beasts are not. However, as great a defender of reason as Wesley was, he specifically discarded this view in favor of what he considered to be a more accurate one: namely, that the capacity for God, the love and worship of the Holy One, is what sets humans apart. In his sermon, *The General Deliverance*, produced in 1781, he comments:

> **What then makes the barrier between men and brutes? The line which they cannot pass? It was not reason .... But it is this: man is capable of God; the inferior creatures are not. We have no ground to believe that they are in any degree capable of knowing, loving, or obeying God. This is the specific difference between man and brute — the great gulf which they cannot pass over.[1]**

If this indeed is the case, that what distinguishes human beings from all other species is their capacity for God, then what of those men and women who knowingly and willfully reject the Supreme Being? "Whoever does not know, or love, or enjoy God, and is not careful about the matter," Wesley warns, "does in effect disclaim the nature of man, and degrade himself into a beast."[2] Likewise, in his sermon *The General Deliverance* Wesley cautions: "It is true they [who don't know God] may have a share of reason — they have speech and they walk erect. But they have not the mark, the only mark, which totally separates man from the brute creation."[3] Interestingly, this last comment may just be one of the few instances in his sermons where Wesley engages in some dry humor or even possibly in some outright sarcasm.

At any rate, this chain of being, the order and harmony established in the creation, reveals two more significant attributes: namely, the wisdom and the goodness of God. "Now the wisdom, as well as the power of God," Wesley notes in his *Wisdom of God's Counsels*, "is abundantly manifested in his creation, in the formation and arrangement of all his works."[4] Moreover, in his sermon, *God's*

---

1. Ibid., 2:441. (The General Deliverance) Wesley's view is quite interesting, especially when considered from a modern perspective. A branch of current scientific research, for example, suggests that some highly developed animals such as chimpanzees are able to use language. This view, however, — and it is hotly debated by other scientists — undermines the idea of human distinctiveness only if that distinctiveness is understood *chiefly* in terms of rational capacity. Wesley's judgment, on the other hand, appears to be much more inclusive and balanced, and it corresponds very closely to our common sense notions on the matter. For example, the Methodist leader's view can be used to affirm that the mentally deficient and children are as completely and unequivocally human as the brightest genius, the noblest and most advanced mind. Why? Because the *humanitas* inheres not in reason alone, however noble it may be, but also in the capacity for God.

2. Ibid., 2:449-50.

3. Ibid., 2:450. Bracketed material is mine.

4. Ibid., 2:552. (The Wisdom of God's Counsels)

Approbation of His Works, produced in 1782, Wesley continues: "His goodness inclined him to make all things good: and this was executed by his power and wisdom."[1] Observe, however, that the thoroughgoing goodness of creation of which Wesley writes refers to creation not in its present state, but at its beginning, that is, before the spoilage of God's handiwork by human sin and evil. In fact, Wesley takes this point so far as to argue that originally there were no such things as earthquakes and volcanoes,[2] that "there was no violent winter or sultry summer ... no weeds, no useless plants,"[3] and that the creatures of the earth did not then preserve their lives by destroying others[4]. Clearly, not all will accept this description just outlined, but in fairness it should be observed that Wesley's purpose here, once again, was not really scientific but apologetic. That is, he hoped to take the force out of the argument used by the agnostics and atheists of his own era that the created order demonstrates neither the goodness of God, nor His wisdom or power — a subject which will receive further treatment below under the heading "theodicy."

Finally, one last way — and perhaps the most important — in which Wesley explores the created order is not merely in material or physical terms (plants, animals, and human beings etc.), but in moral and ethical ones. Thus, the moral law which was promulgated at Sinai, and later at the Sermon on the Mount, displays, among other things, the moral structure which was established by God in the beginning and which was expressed temporally and spatially in creation, in the very nature and fitness of things. Here, then, the will of God takes a definite, concrete form. It is neither amorphous nor unintelligible. Wesley explains:

> **If we survey the law of God in another point of view, it is supreme, unchangeable reason; it is unalterable rectitude; it is the everlasting fitness of all things that are or ever were created.... And it is ... exactly agreeable to the fitness of things, whether essential or accidental.**[5]

This means, therefore, that the structure and harmony of creation as displayed in the moral law is not arbitrary, but serves as an external and objective standard for all creatures, especially in the areas of sexuality, male/female relationships, the family, humanity's use and development of nature, as well as several others. In short, human beings, *as creatures*, are not free to ignore or repudiate, to use Wesley's own language, "the everlasting fitness of all things that are or ever were created."[6] Again, from Wesley's perspective, men and women are not

---

1. Ibid., 2:399. (God's Approbation of His Works)
2. Ibid., 2:391. From a consideration of the omnipotence, omniscience, and infinite perfection of God, Leibniz concluded that this is the best of all possible worlds — a notion upon which Voltaire, a contemporary of Wesley, heaped considerable scorn, especially in his novel *Candide*. Cf. Gottfried Leibniz, *The Philosophical Works of Leibniz*, translated by George Martin Duncan (New Haven: Tuttle, Morehouse and Taylor, 1890), pp.194-226.
3. Outler, *Sermons*, 2:391, 393.
4. Ibid., 2:395.
5. Ibid., 2:10. (Original, Nature, Property, and Use of the Law)
6. Ibid. For more on just how Wesley understood the relation between creation and the moral law, see my earlier book, *Wesley On Salvation* (Grand Rapids, Michigan: Francis Asbury Press, 1989), p. 31 ff. See also Cannon, *Theology*, p. 174.

autonomous, but are — for want of a better term — theonomous beings who are in relation to and dependent upon a good and gracious Creator.

B. Governor

The second major relational attribute which Wesley affirms is that God is a Governor with respect to His creation. This attribute, which is actually a role or office, entails a measure of responsibility and even limitation as noted earlier. Thus, God not only creates, but also preserves and sustains what He has brought into being. This continuing activity of the Deity may be viewed in one sense as the ongoing process of creation and therefore as highlighting God's earlier role as Creator; however, it may also viewed, in another sense, in terms of God's role as Governor. That is, sustaining and preserving are, to a degree, aspects of what it is implied in superintending the creation. Wesley writes:

> On the contrary, we have the fullest evidence that the eternal, omnipresent, almighty, all-wise Spirit, as he created all things, so he continually superintends whatever he has created. He governs all, not only to the bounds of creation, but through the utmost extent of space; and not only through the short time that is measured by the earth and sun, but from everlasting to everlasting.[1]

Moreover, Wesley again distinguishes these two roles of Creator and Governor, but this time in his *Thoughts Upon God's Sovereignty* where he maintains: "Whenever, therefore, God acts as Governor, as a rewarder or punisher he no longer acts as a mere Sovereign, by his own will and pleasure."[2] In other words, here the freedom and sovereignty of God as Creator must not be confused with His role as a Governor, a role which entails, to use Wesley's own words, acting not "according to his own mere sovereign will; but ... according to the invariable rules both of justice and mercy."[3] Again, if these roles are not distinguished, then the issues of reward and punishment can become quite arbitrary and deterministic, a function of Divine freedom and prerogative rather than of justice and mercy. In fact, so concerned was Wesley with this latter possibility that he added: "Let then these two ideas of God the Creator, the sovereign Creator, and God the Governor, the just Governor, be always kept apart."[4]

1. Providence

Since God is not only a Creator, but also a Governor, one who cares for and superintends His creation, then believers can take great comfort in knowing this. Indeed, according to Wesley, events do not happen by mere chance or according

1. Ibid., 4:69. (The Unity of the Divine Being) Wesley refers to God as a Creator, Sustainer, Preserver, and Governor, although these are not four distinct roles, for the second and third are essentially subsumed under the first. For more references on this subject Cf. Outler, *Sermons*, 2:538. (On Divine Providence); 3:50 (Of the Church); 2:411-12. (On the Fall of Man); 2:426-27. (God's Love to Fallen Man); 4:71. (The Unity of the Divine Being); and 3:93. (Spiritual Worship).
2. Jackson, *Wesley's Works*, 10:362.
3. Ibid.
4. Ibid., 10:363.

to a rigid determinism; instead, God is graciously involved in the affairs of human life and is actively concerned about the welfare of all. In a letter to Dr. Conyers Middleton in 1749, for example, Wesley exclaims: "He [the believer] is happy in knowing there is a God, an intelligent cause and Lord of all, and that he is not the produce either of blind chance or inexorable necessity."[1] Elsewhere, in a letter to Ann Bolton, written in 1781, Wesley elaborates:

> It is a great step toward Christian resignation to be thoroughly convinced of that great truth that there is no such thing as chance in the world; that fortune is only another name of Providence, only it is covered Providence. An event the cause of which does not appear we commonly say 'comes by chance.' Oh no: it is guided by an unerring hand; it is the result of infinite wisdom and goodness.[2]

Perhaps the best window, however, on Wesley's understanding of Divine providence is the sermon he produced in the latter part of his career (1786) which is simply entitled, *On Divine Providence*. In this piece, he first of all contends that providence is not the wishful thinking of Christians, but is a teaching clearly affirmed in the Scriptures.[3] After this initial point is established, Wesley proceeds to draw a relationship between some of the attributes already discussed and God's providential care for the world. "The omnipresent God sees and knows all the properties of all the beings that he hath made," Wesley observes, "He knows all the connections, dependencies, and relations, and all the ways wherein one of them can affect another."[4] Accordingly, God knows how the stars, comets, and planets affect the earth; he knows all the powers and qualities of the animals He has made, and he knows, more importantly, "the hearts of the sons of men."[5]

But God's knowledge of these several relations, according to Wesley, is not enough to support a full-blown doctrine of providence. For behind this knowledge, there must also be a good will, a loving and merciful God who actively and purposefully seeks the best for His people. Along these lines, Wesley contends that the Holy One of Israel is indeed merciful as well as omniscient; loving as well as omnipotent, "He is concerned every moment for what befalls every creature upon earth, and more especially for everything that befalls any of the children of men."[6]

However, even some of Wesley's theological opponents were willing to admit that the Deity is concerned in a general way with the creation and is therefore

---

1. John Telford, ed., *The Letters of John Wesley, A.M.* 8 vols. (London: The Epworth Press, 1931), 2:379.

2. Ibid., 7:45-46. Wesley also denies that events happen by mere chance in his homily, *On the Education of Children.* Cf. Outler, *Sermons*, 3:353.

3. Outler, *Sermons*, 2:536. (On Divine Providence) Outler contends that Wesley's understanding of this doctrine was dependent on the earlier work of such Anglicans as Hooker, Pearson, Ussher, and Wilkins. Cf. Outler, *Sermons*, 2:534.

4. Ibid., 2:539.

5. Ibid.

6. Ibid., 2:540.

good, but they were loathe to confess the notion of a particular providence, that the Supreme Being, the Maker of all, would dare to trouble Himself with the small, private, and commonplace troubles of individuals and societies. However, Wesley, for his part, rejected this last view, which essentially was a Deist position, and argued against it in a number of ways. He, first of all, noted in an important sermon that the denial of a particular providence, the assumption that "the little affairs of men are far beneath the regard of the great Creator and Governor," contradicts the Scriptures.[1]   Second, such a view apparently makes no allowance for exceptions to the general laws of nature in the form of miracles.[2] And third Wesley contends that the idea of a general providence exclusive of a particular one is a confused and an ultimately contradictory idea. He reasons:

> You say, 'You allow a *general* providence, but deny a *particular* one.' And what is a general (of whatever kind it be) that includes no particulars? Is not every general necessarily made up of its several particulars? Can you instance in any general that is not? ... What then becomes then of your general providence, exclusive of a particular? Let it be for ever rejected by all rational men as absurd, self-contradictory nonsense.[3]

Observe that Wesley's language used to support Divine providence in both a general and a particular sense is clear, succinct, and perhaps even a bit strident. And it is this last issue of stridency which is most intriguing. Why, for instance, does this Methodist pastor use the terms "absurd" and "nonsense" in this context? Why turn up the emotional heat? What value (or values) is Wesley attempting to safeguard here and why is it deemed so important?

To answer these questions one must have some appreciation of how the activity of the Methodist Revival affected and informed Wesley's theological views. In October of 1743, for instance, while John Wesley was staying at the home of Francis Ward in Wednesbury, a mob arose, surrounded the house, and cried out in angry tones, "Bring out the minister; we will have the minister."[4] Subsequent-

---

1. Ibid., 2:544. For Wesley, the principal effect of a belief in the particular providence of God is serenity as demonstrated in his commentary on Matthew 6:31 in which he writes: "We will not therefore indulge these unnecessary, these useless, these mischievous cares. We will not borrow the anxieties and distresses of the morrow, to aggravate those of the present day. Rather we will cheerfully repose ourselves on that heavenly Father, who knows we have need of these things; who has given us the life, which is more than meat, and the body, which is more than raiment. Cf. John Wesley, *Explanatory Notes Upon the New Testament* (Salem, Ohio: Schmul Publishers), p. 28.

2. Outler, *Sermons*, 2:546.

3. Ibid., 2:548. Wesley also argues for a particular providence in his journal account of 6 July 1781 where he writes: "It is true, the doctrine of a particular providence (and any but a particular providence is no providence at all) is absolutely out of fashion in England; and a prudent author might write this to gain the favour of his gentle readers. Yet I will not say this is real prudence, because he may lose hereby more than he gains; as the majority, even of Britons, to this day retain some sort of respect for the Bible." Cf. Nehemiah Curnock, *The Journal of the Rev. John Wesley, A.M.*, 8 vols. (London: The Epworth Press, 1938), 6:326.

4. Nehemiah Curnock, *The Journal of the Rev. John Wesley, A.M.*, 8 vols. (London: The Epworth Press, 1938), 3:98.

ly, Wesley was dragged from Justice to Justice, had his hair pulled by a wild man, and then, if this weren't enough, many of the crowd began to scream, "knock his brains out; down with him; kill him at once."[1] Yet for all this confusion and danger, the Methodist leader apparently remained remarkably calm. Why?

Elsewhere, when he was in Falmouth in 1745, a similar situation arose and a woman asked the middle-aged cleric, "But, sir, is it not better for you to hide yourself? To get into the closet?" To which Wesley replied, "No. It is best for me to stand just where I am."[2] Moreover, when he was in Ireland in 1750, the rabble at Hammonds Marsh peppered him with insults and with whatever was near at hand. Wesley, however, remained, once again, undaunted and did what was to become for him one of his chief ways of dealing with mobs; that is, he immediately walked into their midst and showed no fear.[3] Once again, why?

In each instance just recounted, Wesley concludes the record in his Journal by noting and giving thanks for the gracious, providential activity of God. Thus, of the Wednesbury affair, he declares: I never saw such a chain of providences before; so many convincing proofs that the hand of God is on every person and thing, overruling all as it seemeth Him good."[4] And of the Falmouth (West Cornwall) incident he adds: "I never saw before, no, not at Walsall itself, the hand of God so plainly shown as here."[5] Similarly, his judgment of the Irish debacle is expressed in his concluding remark that in the welter of it all "God restrained the wild beasts."[6]

For John Wesley, then, the idea of God's providence was not an airy, speculative notion, an idea that fills the pages of learned tomes but never quite makes it into practice. No, for this evangelist, divine providence quite frankly means that God can be trusted during the good, but more importantly, during the bad as well. The sustaining and encouraging grace of the Supreme Being can be counted on in the fields, along the highways, and in the midst of mobs, insults, and bricks. Therefore, Wesley's calm and his sense of assurance in the midst of trial, some of it quite severe, was neither foolhardy nor arrogant. Instead, it was simply the quite demonstration, the practice and enactment, of a gentle man's belief in the goodness and power of his God.

In fact, so important was divine providence to Wesley that he tracked the rippling effects of this grace in three ever-widening circles. In other words, over and above God's care of the whole universe (general providence) God, as Governor, is concerned with three circles of people in a special way (particular providence). Thus, for example, the widest circle, the outermost one, "includes the whole race of mankind, all the human creatures that are dispersed over the face of the earth."[7] This ring "comprises not only the Christian world...," as Wesley points out, "but the Mahometans also, who considerably outnumber even the

1. Ibid., 3:100.
2. Ibid., 3:189.
3. Ibid., 3:471.
4. Ibid., 3:100.
5. Ibid., 3:190.
6. Ibid., 3:471.
7. Outler, *Sermons*, 2:542. (On Divine Providence)

nominal Christians; yea, and [it includes] the heathens likewise."[1] The second circle, a smaller one, of which God takes more immediate care, embraces all who call themselves Christians, "all who profess to believe in Christ."[2] And the third circle, the innermost one, contains "only the real Christians, those that worship God, not in form only, but in spirit and in truth."[3] Of this last group Wesley observes: "Nothing relative to these is too great, nothing too little, for his attention. He has his eye continually, as upon every individual person that is a member of this his family."[4]

In short, Wesley affirms not only a general providence but also a particular one, a gracious care that increases in intensity as the circles become ever smaller, as persons are transformed by the Holy Spirit and are drawn near to the holy throne of love. Such grace and care, then, are the privileges of all humanity, to be sure, but especially of real, vital, altogether Christians. Truly, Wesley had little reason to fear the mob.

2. Theodicy

Though Wesley took great pains to articulate the providence of God, he was honest enough to realize that this benevolent concern was not apparent to all, not even to Christians. Thus, on the one hand, he asserts that the "Lord is loving unto every man, and that his mercy is over all his works."[5] But then, on the other hand, Wesley admits that "we know not how to reconcile this with the present dispensation of his providence."[6] Moreover, in his manuscript sermon *The Promise of Understanding*, this Methodist itinerant questions why God has allowed evil to have a role in his creation at all; "why he, who is so infinitely good himself, who made all things 'very good,'... permitted what is so entirely contrary to his own nature, and so destructive of his noblest works."[7] Beyond this, Wesley ponders why some families are raised to "wealth, honour, and power,"[8] and why others are held back with "poverty and various afflictions."[9]

---

1. Ibid. Bracketed material is mine. It appears that the relationship between the three circles of providence is such that the outer circles include the inner, but not the other way around. Thus, the outermost circle includes the whole human race, that is, all Christians and non-Christians alike; the second circle is composed of all "that are called Christians" (so it must also include real Christians); however, the innermost circle is the most exclusive of all, for it embraces only real Christians, only those who worship God in spirit and truth.

2. Ibid., 2:543.

3. Ibid. Observe that in this context, as late as 1786, Wesley is still making the distinction between nominal Christianity on the one hand and real Christianity on the other. This practice, of course, can be traced back to his sermon *The Almost Christian* written in 1741 — and even earlier. But the main point here is that this kind of judgment, though somewhat modified, never "dropped out."

4. Ibid. Wesley also elucidates the circles of providence in his sermon, *Spiritual Worship*. Cf. Outler, *Sermons*, 3:94.

5. Ibid. 2:578-79. (The Imperfection of Human Knowledge)

6. Ibid.

7. Ibid., 4:285. (The Promise of Understanding)

8. Ibid., 2:581-82. (The Imperfection of Human Knowledge)

9. Ibid.

And why is God pleased to bestow "a measure of virtue and happiness,"[1] on some and "such a measure of suffering"[2] on others? In other words, through these many pointed and difficult questions, John Wesley raises the classic issue of theodicy: how can evil and human suffering exist in the face of a good and all powerful God?

In tackling this problem, Wesley, first of all, makes a distinction between natural and moral evil as found in his *Promise of Understanding*.[3] Of the former, that is, natural evil, he maintains that questioning the goodness of God on this ground entails a fundamental error — a mistake and confusion in thought as revealed by the following consideration:

> ... all the objections which 'vain men who would be wise' make to the goodness or wisdom or God in the creation. All these are grounded upon an entire mistake, namely, that the world is now in the same state it was at the beginning....The world at the beginning was in a totally different state from that wherein we find it now.[4]

What Wesley is implying here and what he states outright elsewhere is that the fall of humanity is the real culprit, the instigator of much of the evil found in the natural world. In its train, for instance, fallen humanity has left sin, death, and "a whole army of evils, totally new, totally unknown till then, broke in upon rebel man, and all other creatures, and overspread the face of the earth."[5] In short, the Fall, as noted earlier, has affected the creation quite adversely; it has disrupted that golden chain let down from heaven. Its consequences, therefore, are felt in every species, and its reach extends to the entire natural realm both animate and inanimate.

Moreover, and with a little more emotion, Wesley contends that the Divine Being does not need to be defended by His guilty, fallen, creatures, no matter how reasonable or well-intended the arguments may be: "Let every sensible infidel then be ashamed of making such miserable excuses for his Creator! He needs none of us to make apologies, either for him or for his creation! 'As for God, his way is perfect.'"[6]

A second way in which Wesley approached the problem of natural evil was to indicate that in some instances, at least, a significant good often emerges out of this evil. "Do not all men know that whatever evil befalls them, it befalls them by God's appointment?" he writes, "And that he appoints every evil of this life to

1. Ibid., 4:286. (The Promise of Understanding)
2. Ibid.
3. Ibid., 4:285. In this sermon, Wesley actually divides evil into three categories: natural, moral, and penal. However, since much of Wesley's material explores only the first two aspects, only these have been treated in this present work.
4. Ibid., 2:397. (God's Approbation of His Works)
5. Ibid., 2:398. It is important to observe here that Wesley attributes the evil present in the animal kingdom to the fall of humanity. Thus, Adam's sin has consequence not only for his own species, as its representative, but for all other species as well. Moreover, such a notion not only suggests the interconnectedness of the animal realm, but it also points to a hierarchical order with humanity at its apex.
6. Ibid., 2:399.

warn men to avoid greater evils?"[1] This apparent didactic purpose of natural evil is also evident in his cautionary remarks, "every uncommon evil is the trumpet of God blown in that place, that the people may be afraid."[2] But Wesley goes even further than this in his sermon *Public Diversions Denounced* and maintains:

> But of any extraordinary affliction, especially when many persons are concerned in it, we may not only say that in this God speaketh to us, but that the God of glory thundereth! This voice of the Lord is in power. This voice of God is in majesty. This demands the deepest attention of all to whom it comes.[3]

For whatever reason, Outler concludes that this sermon "was not the sort of piece that Wesley would have wanted published under his name."[4] Admittedly, *Public Diversions Denounced* was a manuscript sermon, and therefore was never printed during Wesley's lifetime — though he did keep it among his papers. At any rate, perhaps the most convincing explanation for the non-publication of this piece cannot be its association of natural evil and divine judgment, as some scholars suggest, for Wesley subsequently made this very association, but this time in print, in his estimation of the significance of two earthquakes: one on 8 February 1750, the other on 8 March 1750, which rocked London, Gosport, Portsmouth, and the Isle of Wright.[5] Of the first quake, Wesley observes in his Journal: "There were three distinct shakes, or wavings to and fro, attended with an hoarse rumbling noise, like thunder. How gently does God deal with this nation! Oh that our repentance may prevent heavier marks of His displeasure."[6] And exactly a month later he comments on the second series of shocks: "In the evening God rent the rocks again. I wondered at the words He gave me to speak; but He doeth whatsoever pleaseth Him."[7]

---

1. Ibid., 4:319. (Public Diversions Denounced)
2. Ibid., 4:320.
3. Ibid., 4:321.
4. Ibid., 4:318.
5. Luke L. Tyerman, *The Life and Times of the Rev. John Wesley, M.A.*, 3 vols. (New York: Burt Franklin) 2:71. Tyerman points out that the quakes caused so much fear among the people of London that the women of that city made "earthquake gowns," garments suitable to wear as they sat outside all night long, away from falling ceilings and from harm's way. Cf. p. 72.
6. Curnock, Journal, 3:453.
7. Ibid., 3:456. The modern view of nature and natural occurrences is that they can be utterly explained by the laws of an objective, positivistic science; no other kinds of interpretive schemes — theological, aesthetic, or otherwise — are given much credence. In other words, in the modern mentality, nature is opaque — unsuitable and unable to reveal the activity of God. Again, in this scheme, nature is deemed ultimately without purpose; it is, to borrow a phrase from Shakespeare, "a tale told by an idiot, full of sound and fury, and signifying nothing." What is truly remarkable, however, is that this view of nature, for the most part, is shared by some Neo-orthodox Protestants who in the name of *sola gratia* and *sola fide* discount the notion that nature displays the goodness, wisdom, power, and activity of the Creator. Here as well nature is dark. But Wesley thought otherwise and wrote: "Do not all men know that whatever evil befalls them, it befalls them by God's appointment? And that he appoints every evil of this life to warn men to avoid greater evils? That he sends these lighter marks of his anger to awaken men, that they may shun his heavier vengeance." Cf. Outler, *Sermons*, 4:319-20.

In light of the preceding, though Wesley does in some sense associate natural evil and Divine judgment, he by no means draws an *exact* equation between them, for these realities are much too complex for that. To be sure, Wesley knew that the innocent suffer by natural catastrophe and the like, and in a way that can only provoke both human sympathy and puzzlement. Consequently, it is safe to affirm that there was still a healthy role for mystery in Wesley's attempts at theodicy.

Obviously, an appeal to natural evil is insufficient to explain the full range of suffering that human beings experience. Wesley, therefore, postulated a second category, namely, moral evil. During the decade, for example, when many of his later sermons were written, that is, during the 1780's, the American Revolution was still raging (it ended 1783), Turkey declared war on Russia (1787), Austria declared war on Turkey (1788), and the French Revolution, with all its later carnage and obscene butchery, was just getting under way (1789). In their wake, these internecine struggles left widows, orphans, and the disabled to fend for themselves. Again, these wars spawned pain and suffering of an almost unspeakable order. But why? Why does a good, loving, and omnipotent God permit these horrors to occur? This is to pose the question of theodicy not in natural terms, but in moral ones.

One answer, and perhaps the most convincing, that Wesley offers to this dilemma is that God as Governor of the world governs men and women "so as not to destroy either their understanding, will, or liberty."[1] The sovereignty and omnipotence of God, then, are in no way threatened by this prospect of encountering true agents, creatures who are in some sense independent, and who therefore have moral freedom and the possibility for either virtue or vice. Wesley elaborates:

> **Were human liberty taken away men would be as incapable of virtue as stones. Therefore, the Almighty himself cannot do this thing. He cannot thus contradict himself, or undo what he has done. He cannot destroy out of the soul of man that image of himself wherein he made him and without doing this he cannot abolish sin and pain out of the world.**[2]

Three things are important in this context. First, Wesley rejects the notion of a *natural* free will; instead, he considers human moral liberty, restored in some measure, and its resultant responsibility as fruits of the prevenient grace of God, a grace which mitigates some of the worst effects of the Fall. Observe the words of the leader of the English Revival in his treatise, *Predestination Calmly Considered*: "there is a measure of free-will supernaturally restored to every man, together with that supernatural light which 'enlightens every man that cometh into the world.'"[3] It is this grace, then — not natural ability — which renders men and women both free and accountable.

1. Ibid., 2:541. (On Divine Providence)
2. Ibid.
3. Jackson, *Wesley's Works*, 10:229-30. For another reference of Wesley's association of free-will and prevenient grace, Cf. Jackson, *Wesley's Works*, 10:232-232.

Second, God cannot be a just and fair Judge — an aspect of what it means to be a Governor — unless His creatures are morally free. "All reward, as well as all punishment," Wesley maintains, "pre-supposes free-agency; and whatever creature is incapable of choice, is incapable of either one or the other."[1] Again, "if man be capable of choosing good or evil," Wesley continues "then he is a proper object of the justice of God, ... but otherwise he is not."[2] Indeed, the very wisdom of God and the dignity of humanity are affirmed in showing that the Lord God redeems humanity in a way so as not to destroy its nature, nor to revoke the liberty which He has given it.[3]

Third, notice that in Wesley's comments just cited in the block quotation above he offers a theodicy by calling for a rethinking of what is meant by Divine omnipotence. According to this Oxford don, the all-powerful character of God does not mean that He is either coercive or that He has the power to contradict Himself. God simply will not countermand His earlier decree to create free, sentient, responsible, moral beings. This means, of course, that those who have called the Most High into account due to moral evil have probably failed to consider in a proper fashion just what Divine omnipotence entails: that is, what it can do, but more importantly, what it cannot do. Remember, not even God can contradict Himself, not even the Supreme Being can create a world in which their are free moral beings without running the risk of evil.

Once again, the freedom to choose evil is a necessary though undesirable consequence of the freedom to choose the good. But just what is this great good that admittedly comes at so high a price according to Wesley? It is nothing less than the immeasurable good of loving God and our neighbor, the realization of the two great commandments of which Jesus spoke. Therefore, to ask for a world where there is not even the slightest possibility for freedom and for the moral evil which is based upon it, is to ask for a world in which there is also not the slightest possibility for the good, for the love of God and neighbor. This is, in actuality, to ask for less, much less, and not more.

Moreover, Wesley takes this last point so far as to claim that were it not for the Fall of Adam, with all its freedom and evil, we would not then know some of the deepest riches of God's love and grace. He states:

> Unless the many had been made sinners by the disobedience of one, by the obedience of one many would not have been 'made righteous.' So there would have been no room for that amazing display of the Son of God's love to mankind. There would have been no occasion for his 'being obedient unto death, even the death of the cross.' It could not then have been said, to the astonishment of all the hosts of heaven, 'God so loved the world,... We might have loved the Author of our being, the Father of angels and men, as our Creator and Preserver;... But we could not have loved him under the nearest and dearest relation, as 'delivering up his Son for us all."[4]

1. Ibid., 10:362.
2. Ibid., 10:233-34.
3. Outler, *Sermons*, 2:553. (The Wisdom of God's Counsels)
4. Ibid., 2:425,426-27. (God's Love to Fallen Man)

Observe in Wesley's comments above the immense wisdom and goodness of God, that the Almighty is astonishingly able to bring goodness out of evil. Here theodicy is informed, quite interestingly, by the providence, wisdom, and goodness of God.

Though Wesley's attempts at theodicy are both well-argued and impressive, he did not for a moment believe that he had successfully addressed all the pertinent issues. In his honesty and candor, this Methodist leader knew quite well that such matters will continue to be troubling for most people, but that this situation itself should perhaps goad them to a Job-like humility.[1] But even after such lessons are learned, even after one has made the distinction between natural and moral evil, the questions linger. And apparently Wesley himself was still perplexed and wrote on one occasion — no doubt with some difficulty and pain — "Who can explain why Christianity is not spread as far as sin? Why is not the medicine sent to every place where the disease is found?[2] The Calvinistic Methodists had a fairly straightforward answer to this question; Wesley, the Arminian, did not.

1. Ibid., 4:287. (The Promise of Understanding)
2. Ibid., 2:581. (The Imperfection of Human Knowledge)

CHAPTER TWO

CHRISTOLOGY
"And in Jesus Christ his only Son our Lord..."

At the center of the Christian faith, the bedrock which sustains so much of its teaching and practice, now as in the past, is the person of Jesus Christ. Indeed, throughout history councils have met, creeds have been written, and religious leaders have been deposed — all with respect to the important matter of Christology. How one considers Christ then ("Who do you say I am?" Mark 8:29) is neither an incidental nor an indifferent matter, but has great consequence for the Christian faith, its life, and its practice.

Accordingly, John Wesley wrote several occasional pieces, many of them sermons, in which the theme of the doctrine of Christ was either the main emphasis (*On Knowing Christ after the Flesh*) or at least a significant part of some other issue (*What is Man?*). Granted, the Methodist leader never wrote a full-length, penetrating, and systematic treatment on this subject, but when his numerous references are gathered together, especially from his entire sermon corpus, a remarkably clear picture does emerge. Normally, treatments of Christology are arranged under the broad headings of the person, states, and work of Christ. However, due to the nature and the amount of material present in Wesley's writings, the following discussion will order its material under the categories of the person and work of Christ and these two headings will include all the material from the usual, additional category of the states of Christ. Such a procedure should make for a more intelligible and profitable reading in this area.

I. The Person of Christ

A. The Divine Nature
In the same year (1780) that Wesley pleaded with the Bishop of London, Dr. Lowth, to send more spiritual laborers to reap the American harvest, he also composed a very readable homily, *Spiritual Worship*, which contains some prominent Christological sections. Taking 1 John 5:20 as his text (He is the true God, and eternal life), Wesley underscores the divinity of Christ in this sermon under seven main headings and thereby applies many of the titles, attributes, and works of the most high God, which we have already encountered in Chapter

One, to the Son.[1] To illustrate, Wesley first of all maintains in this piece, that Jesus Christ is eternal,[2] that He has existed before the foundations of the earth — before all worlds, and before all time. And elsewhere, in his work *On Eternity* the Methodist pastor copies a poem, with a few modifications, from his brother Samuel, Jr. which reads as follows:

> Hail, God the Son, with glory crowned,
>   E'er time began to be
> Throned with thy Sire through half the round
>   of wide eternity
>
> Hail, God the Son, with glory crowned,
>   When time shall cease to be;
> Throned with the Father through the round
>   of whole eternity[3]

Observe that the two stanzas just cited display the eternity of the Son in terms of the important distinction of *a parte ante* (first stanza) and *a parte post* (second stanza) which was described in detail earlier. Remember also from this previous discussion that it is God alone, not any created being or thing, who is eternal *a parte ante*. This, then, is a unique characteristic, a divine trait. And since the Son, according to Wesley, is eternal in precisely this way, Jesus Christ is therefore truly and fully God.

Second, in the homily *Spiritual Worship*, the Son is intimately involved in the creation of the world; He is "the true God, the only Cause, the sole Creator of all things."[4] Wesley, however, does not limit the Son's role in creation simply to an instrumental one — as in some other christologies — in which the Father creates *through* the Son. On the contrary, in his sermon *What is Man*, the Oxford don affirms that "We cannot doubt but when the Son of God had finished all the work which *he created and made*, he said 'These be thy bounds! This be thy just circumference, O world!"[5] More to the point, Wesley contends that it was the only-begotten Son of God who pronounced the very words of Genesis, "Let there be light."[6]

Third, the Son as 'the true God' is also the "*Supporter* of all things that he hath made."[7] That is, He sustains all things by the word of his power, "by the same powerful word which brought them out of nothing."[8] And fourth, the Son

1. Albert C. Outler, ed., *The Works of John Wesley, The Sermons* 4 vols. (Nashville: Abingdon Press, 1984), 3:91 (Spiritual Worship)
2. Ibid., 3:90.
3. Ibid., 2:359-60. And see Outler's note # 5 p. 359 for more information on this poem. (On Eternity)
4. Ibid., 3:91. (Spiritual Worship)
5. Ibid., 3:457. (What is Man?) Emphasis is mine.
6. Ibid., 2:478. (The End of Christ's Coming)
7. Ibid., 3: 91 (Spiritual Worship)
8. Ibid.

of God is likewise "the *Preserver* of all things."[1] In other words, He is not only the Author of all motion in the universe[2], but also "the life of everything that lives ... [as well as] the fountain of all the life which man possesses."[3] Wesley elaborates:

> He not only keeps them in being, but preserves them in that degree of well-being which is suitable to their natures. He preserves them in their several relations, connections, and dependences, so as to compose one system of beings, to form one entire universe, according to the counsel of his will.[4]

Fifth, the two preceding roles highlight the active care, the superintendency, which is required to maintain the world and its established order. Here the Son is, to use Wesley's own words, "the Lord and Disposer of the whole creation, and every part of it."[5] Again, the Son is the "Governor of all things"[6] that are or ever were created, a role which includes, like the Father's, a "providential government over the children of men."[7] In fact, the same three circles of providence which we have already encountered in the sermon *On Divine Providence* under the heading of the doctrine of God are also present in this earlier "Christological" sermon, *Spiritual Worship*.[8] Providential intent and care, then, is a part of the Son's work as well.

Furthermore, the teleological thrust, the goal orientation of much of Wesley's theology, is aptly mirrored in his sixth title for the Son of God. Wesley states: "being the true God he is the *End* of all things, according to that solemn declaration of the Apostle: 'Of him, and through him, and to him, are all things.'" Moreover, the Oxford don adds to these designations, tying the various roles together, "of him as the Creator; through him as the Sustainer and Preserver; and to him as the ultimate End of all."[9] Thus, the Son of God is the goal, the τελος (telos), the perfection in love to which human beings are directed.

1. Ibid. For more on the creating, supporting, and preserving activity of Christ, that is, on His non-mediatorial work Cf. John Deschner, *Wesley's Christology* (Dallas: Southern Methodist University Press, 1960), p. 65-68.

2. Ibid., 3:92.

3. Ibid., 3:95. In this sermon, Wesley maintains that Jesus Christ is the life of everything that lives: vegetables, animals, and rational beings. See also Outler's note, number 37, on this particular progression.

4. Ibid., 3:91.

5. Ibid., 3:93

6. Ibid. For another reference to the Son's work as Governor, see *The Duty of Constant Communion* where Wesley states: God, our Mediator and Governor, ... declares to us that all who obey his commands shall be eternally happy; all who do not shall be eternally miserable. Now one of these commands is, 'Do this in remembrance of me.'" 3:431.

7. Ibid., 3:94. (Spiritual Worship)

8. Ibid. And compare with *On Divine Providence*, 2:542-43. Observe also that when Wesley refers to the innermost circle of providence in the sermon *Spiritual Worship*, he indicates that it includes only "the invisible church of Christ — all real Christians, wherever dispersed in all corners of the earth." (3:94) As noted in the last chapter, this kind of distinction, though slightly modified, was repeatedly employed by the mature Wesley.

9. Ibid., 3:94-95. (Spiritual Worship)

And last, but obviously not least, the Son of God is "the Redeemer of all the children of men."[1] Jesus Christ saves humanity from the guilt and power of sin and ushers in a freedom unexcelled and unequaled: the freedom to love God and neighbor. This role of the Redeemer whereby forgiveness and new life are mediated to the faithful is perhaps the best known and, in some people's minds at least, the only principal role for the Son of God. Indeed, the division of labor, if you will, among persons of the Trinity is sometimes divided along these lines: the Father is the Creator, the Son is the Redeemer, and the Holy Spirit is the Sanctifier. However, such views do not adequately represent Wesley's Christology (or his doctrines of God and the Holy Spirit for that matter). In short, for the leader of the British Revival, the Son of God is suitably and accurately described in all the following ways: as the Redeemer, of course, but also as the Creator, Sustainer, Preserver, and Governor. No single function, in other words, is exclusive to the Father — or to the Son or to the Holy Spirit. And it will become apparent as this work progresses that one of the chief ways that Wesley emphasized the unity of the Godhead was by articulating the interpenetration of roles by each person of the Trinity.

In good Protestant fashion, Wesley's descriptions of the roles and titles of the Son of God were richly supported by his careful use of Scripture. Wesley, however, also affirmed the divinity of Jesus Christ by an appeal to Church tradition. In his sermon, *What is Man?*, for instance, he cites approvingly the language of the Council of Nicea: "The Son of God, that was *God of God, Light of light, very God of very God*, in glory equal with the Father, in majesty co-eternal, emptied himself etc."[2] This exact language, by the way, also reverberates in the sermon under review, *Spiritual Worship*.[3] Beyond this, Wesley concurred with the teaching of his own Anglican Church which in its Second Article of Religion stated that "The Son, who is the Word of the Father, the very and eternal God, [is] of one substance with the Father."[4] In all this material, then, in affirming that the Son is consubstantial (of the same substance) with the Father, Wesley rejects even the slightest hint of subordinationism (that the Son is not equal to the Father), and in his *On Knowing Christ After the Flesh*, produced in 1789, he repudiates Arianism and other low Christologies, Socinianism in particular.[5]

1. Ibid. 3:93.

2. Ibid., 3:460. (What is Man?) Emphasis is mine.

3. Ibid., 3:91. (Spiritual Worship) For yet another reference to the language of Nicea, Cf. *Letter to a Roman Catholic* in Thomas Jackson, ed., *The Works of John Wesley*, 14 vols. (Grand Rapids, Michigan: Baker Book House, 1978), 10:81.

4. John Wesley, *Sunday Service of the Methodists in North America* (Nashville: The United Methodist Publishing House, 1984), p. 306.

5. Outler, *Sermons*, 4:99-100. (On Knowing Christ After the Flesh) Socinianism, which developed from the thought of Lelio Sozzini (1525-62) and Fausto (1539-1604), taught that Jesus is the revelation of God, but that He is merely a man. Some scholars see in this movement the early strains of what later became known as Unitarianism. Cf. A. J. McLachlan, *Socinianism in Seventeenth-Century England*, 1951.

So impressed was Wesley with the divinity of Jesus that he even balked at the use of familiar, sentimental, and what he called "fondling kind of expressions," to describe[1] or address Christ as evidenced by the following:

> Some will probably think that I have been over-scrupulous with regard to one particular word, which I never use myself either in verse or prose, in praying or preaching, ... It is the word 'dear.' Many of these frequently say, both in preaching, in prayer, and in giving thanks, 'dear Lord', or 'dear Saviour'; and my brother used the same in many of his hymns, even as long as he lived. But may I not ask, Is not this using too much familiarity with the great Lord of heaven and earth?[2]

One may question whether or not Wesley, in fact, is being over-scrupulous here. However, the Methodist pastor also knew, as the saying goes, "familiarity breeds contempt." Of course, not that believers would actually go so far as to disdain Christ, but language creates an atmosphere: it fosters images and impressions that can move the heart and mind down paths they should not go. Quite simply, to think or even to claim that one knows Christ in this familiar and common way suggests, in Wesley's mind at least, that perhaps one has underestimated the Savior and has taken His divinity for granted. This is not a thing of a "purely indifferent nature,"[3] Wesley cautions, "We are to honour the Son even as we honour the Father."[4] But why are believers to revere the Son so? Because Jesus Christ is divine and glorious. "The Son," Wesley continues, "[is] the Creator of all! A God, a God appears! Yes, 'O''ΩN, the Being of beings, Jehovah, the Self-existent, the Supreme, the God who is over all blessed for ever."[5] Reverence, then, not familiarity is in order.

B. The Human Nature

But Jesus Christ is not simply divine; he is also human. And this teaching was fully appreciated by Wesley in his many writings. For instance, in his commentary on 1 John 2:22, a good window on the humanity of Christ, Wesley affirms that "Jesus is the Christ; that he is the Son of God; that he came *in the flesh* is one undivided truth."[6] Elsewhere, in the Articles of Religion which he edited for the American Methodists, Wesley reaffirms the doctrine of the English Church. Article two, for example, reads in part:

> The Son, who is the Word of the Father, the very and eternal God, of one substance with the Father, took man's nature in the womb of the blessed Virgin; so that two whole and perfect natures — that is to say,

1. Ibid., 4:105.
2. Ibid., 4:102.
3. Ibid., 4:104.
4. Ibid., 4:106.
5. Ibid., 1:474. (Upon Our Lord's Sermon on the Mount, Discourse I).
6. John Wesley, *Explanatory Notes Upon the New Testament* (Salem, Ohio: Schmul Publishers), p. 634. Emphasis is mine.

the Godhead and manhood — were joined together in one person, never to be divided, whereof is one Christ, very God and very man ...[1]

Moreover, in his sermon, *The End of Christ's Coming*, produced in 1781, Wesley adds: "It was in the fullness of time ... that God 'brought his first begotten into the world, made of a a woman,' by the power of the Highest overshadowing her."[2]

Just how the true God, the Creator, Sustainer, Preserver, Governor, and Redeemer becomes man, takes on a human nature, and thereby becomes particularized is a question for which Wesley has no satisfactory answer. And in order to understand more clearly the issues which are involved here, it is helpful to call to mind an important distinction which Wesley makes with respect to this topic in his sermon *On the Trinity*: "The Bible barely requires you to believe such *facts*, not the manner of them. Now the mystery does not lie in the *fact*, but altogether in the *manner*.[3] Again, in this same sermon, Wesley contends that he knows nothing about the manner of the incarnation and therefore believes nothing about it.[4] What he does know is that it has occurred, and that the "word was made flesh."

Though Wesley cannot fathom how the eternal can become temporal, how the omnipresent can be localized, he does attend to many of the issues surrounding the birth of Christ, especially in relation to the Virgin Mary. Thus, in his comments on Luke 1:47 he asserts that Mary was the mother of Christ "*after the flesh* which was an honour peculiar to her."[5] Such an assertion has led Deschner to query: "is Mary the mother of Jesus Christ in both natures?" and he continues: "At this point, where Nestorianism foundered, Wesley lacks precise indications."[6]

The issue which Deschner has raised is a technical — though important — one and goes back to the great Christological debates of the fifth century when Nestorius, who was then bishop of Constantinople, maintained that Mary was not the mother of God (theotokos), but was only mother of the human nature of Christ. In other words, Nestorius so separated the two natures of Christ, the divine and the human, that the unity of the person of Christ was eclipsed. Moreover, in his Christology, Nestorius obviously rejected the notion of a *communicatio idiomatum*, that the attributes of the two natures interpenetrated one another. Mary therefore could not have been the "Bearer of God," but only the bearer of the

---

1. John Wesley, *Sunday Service*, p. 306. Note that a line from the original article reads, "in the womb of the blessed Virgin, of her substance..." Wesley, as Deschner correctly points out, deletes the phrase "of her substance" for whatever reason. Cf. John Deschner, *Wesley's Christology* (Dallas: Southern Methodist University Press, 1960), p. 25.

2. Outler, *Sermons*, 2:479. (The End of Christ's Coming)

3. Ibid., 2:383. (On the Trinity)

3. Ibid., 2:384.

4. Wesley, *N.T. Notes* p. 143. Emphasis is mine.

6. Deschner, *Christology*, p. 30.

human nature. Such views ultimately led to the condemnation of Nestorius at the Council of Ephesus in 431.[1]

Even though Deschner concedes that Wesley's Christology is in line with orthodoxy, with the council of Chalcedon in particular [2]— which by the way offered the formula "two natures in one person" — he nevertheless has raised some doubts concerning the soundness of Wesley's Christology. Deschner, for instance, notes concerning the issue of Mary as the mother of God: "does he [Wesley] ... also make a reservation or qualification with respect to the personal union?" and he adds, "There is no need to make a Nestorian of Wesley for this question to have interest and point for this study."[3] In addition, though Deschner claims "It is too much to say that Wesley's is a docetic Christology,"[4] the direction of his argument seems to lead elsewhere — not to a claim of docetism, of course, but to an underestimation of Wesley's conception of the humanity of Christ — an underestimation that can be called into question in two key ways.

First of all, though Wesley's favorite way of referring to the role of Mary in the incarnation was as "mother after the flesh," as noted earlier, this is not evidence for an incipient Nestorian Christology. Why? Simply because Wesley, unlike Nestorius, affirmed, taught, and expounded the communication of properties, the *communicatio idiomatum*, between the divine and human natures. There is really no depreciation of the human nature here. Wesley explains:

> **Therefore he [Christ] is omnipresent; else he could not be in heaven and on earth at once. This is a plain instance of what is usually termed the communication of properties between the Divine and human nature; whereby what is proper to the Divine nature is spoken concerning the human, and what is proper to the human is, as here, spoken of the Divine.[5]**

In other words, the deemphasis of the humanity of Christ in the Christology of Nestorius grew out of his separation of the two natures and out of his denial of the *communicatio idiomatum*. Wesley, on the other hand, neither devalued the human nature of Christ nor did he reject "a communication of properties."

Second, the point under consideration is subtle but no less vital. Yes, Wesley does indeed underscore the divinity of Christ as Deschner argues, but this should not be taken as proof that Wesley failed to appreciate fully the humanity of Christ. Instead, this Christological tendency must be viewed against the back-

---

1. Philip Schaff, *History of the Christian Church* 8 vols. (Grand Rapids, Michigan: Wm. B. Eerdmans Publishing Co., 1981), 3:714-28.
2. Deschner, *Christology*, p. 30.
3. Ibid.
4. Ibid., 28. That Deschner has suspicions concerning Wesley's estimation of the humanity of Christ is revealed in his following comment: "Somewhere in the background of Wesley's thought there must lie an attitude toward human nature, as such, which forbids him from taking with final seriousness the idea that the incarnation means an affirmation of human nature, not simply subjection to it." Cf. Deschner, *Christology*, p. 31-32.
5. Wesley, *N.T. Notes*, p. 219

drop of Wesley's prior commitment to the language of the Anglican second article which affirms "one Christ, very God and very man,"[1] as well as in terms of his own commentary on the pertinent biblical material, especially John 3:13.[2] And perhaps it is precisely the reverence and respect which Wesley felt as he pondered the full implications of the deity of Christ — and who has done this well? — which has led modern commentators to question his views on the humanity of Christ. Simply put, for Wesley, Jesus Christ as the God/Man, though true man, deserves more respect than mere man.

Another noteworthy issue which surrounds the humanity of Christ is the nature and mode of His birth. That Wesley affirms Jesus was born of a virgin comes as no surprise, especially since the Methodist leader seldom departed from orthodoxy, but that he goes on to claim that Mary, even after this birth, "continued a pure and unspotted virgin,"[3] does indeed come as a surprise, especially to Protestant ears. But how then does Wesley interpret the important scriptural passage, "Isn't his [Jesus'] mother's name Mary, and aren't his brothers James, Joseph, Simon, and Judas? Aren't all his sisters with us?" (Matt 13:55-56). Interestingly, Wesley resuscitates a teaching that went back as far as Jerome and which worked its way into some of the corridors of Anglicanism. For instance, concerning this verse, Wesley writes in his *Notes Upon the New Testament*: "*His brethren* — Our kinsmen. They were the sons of Mary, sister to the virgin, and wife of Cleophas or Alpheus."[4] In other words, this Mary was not his mother, but his aunt; James, Joseph, Simon, and Judas were not his brothers, but his cousins! This interpretation, by the way, is reiterated in Wesley's commentary on Matthew 12:46 and John 7:03. and stands as a novelty in his otherwise very Protestant theology.

Clearly, the very act of the incarnation of Christ entailed a condescension, a renunciation and veiling of the glories of the divine nature (morphe theou). And Wesley was quick to note these points as well, especially in his late sermon, *God's Love to Fallen Man*, where he states:

1. Wesley, *Sunday Service*, p. 306.

2. Wesley, *N.T. Notes*, p. 219.

3. Jackson, *Wesley's Works*, 10:81. The notion of the perpetual virginity of Mary lacks Scriptural support. In fact, the Bible is quite frank in its discussion about the brothers (and sisters Matt 13:56) of Christ: James, Joseph, Simon, and Judas in particular. Cf. Matt. 12:46, Matt 13:55, and John 7:03-05. Nevertheless, sometimes it is argued that the brothers of Matthew 12:46 are not the flesh and blood brothers of Christ, but are just very good friends. However, such an interpretation is evasive and belies the whole point of Jesus' question, "Who is my mother and who are my brothers?" Matt 12:48. The implication here, of course, is that the flesh and blood relatives, like Mary and the brothers of Jesus, are contrasted with those people who *lack such a familial relation*. But since the latter, as their chief characteristic, do the will of the Father, they are indeed judged the "family" of Christ. Moreover, the idea of the perpetual virginity of Mary unduly elevates the status of Mary, and it eventually led to the creation of an atmosphere in which a full-blown Maryology could emerge, most notably in terms of the proclamation of the Immaculate Conception of Mary in 1854 by the Roman Catholic Church.

4. Wesley, *N.T. Notes*, p. 51.

> What manner of love is this wherewith the only-begotten Son of God
> hath loved us! So as to 'empty himself,' as far as possible, of his eter-
> nal Godhead! As to divest himself of that glory which he had with the
> Father before the world began. As to take the form of a servant, being
> found in fashion as a man! And to humble himself still farther, 'being
> obedient unto death, yea, the death of the cross'![1]

This passage just cited and others have led Deschner to claim that Wesley's
understanding of the humiliation of Christ moves quickly from a position of
'renouncing' to one of 'veiling' such that, "One cannot avoid the impression of
a certain uneasiness in Wesley about the humiliation as a whole."[2] Admittedly,
Wesley does at times use the term 'veiling' without mentioning the other term,
'renouncing,' as in his sermon *On Working Out Our Own Salvation.*[3] And he
does, after all, continue to affirm the dignity and excellency of Christ even in the
Redeemer's most humbled state. However, the Anglican cleric by no means soft-
pedals the humiliation of Christ as demonstrated in a pertinent homily which
reads in part: "he [Christ] humbled himself to a still greater degree, 'becoming
obedient' to God, though equal with him, 'even unto death, yea the death of the
cross'— *the greatest instance of humiliation and obedience.*[4] And elsewhere, in
his comments on Philippians 2:7, Wesley declares:

> He [Christ] was content to forego the glories of the Creator, and to
> appear in the form of a creature: nay, to be made in the likeness of the
> fallen creatures; and not only to *share the disgrace*, but to suffer the
> punishment due to *the meanest and vilest among them all.*[5]

Humiliation, then, is neither an absent nor a muted note in Wesley's doctrine
of Christ. In fact, in his Christology, Wesley appears to hold the ideas of divinity and humanity, exaltation and humiliation, in concert. *Both* the excellency of
Christ *and* his abasement are often affirmed simultaneously, especially in the
Methodist leader's comments on Calvary; neither aspect, therefore, is or should
be discounted.

One place, however, where there is a break, a discontinuity, in Jesus' form as
a servant is, of course, at His transfiguration as recorded in Mark 9:2 and elsewhere. Here, Wesley marks this transition and observes that "the Divine rays,
which God let out on this occasion, made the glorious change from one of these
[forms] into the other."[6] Otherwise, according to Wesley, Jesus remained in the
form of a servant until his glorification.

---

1. Outler, *Sermons*, 2:428. (God's Love to Fallen Man)
2. Deschner, *Wesley's Christology*, p. 58.
3. Outler, *Sermons*, 3:201. (On Working Out Our Own Salvation)
4. Ibid., 3:201-02. Bracketed material is mine. Emphasis is mine.
5. Wesley, *N.T. Notes*, p. 509.
6. Ibid., p. 117. Also realize that Wesley took issue with the notion that the humanity of Christ
existed before the world began, as held by Dr. Watts. Cf. Outler, *Sermons*, 2:478. (The End of
Christ's Coming). Bracketed material is mine.

II. The Work of Christ

With respect to the work of Christ, it should first of all be noted that Wesley makes a distinction between the God/Man's mediatorial and non-mediatorial activity[1]. Actually, this is a distinction with which the reader is already familiar. In other words, under the topic of the person of Christ, it has already been noted that Jesus Christ is not merely a redeemer, but that He also participates quite actively in the creating, preserving, sustaining, and governing of the world — and all of this in a providential fashion, ever seeking to improve the goodness of creation and the state of all beings.[2] This non-mediatorial work, therefore, will not be treated again, and the discussion will now move to a consideration of the mediatorial activity of the Messiah.

The flow of the following argument can be presented in at least two ways: on the one hand, we can follow the order of Deschner and explore the mediatorial functions of Christ under the headings prophet, king, and priest. In this view, the priesthood of the Redeemer is considered last in order to highlight the priority of this role — that it undergirds and is the foundation for the other two. On the other hand, we can follow the traditional order of prophet, priest, and king which is duplicated in the Christologies of several major theologians, both past and present.[3]

Although there is much merit to Deschner's order, he nevertheless intends to overcome a supposed "two-sidedness" (moralistic/evangelical) in *Wesley's* theology — not in the interpretations of it — by means of this device.[4] However, since the present writer does not accept the diagnosis (as will become apparent in the chapter on soteriology), he likewise does not accept the cure. Therefore, the traditional arrangement of prophet, priest, and king will be maintained in the subsequent discussion.

A. Prophet

For Wesley, the prophetic office of Christ embraces an unexcelled teaching role. "Now here we want Christ in his prophetic office," he writes, "to enlighten our minds, and teach us the whole will of God."[5] And one of the best sermons through which we can gain insight in this area is the piece *Upon our Lord's Sermon on the Mount, Discourse the First.* In it, the Methodist leader poses four vital questions: First, who is it that is speaking here, that is, who is this person,

1. Deschner, *Christology*, p. 65.
2. For further references in this area Cf. Outler, *Sermons*, 4:199., Creator and Sustainer (On Faith); 3:92., Author of all motion that is in the universe., (Spiritual Worship); 3:91., Creator, Supporter, and Preserver (Spiritual Worship).
3. One of the best contemporary expositions of the work of Christ is Emil Brunner's *The Mediator*, which, by the way, has had a significant impact on this present writer's thinking. And Brunner's treatment follows the order of prophet, priest, and king. Cf. Emil Brunner, *The Mediator*, (Philadelphia: The Westminster Press), p. 399 ff.
4. Deschner, *Christology*, p. 79.
5. Wesley, *N.T. Notes*, p. 11.

and what is His nature, who delivers the Sermon on the Mount? And in partial response to this question, Wesley affirms that this preacher is none other than:

"the Lord of heaven and earth, the Creator of all, who, as such, has a right to dispose of all his creatures; the Lord our Governor, whose kingdom is from everlasting, and ruleth over all; the great Lawgiver, who can well enforce all his laws, 'being able to save and to destroy'; yea, to punish with everlasting destruction from his presence and from the glory of his power."[1]

Second, what does the Lord teach? What is the heart of the message which he seeks to communicate? According to Wesley, Jesus Christ in this setting is fulfilling the prophetic office, completing its intent, by revealing the way to heaven. "He is teaching us the true way to life everlasting, the royal way which leads to the kingdom," Wesley observes, "And the only true way; for there is none besides — all other paths lead to destruction."[2] Again, the Redeemer's teaching is succinct, offering neither more nor less than He has received from the Father.[3] And it is corrective: that is, this teaching refutes the errors of the contemporary scribes and Pharisees as well as "all the practical mistakes that are inconsistent with salvation which should ever arise in the Christian Church."[4] In short, in terms of the past, our Lord's sermon fulfills the prior prophetic movement; in terms of the present, it instructs and corrects; and in terms of the future, it guides and encourages. There is no lack here.

Third, to whom is the Sermon on the Mount addressed? Not merely to the disciples alone. Otherwise, Wesley reasons, Jesus would have had no need to go "up into the mountain."[5] The crowds, the multitude surrounding the mount, are also instructed in the holy way. But the reach of Christ's teaching lies even beyond this larger assembly and includes, in Wesley's words, "all the children of men, the whole race of mankind."[6] This means, of course, that the wisdom expressed in the Sermon on the Mount does not constitute what are sometimes referred to as the "counsels of perfection" and which are, for that reason, limited to a spiritual elite. Instead, all may embark upon this path; meekness, peace-making, and even purity of heart are possibilities, through the grace of God, for everyone who believes. As there is no lack in this teaching, so also are none excluded.

And last, in what manner does Jesus Christ teach here? Though the Sermon on the Mount is similar to the Decalogue given at Mount Sinai, both expressing the nature of true religion and the worship of the one God, Wesley nevertheless

1. Outler, *Sermons*, 1:470 (Upon our Lord's Sermon on the Mount, Discourse the First)
2. Ibid.
3. Ibid., 1:470-71.
4. Ibid., 1:471. And some of the "practical mistakes" with respect to soteriology which Wesley encountered are quietism and antinomianism. For his comments and observations on the former see Outler's notes on the following pages: 1:214, 215, 380, 384, 392, 539, 545, and 604; for more on the latter see 1:219, 252, 323, 554, and 2:21.
5. Ibid., 1:471.
6. Ibid., 1:472.

calls attention to the differences between these discourses, especially in terms of their respective settings. At the Sermon on the Mount, for example, there is neither fire, darkness, tempest, thunder, nor a quaking mountain — all of which formed the backdrop of Sinai. Instead, Jesus speaks with such "amazing love," Wesley writes, "He now addresses us with his still, small voice."[1] The former address evoked the fear of the Lord; the latter a response of love.

Another way in which Wesley explores the prophetic office of Christ is to view the Savior not simply as a teacher, but also as a lawgiver. This may come as a surprise to those Protestants who, in the name of *sola fide*, have minimized the significance of the moral law, or worse yet, who have relegated it largely to the covenant of Moses — a covenant which has been surpassed by the grace of Christ. But the contrast need not be drawn so sharply. Though the new covenant is indeed superior to the old, Wesley never underestimates the continuing value of the moral law which was expressed under the old covenant. In fact, in this Anglican cleric's view, Christ affirms, teaches, and highlights the lasting significance of the moral law as revealed in the following:

> **Yet was it [the moral law] never so fully explained nor so thoroughly understood till the great Author of it himself [Christ] condescended to give mankind this authentic comment on all the essential branches of it; at the same time declaring it should never be changed, but remain in force to the end of the world.[2]**

However, Martin Luther often spoke of a "time of the law" and a "time of the gospel." Consequently, one of this German Reformer's central emphases was that the process of salvation entails a movement from the law to the gospel, but not really back again. Thus, he states in his *Lectures on Galatians*: "Then let the Law withdraw; for it was indeed added for the sake of disclosing and increasing transgressions, but only until the point when the offspring would come. Once He is present, let the Law stop.[3] Wesley, on the other hand, of course underscored

1. Ibid., 1:474

2. Ibid., 1:553. (Upon our Lord's Sermon on the Mount, Discourse the Fifth) Commenting on this specific sermon of Wesley's, Charles Dillman claims that although "love was central to Wesley's thought ... that principle is drowned out with an extreme legalism." However, in every place where Wesley underscores the law, he does so in terms of the rich grace of God as perhaps best revealed in his dictum, "faith working by love." Legalism, in actuality, is therefore a phantom charge, and indicates a lack of understanding of Wesley's vital doctrine of grace and the role which moral law plays *within* that context. Cf. Charles N. Dillman, "Wesley's Approach to the Law in Discourse V, on the Sermon on the Mount," *Wesleyan Theological Journal* 12 (Spring 1977), p. 64. Bracketed material is mine.

3. Martin Luther, *Luther's Works*, ed., Jaroslav Pelikan, Vol. 26: *Lectures on Galatians 1535* (Saint Louis: Concordia Publishing House, 1963), p. 317. Note also in these lectures that Luther offers only two uses, not three, in which the law serves (*duplex usus legis*): that is, a political use (*usus politicus*) and a theological one (usus theologicus). Moreover, this German reformer deemed the theological use (accusatory force, driving the believer to Christ) to be primary. Wesley and Calvin, on the other hand, have a fully developed third use (tertius usus) of the law whereby it guides, informs, and instructs concerning the contours of the Christian life. Such a *prescriptive* use is largely lacking in Luther's theology and is not listed among his other uses in the *Lectures on Galatians*. Cf. Kenneth J. Collins, "John Wesley's Theology of Law (Ph.D. dissertation, Drew University, 1984), p. 181-90.

the movement from the law to the gospel, but he did not leave it at that. Instead, he writes, "the law continually makes way for and points us to the gospel; ... [and] the gospel continually leads us to a more exact fulfilling of the law."[1] Both movements are affirmed; neither is minimized. Wesley elaborates:

> **From all this we may learn that there is no contrarity at all between the law and the gospel; that there is no need for the law to pass away in order to the establishing of the gospel. Indeed neither of them supersedes the other, but they agree perfectly well together. Yea, the very same words, considered in different respects, are parts both of the law and of the gospel. If they are considered as commandments, they are parts of the law: if as promises, of the gospel...the gospel being no other than the commands of the law proposed by way of promises.[2]**

Again, in a sermon which takes Matthew 5:17-20 as its principal text ("Anyone who breaks one of the least of these commandments and teaches others to do the same will be called the least in the kingdom of heaven") Wesley accentuates the role of Jesus as a lawgiver: "For did ever any may preach the law like him?... Can any 'preach the law' more expressly, more vigorously, than Christ does in these words?"[3] Therefore, the Methodist preachers under Wesley, both lay and ordained, were to "preach [the law] in its whole extent, to explain and enforce every part of it in the same manner, as our great Teacher did while upon earth."[4] Nothing less is gospel preaching.

Indeed, so concerned was Wesley with the specter of antinomianism (making void the law through faith) as he had experienced it in the joint Moravian - Methodist Society in Fetter Lane during July of 1740 that he took most every occasion to punctuate the grace of the gospel *and* the abiding nature of the moral law. Therefore, to make light of the law in the name of the gospel, to teach that less obedience is required now than before one believes, are conclusions that do not follow. "Nor indeed can anyone escape this charge," Wesley warns, "who preaches faith in any such manner as either directly or indirectly tends to set aside any branch of obedience; who preaches Christ so as to disannul or weaken in any wise the least of the commandments of God."[5]

One last point should be noted. From the preceding discussion, it should be apparent that Wesley never viewed the law in isolation, that is, as fuel for scrupulosity — that bane of spirituality — or for legalism. On the contrary, as Deschner notes as well, the Methodist leader attempted to provide, especially through the teaching and lawgiving roles of Christ, an "explicit Christological

·

1. Outler, *Sermons*, 1:554. (Upon Our Lord's Sermon on the Mount, Discourse the Fifth). Bracketed material is mine.

2. Ibid.

3. Ibid., 1:555.

4. Ibid., 2:34. (The Law Established through Faith, Discourse II) Bracketed material is mine.

5. Outler, *Sermons*, 1:559. (Upon Our Lord's Sermon on the Mount, Discourse the Fifth). For a further discussion of Wesley's rejection of antinomianism Cf. *A Blow at the Root or Christ Stabbed in the House of His Friends* in Jackson, *Wesley's Works*, 10:364-69.

foundation"[1] to his formulations. Christ is the "Author of the law,"[2] the "giver of the Decalogue to Moses,"[3] and at the end of time "will judge the world by the law."[4] Add to this Wesley's doctrine of grace in which the law is conceived as a blessed promise to be fulfilled in the life of the believer, as noted earlier, and the picture which begins to emerge is one of balance and nuance — one which avoids the Scylla of Fetter Lane solafidianism (enlarging faith out of all proportion) on the one hand, and the Charybdis of legalism and self-justification on the other.

B. Priest

The priestly office of Christ, according to Wesley, embraces two major roles: sacrifice and intercession. For example, in his sermon, *The Law Established Through Faith: Discourse II*, produced in 1750, he writes: "to preach him [Christ] ... as our great High Priest ... reconciling us to God by his blood, and ever living to make intercession for us," is the principal task of a gospel preacher.[5] And elsewhere, in his *Letter to a Roman Catholic*, written a year earlier in 1749, Wesley declares: "he was a Priest, who gave himself [as] a sacrifice for sin, and still makes intercession for transgressors."[6] In addition, it should be noted that the latter role of intercession is dependent upon the prior work of sacrifice. Jesus Christ can intercede on the world's behalf precisely because He sacrificed Himself even unto death.

One of Wesley's favorite ways of considering the priestly office of Christ was to view it anthropologically: that is, from a human perspective, in terms of people's needs. Here, in a few sermons written during the 1780's, Christ surfaces as "the remedy" provided for the disease of sin. "Behold then both the justice and mercy of God," Wesley exclaims, "... And his mercy in providing an universal remedy for an universal evil!"[7] Again, "Here is a remedy provided for all our guilt, here is a remedy for all our disease, all the corruption of our nature."[8] Naturally, Wesley's images of disease and remedy easily led to a discussion of Christ as the great Physician, especially in his sermon *The Mystery of Iniquity*.[9] However, one of his clearest expressions of this teaching is found in an early manuscript sermon, *The Trouble and Rest of Good Men*, produced in 1735, in which it is affirmed:

The whole world is indeed, in its present state, only one great infirmary: ... And for this very end the great Physician of souls is continu-

1. Deschner, *Christology*, p. 101.
2. Ibid., p. 100.
3. Ibid., p. 101.
4. Ibid.
5. Outler, *Sermons*, 2:37. (The Law Established through Faith: Discourse II) Bracketed material is mine.
6. Jackson, *Wesley's Works*, 10:81. Bracketed material is mine.
7. Outler, *Sermons*, 2:411. (On the Fall of Man)
8. Ibid., 2:410.
9. Ibid., 2:452. (The Mystery of Iniquity)

ally present with them, marking all the diseases of every soul, and giving medicines to heal its sickness.[1]

1. Wesley's Doctrine of the Atonement

Whether Wesley is describing the sacrificial or the intercessory roles of Christ, the reader of his homilies cannot fail to be impressed with the voice of Scripture that permeates these discussions. To be sure, it seems that Wesley took great pains to develop his doctrine of the Atonement precisely in terms of a biblical vocabulary. And the following passage is typical of his language and style:

> Unless then many had been made sinners by the disobedience of one ... there would have been no occasion for his 'being obedient unto death, even the death of the cross' (Phil. 2:8).... Neither could we then have said, 'God was in Christ reconciling the world unto himself; (2 Cor. 5:19) or that he 'made him to be sin for us who knew no sin, that we might be made the righteousness of God through him.' (2 Cor. 5:21.)[2]

Beyond this, Wesley appealed to the doctrinal formulations of his own church, especially as reflected in *The Book of Common Prayer*. In his sermon *God's Love to Fallen Man*, for instance, he declares: "But we could not have loved him as 'bearing our sins in his own body on the tree,' and by that one oblation of himself once offered making a full oblation, sacrifice, and satisfaction for the sins of the whole world.'"[3] Compare this with the language of Wesley's *Sunday Service* which followed *The Book of Common Prayer* in considerable detail:

> Almighty God, our heavenly Father, who, of thy tender mercy, didst give thine only Son Jesus Christ to suffer death upon the cross for our redemption; who made there (by his oblation of himself once offered) a full, perfect, and sufficient sacrifice, oblation, and satisfaction for the sins of the whole world;..."[4]

And this exact language, which functions as a kind of formula for Wesley, is likewise found in his sermons, *The End of Christ's Coming* and *Spiritual Worship*.[5]

But just what does this language mean? What does it suggest about Wesley's view of the atonement? First of all, the terms "full" and "perfect" reveal that Christ's sacrifice is not partial, but complete; not imperfect — requiring yet further work but perfect, needing no addition or repetition. And commenting on

---

1. Ibid., 3:533. (The Trouble and Rest of Good Men)
2. Ibid., 2:425. (God's Love to Fallen Man) The material in parenthesis is mine. An interesting project in the field of Wesley studies would be to explore the English evangelical's use of Scripture in his theological writings. One study in particular that interests this present writer is Wesley's use of 1 John as he explores the doctrine of salvation in his sermons. The references are simply too numerous not to receive at least some treatment at the hand of Methodist scholars.
3. Ibid., 2:427.
4. John Wesley, *Sunday Service*, p. 135-36.
5. Cf. *The End of Christ's Coming*, 2:480; and, *Spiritual Worship*, 3:93.

John 30:19 ("It is finished"), the Methodist leader reveals that the suffering of Christ *purchased* humanity's redemption.[1] There is no further price to pay.

Second, the language of "sufficient sacrifice and oblation" as found in his *Sunday Service* not only underscores, once again, the adequacy of this work, but it also demonstrates that the atonement is a sacrifice, that the loss of a great and inestimable value is involved here. "God made him who had no sin to be sin for us, so that in him we might become the righteousness of God" (2 Cor 5:21). Accordingly, the reconciliation of God and humanity comes at a great price. Forgiveness, then, though it is marked by grace and love is neither cheap nor easy: it requires nothing less than the death of the only begotten Son of God.[2]

Third, the life and death of Christ, for Wesley, entails a "satisfaction for the sins of the whole world" 1 John 2:2. Actually, the exact word for satisfaction used in this verse, and the one which Wesley read in his Bible, is "propitiation." Many modern biblical scholars, however, translate the original Greek term, ἱλασμος (hilasmos) not as satisfaction or propitiation, but as "expiation." The Revised Standard Version, for instance, reads: "and he is the expiation for our sin, and not for ours only but also for the sins of the whole world." But Wesley much preferred the term propitiation to that of expiation. Thus, in his sermon, *On Working Out Our Own Salvation* he declares that Jesus Christ gave himself to be "'a propitiation for the sins of the whole world.'"[3] And elsewhere, in his *Mystery of Iniquity* the Oxford fellow uses exactly the same language.[4]

Continuing this line of thought, many modern commentators reject the term propitiation because it suggests the idea of an angry God, that the punitive justice of the Most High must be satisfied before reconciliation can take place. However, such a theological and exegetical judgment, the removal of all anger from the Godhead, is not indicative of Wesley's thinking on this matter as revealed in a letter which he wrote to Mary Bishop in 1778, part of which reads as follows:

> But it is certain, had God never been angry, He could never have been reconciled. So that, in affirming this, Mr. Law strikes at the very root of the atonement, and finds a very short method of converting Deists. Although, therefore, I do not term God, as Mr. Law supposes, 'a wrathful Being,' which conveys a wrong idea; yet I firmly believe He was angry with all mankind, and that He was reconciled to them by the death of His Son. And I know He was angry with me till I believed in the Son of His love.[5]

1. Wesley, *N.T. Notes*, p. 268. Bracketed material is mine.

2. Most people are familiar with the maxim, "To err is human; to forgive divine." However, this proverb must not issue in the notion — as so often happens — that forgiveness is expected, that it can be counted on, that we can, therefore, take the grace of God, which comes at a significant sacrifice, for granted. There is no warrant for this "cheap grace" — to borrow a phrase from Bonhoeffer — either in the Bible or in Wesley's writings.

3. Outler, *Sermons*, 3:200. (On Working Out Our Own Salvation)

4. Ibid., 2:452. (The Mystery of Iniquity)

5. John Telford, ed., *The Letters of John Wesley, A.M.* 8 vols. (London: The Epworth Press, 1931), 6:298.

Wesley, however, does not mistake divine anger for human wrath, as is so often done. The anger of humanity, for instance, is often wild, animated, and vengeful — consumed in hateful passions that are anything but holy. God's anger, on the other hand, is not like this. Consequently, Wesley cautions his readers that the "wrath" of the Most High must never be confused with human anger nor, more importantly, conceived apart from His love — a love which remains His "darling, his reigning attribute."[1] Indeed, God's punitive anger, which in one sense is a function of His justice, grows out of and can only be understood in terms of the divine love. Wesley cautions:

> **Is not wrath a human passion? And how can this human passion be in God? We may answer this by another question: is not love a human passion? And how can this human passion be in God? But to answer directly: wrath in man, and so love in man, is a human passion. But wrath in God is not a human passion; nor is love, as it is in God. Therefore the inspired writers ascribe both the one and the other to God, *only in an analogical sense.*[2]**

And this relation which Wesley establishes between divine love and wrath can also be viewed in the other direction: that is, the love of God itself is not properly appreciated except in terms of divine wrath. Both characteristics, then, are to be seen in tandem. And such an association keeps Wesley's notion of God's love free from both sentimentality and indulgence. In short, as the sacrifice of the atonement is costly, so also is the love of God which is revealed through it.

In a real sense, Wesley's doctrine of the atonement in its emphasis on penal substitution is similar to the satisfaction theory of Anselm of Canterbury first put forth in the eleventh century. The heart of this medieval theory may be summarized as follows:

> **1. Humanity ought to make satisfaction for sin but cannot. (Men and women owe all their obedience to God anyway, so there is nothing "extra" to offer up to satisfy for past sins.)**

> **2. God can make satisfaction for sin, but ought not. (Since God has not sinned.)**

Therefore

> **3. Only the God/Man both can and ought to make satisfaction for sin.[3]**

Compare the first premise of this syllogism with Wesley's description of human inability to bring about the atonement in the following selection:

> **How shall he pay him that he oweth? Were he from this moment to perform the most perfect obedience to every command of God, this**

1. Wesley, *N. T. Notes*, p. 637.
2. Ibid., p. 374. Emphasis is mine.
3. I acknowledge debt to Joseph M. Colleran for this perceptive syllogism. Cf. Joseph M. Colleran, trans., *Cur Deus Homo* (Albany, New York: Magi Books) p. 27.

would make no amends for a single sin, for any one act of past disobedience: seeing he owes God all the service he is able to perform from this moment to all eternity.[1]

Moreover, Wesley continues in an Anselmic vein in a letter to William Law in 1756 where he writes: "Is not man here represented as having contracted a debt with God which he cannot pay? and God as having, nevertheless a right to insist upon payment of it?"[2] This and other kinds of language have led Lindström to the conclusion that "orthodox satisfaction would seem to be the dominant conception in [Wesley's] view of atonement ... the legal order and the judicial system emerge as the governing principle."[3] Likewise, Deschner maintains that "penal satisfaction, not victory, is emphasized when Wesley thinks of the atonement."[4]

Though these judgments just cited are accurate, it would be a mistake to conclude that Wesley's understanding of the atonement cannot resonate with other major views such as the moral influence theory first put forth by Abelard. Thus, for example, in his sermon *On the Fall of Man* Wesley highlights the consequences, the "subjective effects," which the display of God's sacrificial love has on the believer:

We may now attain both higher degrees of holiness and higher degrees of glory than it would have been possible for us to attain if Adam had not sinned. For if Adam had not sinned, the Son of God had not died. Consequently, that amazing instance of the love of God to man had never existed which has in all ages excited the highest joy, and love, and gratitude from his children.[5]

Nevertheless, both Lindström and Deschner are correct, penal substitution in some form or other was, in the end, the motif to which Wesley continually returned.[6] But penal substitution itself can be understood in a number of ways, and so here a few distinctions are in order. First of all, for Wesley, Christ was a substitute for us "only in suffering punishment, not in His fulfilling of the law."[7] Or to use Deschner's words, "God's positive justice is never judged as 'satis-

1. Outler, *Sermons*, 1:478. (Upon Our Lord's Sermon on the Mount, Discourse the First)

2. Telford, *Letters*, 3:352.

3. Harald Lindström , *Wesley and Sanctification* (Wilmore, Kentucky: Francis Asbury Publishing Co., Inc.,), p. 61. Bracketed material is mine.

4. Deschner, *Christology*, p. 121. Note also that Deschner is correct in pointing out that Wesley rejected the idea that Christ descended into hell and the Methodist leader, therefore, "omitted reference to it from his Twenty-five Articles." Cf. p. 50-51.

5. Outler, *Sermons*, 2:411-12.

6. Several Methodist scholars have suggested that Wesley's views on the atonement may be Grotian: that is, involving not a satisfaction to an internal principle in God (love, justice) but involving the maintenance of the necessities of the government of the universe. For a discussion which argues why Wesley's views are not Grotian Cf. William Cannon, *The Theology of John Wesley* (Nashville: Abingdon Press, 1946), p. 209.

7. Lindström , Sanctification, p. 73.

fied,' i.e., the positive demand of the law is never, strictly speaking, fulfilled."[1] Again, though Christ suffered the penalty for our past sins, He did not fulfill the moral law for us. The fulfillment of the law, then, occurs not in justification by means of imputation, but in the process of sanctification through cooperation with the rich grace of God. In fact, so concerned was Wesley with the threat of antinomianism (making void the law through faith) that he deleted key passages in Cranmer's *Homily on Salvation* when he reproduced this work in his own sermons. The Archbishop of Canterbury, for example, wrote:

> **In these places the apostle toucheth especially three things which must go together in our justification: upon God's part, his great mercy and grace: upon Christ's part, the satisfaction of God's justice by the offering his body and shedding his blood, with the fulfilling of the law perfectly and thoroughly; and upon our part, true and lively faith in the merits of Jesus Christ....He for them fulfilled the law in his life, so that now in him and by him every Christian may be called a fulfiller of the law, forasmuch as that which their infirmity lacked, Christ's [righteousness] hath supplied.[2]**

But Wesley edits this material in his sermon *The Lord Our Righteousness* and the following is all that remains of the original passage:

> **These things must necessarily go together in our justification: upon God's part his great mercy and grace, upon Christ's part the satisfaction of God's justice .... and on our part faith in the merits of [Jesus] Christ...**
> **..**
> **..[3]**

Second, though Wesley considered both the active (incarnation, life, and ministry) and the passive (death on the cross) righteousness of Christ to be entailed in the work of atonement,[4] his fear of the depreciation of the moral law and holiness, which often result from overemphasizing certain aspects of the active righteousness (Christ fulfilled the law for us), kept his own emphasis on the passive righteousness of Christ. "Though Wesley can include both the active and passive

---

1. Deschner, *Christology*, p. 175.

2. Albert Outler ed., *John Wesley* (New York: Oxford University Press, 1964), p. 125-26.

3. Outler, *Sermons*, 1:456. (The Lord Our Righteousness) I am dependent, in part, on Deschner for this insight. Cf. Deschner, *Christology*, p. 210-211. Notice that Wesley was willing "to correct" his own Anglican tradition on occasion. Not only did he at times mute the language of the Homilies, but he edited out what he found troubling in the *Thirty-Nine Articles* as well. Cf. Paul Blankenship, "The Significance of John Wesley's Abridgment of the Thirty-Nine Articles as Seen from His Deletions." *Methodist History* 2, 3 (April 1964) 35-47. Moreover, this editorial tendency is problematic especially for those scholars who wish to paint Wesley as "Mr. Anglican Church." The dotted lines in the passage 1:456 are mine in order to indicate omissions.

4. Ibid., *Sermons*, 1:453.

obedience of Christ in the work of atonement," Lindström writes, "the stress nevertheless lies on the latter."[1] In a similar vein, Deschner observes that "Wesley's dislike of the antinomian understanding of imputed holiness ... led him to play down Christ's active obedience."[2] In fact, so concerned was the Anglican cleric in this area that he cautioned his followers — indeed pleaded with them — along the following lines:

> **Warn them against making 'Christ the minister of sin'! Against making void that solemn decree of God, 'without holiness no man shall see the Lord,' by a vain imagination of being holy in Christ. O warn them that if they remain unrighteous, the righteousness of Christ will profit them nothing.**[3]

In short, Wesley understood the atonement as not only providing the basis for the forgiveness of sins (justification) through the sacrificial and substitutionary death of Christ, but also as providing the foundation for the holy life, the actual and inherent restoration of the image of God in the believer through grace. And this last aspect, interestingly enough, is yet another way in which Wesley highlights the never-to-be-minimized process of sanctification. Here, as elsewhere in Wesley's theology, it is a matter of justification (forgiveness) by faith *and* holy living (renewal).

C. King

The kingly office of Christ embraces three principal roles, that of lawgiver, victor, and sanctifier, as revealed in the following homiletical material:

> **To preach Christ as a workman that needeth not to be ashamed is to preach him ... as remaining a King for ever; as *giving laws* to all whom he has brought with his blood; as *restoring* those to the image of God whom he had first reinstated in his favour; as *reigning* in all believing**

---

1. Lindström, *Sanctification*, p. 72-73. In describing Wesley's conception of the atonement Williams observes: "If in faith we rely upon the merit of Christ's atonement, we are taken out of the covenant of works and the order of merit into the covenant of grace and the order of faith. The Christian is no longer judged on a legal basis." (p.85) However, Wesley actually states that all people are under a gracious covenant; the only one ever under a covenant of works was Adam. The Methodist leader explains: "The Apostle does not here oppose the covenant given by Moses to the covenant given by Christ....But it is the covenant of grace which God through Christ hath established with men in all ages ... which St. Paul here opposes to the covenant of *works*, made with Adam in paradise." (The Righteousness of Faith) 1:202-03. Moreover, when Williams notes, in addition, that "the Christian is no longer judged on a legal basis," (p. 85) there is a certain sense in which this is true; nevertheless, for Wesley, at least, the moral law *will be* the standard at the judgment seat of Christ as Deschner correctly points out (p. 100); it has not faded away. Indeed, in answering those who spoke evil of this law, Wesley wrote on one occasion: "So thou hast set thyself in the judgment-seat of Christ, and cast down the rule whereby he will judge the world." (Original, Nature, Property, and Use of the Law) 2:18.

2. Deschner, *Christology*, p. 167.

3. Outler, *Sermons*, 1:463 (The Lord Our Righteousness)

**hearts until he has subdued all things to; until he hath utterly cast out
all sin, and brought in everlasting righteousness.[1]**

Deschner, on the other hand, has considered only two of these roles: namely, that
of sanctifier and victor, and the work of Christ as lawgiver, as an instance of His
kingship, is simply left out.[2] Granted, Wesley seldom mentions this third aspect
as an instance of the royal work; nevertheless, it is apparent in a few of his writings and for that reason must be included in any discussion of this nature. For as
Creator and Governor, the same Christ who spoke the words, "Let there be light,"
as noted earlier, is also the origin of the moral law, and in the exercise of His
royal function, its chief proclaimer. Thus, Christ's relation to the law cannot be
thoroughly explored simply by appealing to His prophetic work; the kingly must
be included as well.

The second principal role of Christ's royal work, that of victory, entails conquering the evils which plague the human community. "Christ, when he engaged
with these enemies," Wesley writes, "first conquered Satan; then sin, ... and lastly death in his resurrection."[3] Concerning this first liberating activity, Wesley
maintains that Christ defeated Satan by dissolving "the dominion and power
which [he] had over us through our sins."[4] Observe, however, that here Satan
has neither rights nor is he owed a debt, as some of the early Church Fathers had
maintained, but simply has raw evil power — a power, however, which is ultimately destroyed by Christ Himself.

In addition, Christ's triumph includes conquering death by the power of his
resurrection, as well as destroying death's fearful rule over the minds of believers. "Every man who fears death is subject to bondage; is in a slavish, uncom-
fortable state," Wesley notes, "But [Christ] delivers all true believers from this
bondage."[5] However, it should be added that though Christ conquers death and
the fear of it for believers, He never enters hell. The crucifixion, apparently, is
the lowest point of the incarnational movement according to Wesley. Christ
entered Hades "which is the receptacle of separate spirits,"[6] but He never entered
a place of torment (more on this in the chapter on eschatology).

The last component of the victory motif, that is, conquering sin and bringing
about moral and spiritual renewal, actually overlaps with the third major kingly
office, that of sanctifier, and so the two will be treated together. On this head,
Wesley writes in his sermon *The End of Christ's Coming*:

> **At the same time the Son of God strikes at the root of that grand
> work of the devil, pride; causing the sinner to humble himself before**

---

1. Ibid., 2:38. (The Law Established through Faith, Discourse II) Emphasis is mine.
2. Deschner, *Christology*, p. 75.
3. Wesley, *N.T. Notes*, p. 442.
4. Ibid., p. 518. Bracketed material is mine.
5. Ibid., p. 568. Bracketed material is mine.
6. Outler, *Sermons*, 4:189. (On Faith) And elsewhere Wesley affirms: "But it does not appear, that
ever our Lord went into hell. His soul, when it was separated from the body, did not go thither, but
to paradise." Cf. Wesley, *N.T. Notes*, p. 279.

the Lord, to abhor himself as it were in dust and ashes. He strikes at the root of self-will, enabling the humbled sinner to say in all things, 'Not as I will, but as thou wilt.' He destroys the love of the world, delivering them that believe in him from every foolish and hurtful desire'; from 'the desire of the flesh, the desire of the eyes, and the pride of life.[1]

Beyond this, Wesley declares in his commentary on Matthew 1:16 that "we want Christ in his royal character to reign in our hearts, and subdue all things to himself."[2] And in his sermon *The Repentance of Believers* he adds:

"a deep conviction of our utter helplessness ... teaches us truly to live upon Christ by faith ... as our King. Hereby we are brought to magnify him, indeed, to give him all the glory of his grace, to make him a whole Christ, an entire Saviour, and truly to set the crown upon his head."[3]

In other words, the victory motif, according to Wesley, is not so much associated with Christ's priestly work, that is, with what He does for us (justification), as it is with his kingly work, what He does in us as a Savior and Sanctifier (sanctification).[4] How is this to be understood? Recall that real change, the impartation of holiness as opposed to its imputation, the transformation of human dispositions and affections, as well as growth in love towards God and neighbor, were all favorably apprised by Wesley as a young man, and increasingly so throughout the remainder of his career. It is not astonishing to learn, then, that these emphases influenced his Christology to a considerable degree and gave it a flavor much different from that of others.

Moreover, though Wesley does indeed underscore the elements of sanctification in his Christology, he never neglects the significance of justification. Accordingly, justification is ever the basis of sanctification in his writings, and these two works, therefore, should always be viewed in association. In fact, Wesley's favorite Christological text amply demonstrates the fullness and sufficiency of Christ's salvific work by tying together these two broad, gracious movements: Jesus Christ is our "wisdom, and righteousness, *and* [our] sanctification and redemption"[5] (KJV). In His person, then, are united the graces sufficient for the restoration of humanity; through His work provision has been made for both pardon and renewal; and by His grace may all be redeemed. Little wonder Wesley's Christology was so reverential.

---

1. Ibid., 2:481. (The End of Christ's Coming) Though Wesley by and large is treating the priestly role of Christ in this sermon, this material is also descriptive of the Savior's kingly functions.

2. Wesley, *N. T. Notes*, p. 11.

3. Outler, *Sermons*, 1:352. (The Repentance of Believers)

4. Deschner, *Christology*, p. 72.

5. This text was a favorite of Wesley's as demonstrated by the number of times it surfaced in his sermons. For a complete listing of these references Cf. Outler, *Sermons*, 4:674.

CHAPTER THREE

THE DOCTRINE OF THE HOLY SPIRIT
"I believe in the Holy Spirit..."

One of the more intriguing characteristics of the Christian faith, that which
sets it apart from mere ideology and a simple subscription to doctrine, is its
emphasis on the Holy Spirit — a conscious, active, willful, and directing person.
Indeed, the believer's understanding of the fact of Christ's death, for instance, is
not purely a casual reminiscence of a past event, like noting that Cicero died in
43 B.C., but instead is filled out and given meaningful depth by the present activity of the Spirit of God. Christians, in other words, are not left to the limits of
nature, reason, or the best that their religious imaginations have to offer. Rather,
in contemplating the crucifixion and other spiritual truths, they often encounter a
subtle, mysterious, other: a Spirit, a Real Presence, who glorifies Christ and who
makes these and other truths known in a way that goes beyond human expression.

During the eighteenth century, an age that took special note of the earlier
excesses of the Puritans, Quakers, and Ranters,[1] it became increasingly difficult
to show, in a convincing way, the importance of the testimony, fruits, and gifts of
the Spirit. Such emphases were often met with the charge of enthusiasm or
fanaticism by a learned, overly rational, and well-positioned Anglican clergy.
For example, on this topic, Wesley sparred with Joseph Butler who penned the
famous *Analogy of Religion*, Edmund Gibson who was then the bishop of London, and Rev. Charles Wheatly who painted the Methodists, among other things,
as "rapturous enthusiasts."[2] Yet Wesley remained undaunted in the face of these
attacks and continued to preach in a way that underscored the activity of the Holy
Spirit, not as some impersonal force or energy, but as a Spiritual Counselor who
is to be sought and, more importantly, obeyed. And it was precisely this emphasis on the Spirit which kept the Oxonian's life and thought beyond the shoals of
dead orthodoxy and formalism. Simply put, for Wesley, Christianity consists in
neither the mere assent to propositions nor in correct ritual practice; instead, it

---

1. Albert C. Outler, ed., *The Works of John Wesley*, *The Sermons* 4 vols. (Nashville: Abingdon
Press, 1984), 2:44.
2. Ibid., p. 45.

entails a graciously transformed life — a life lived in the power and presence of a Holy God.

I. The Person of the Holy Spirit

A. Trinitarian Formulations

One of the chief ways in which Wesley explored the doctrine of the Holy Spirit was in terms of a Trinitarian context, that is, in terms of both Jesus Christ and the Father. "I know there are *three* that bear record in heaven," the Anglican cleric writes, "the Father, the Word, and the Holy Spirit, and that these three are one."[1] At times, this Three-One language appears in the homilies at the end as a kind of brief doxology as in the sermon, *Knowing Christ After the Flesh* which reads: "to the Three-One God, Father, Son, and Spirit, world without end!"[2] At other times, however, as in his commentary on 1 John 5:8, Wesley underscores the unity of the Spirit with the Father and the Son, and observes that all three are of the one same nature, that they are — to use the technical language — consubstantial. He elaborates:

> *And these three are one* — Even as those two, the Father and the Son, are one, John x, 30. Nothing can separate the Spirit from the Father and the Son. If he were not one with the Father and the Son, the apostle ought to have said, the Father and the Word (who are one) and the Spirit are two. But this is contrary to the whole tenor of revelation. It remains, that these three are one. They are one in essence, in knowledge, in will, and in their testimony.[3]

The last line just cited is particularly significant in revealing Wesley's thinking on this score. In this passage, for example, the Holy Spirit is presented as one in essence with the Father and the Son and consequently is truly and fully divine — which means, of course, that there is no hint of subordinationism (the Spirit is somewhat less than the Father or Son) here. Again, the Spirit is one in knowledge; there is nothing hidden from His domain, vision, or competence. And last, the Three are One both in will and testimony; that is, there is no division or contradiction within the Godhead; all aim at the very same goal and purpose.

Yet another way in which Wesley highlighted the unity of the Spirit with the Father and the Son — which among other things kept his thought free from all charges of polytheism — was in terms of the divine love itself, God's reigning attribute. He notes in an early manuscript sermon:

1. Ibid., 4:31 (The Discoveries of Faith) A case can be made for exploring the doctrine of the Trinity under the doctrine of God. However, since Wesley like the early church realized that the doctrine of the Trinity emerges out of a consideration of the new testament revelation of and witness to the deity of the Son *and* the Holy Spirit — that it is, in a sense, a historical construct, though Biblically based — then the Trinity is perhaps best handled within the present context.

2. Ibid., 4:106. (Knowing Christ After the Flesh)

3. John Wesley, *Explanatory Notes Upon the New Testament* (Salem, Ohio: Schmul Publishers), p. 639-40.

Unto God the Father, who first loved us, and made us accepted in the Beloved; unto God the Son, who loved us, and washed us from our own sins in his blood; unto God the Holy Ghost, who sheddeth the love of God abroad in our hearts, be all love and all glory for time and for eternity.[1]

In light of the proceeding, it is apparent that Wesley's doctrine of the Holy Spirit and his understanding of the Trinity were orthodox and, to a large extent, traditional. Accordingly, his thought moved easily down the early corridors of Nicea and Chalcedon. In addition, Wesley clearly had no trouble in affirming the first of the Anglican *Thirty-Nine Articles* entitled, "Of Faith in the Holy Trinity," which he later reprinted for American Methodist consumption in his *Sunday Service*. Nevertheless, in this area, though Wesley greatly appreciated the historic creeds of the church, whether it was the Nicene or Athanasian confession, he never claimed that believers would be damned if they did not assent to their exact formulations. "I insist upon no explication at all;" he declares, "no, not even on the best I ever saw I mean that which is given us in the creed commonly ascribed to Athanasius." More to the point, the Methodist leader adds: "I am far from saying, he who does not assent to this 'shall without doubt perish everlastingly.'"[2]

Likewise, though Wesley often employed the Three-One language which is the staple of Trinitarian formulas, he never insisted on, as John Calvin did to the demise of Servetus,[3] the precise use of the term "Trinity" (or the term "person" for that matter) even though he himself used it on occasion in his writings.[4] In his sermon *On the Trinity*, produced in 1775, Wesley explains:

I dare not insist upon anyone's using the word 'Trinity' or 'Person.' I use them myself without any scruple, because I know of none better.

1. Outler, *Sermons*, 4:345. (The Love of God)
2. Ibid., 2:377. (On the Trinity)
3. Ibid., 4:289. (The Promise of Understanding) In this unpublished manuscript sermon Wesley writes: "To him who dwelleth in the light which no mortal can approach to, whom flesh and blood hath not seen nor can see, to the ever-blessed Trinity, be glory and praise, might and majesty, now and for ever!"
4. One of the more disappointing chapters in Protestant history entails the treatment of Michael Servetus, a well-known anti-Trinitarian, at the hands of the Genevan courts. Servetus had the supreme misfortune of not only denying a doctrine cherished by the majority of Christians, but he also wrote against Calvin's *Institutes of the Christian Religion* in his own *Restitutio Christianismi*. Not surprisingly, while Servetus was in Geneva in 1553 — he was simply passing through — he was arrested at Calvin's demand who subsequently composed a list of accusations. On 27 October 1553, the unfortunate man was condemned to death, though Calvin requested that Servetus be spared burning at the stake and be summarily beheaded instead. But after one more painful encounter with Calvin, Servetus was in fact burned, and when the flames hit his face he screamed in agony until his death nearly half an hour later. This violation of Christian love and decency did not go unnoticed by modern secular historians. Will Durant, for example, in his mammoth work *The Story of Civilization*, concludes the section on John Calvin with this last observation: "We are grateful to be so reassured, and we will agree that even error lives because it serves some vital need. But we shall always find it hard to love the man who darkened the human soul with the most absurd and blasphemous conception of God in all the long and honored history of nonsense." Cf. T.H.L. Parker, *John Calvin* (Philadelphia: The Westminster Press, 1975), p. 121-23; and Will Durant, *The Story of Civilization* Vol. VI. *The Reformation* (New York: Simon and Schuster, 1957), p. 490.

But if any man has any scruple concerning them, who shall constrain him to use them? I cannot; much less would I burn a man alive — and that with moist, green wood — for saying, 'though I believe the Father is God, the Son is God, and the Holy Ghost is God, yet I scruple using the words 'Trinity' and 'Persons' because I do not find those terms in the Bible.[1]

Once again, Wesley's idiom was informed by his rich and impressive knowledge of Scripture. The language he prefers, therefore, the phrases on which he does insist, are not drawn from creeds or from church tradition, though his thought clearly resonates with them, but from the pages of the Bible itself. To be sure, Wesley's favorite way of referring to the Trinity was in terms of the expression already encountered: "There are three that bear record in heaven, the Father, the Word, and the Holy Ghost: and these three are one."(I John 5:7)[2] "I would insist only on the direct words unexplained," he adds, "just as they lie in the text."[3]

Clearly, Wesley's caution concerning Trinitarian language predisposed the revival leader to look askance at much of the speculation which surrounded this doctrine throughout the history of the church. Consequently, just how the Three are truly One is a question which the Methodist leader never really asked. "The Bible," he writes, "barely requires you to believe such *facts*, not the manner of them.... the mystery does not lie in the *fact*, but altogether in the *manner*.[4] And Wesley also points out in his sermon *On the Trinity* that it would be absurd for him to deny the fact of the Three-One God which has been revealed in Scripture, because he cannot understand the manner of it, which of course has not been revealed.[5]

However, Wesley's reluctance to insist on the precise words "Trinity" or "person" coupled with his distaste for speculation about the manner of what is disclosed in revelation should not be interpreted as evidence of theological laxity. It is quite the contrary. Though the Methodist evangelist was tolerant in terms of purely human theological constructions, created to come to terms with these important truths, he knew full well that the "Three-One God" — a phrase actually borrowed from his father Samuel — is "interwoven with all true Christian faith, with all vital religion."[6] In short, the Christian life is simply impossible without the Three-One God. And Wesley elaborates on this point late in his career:

1. Outler, *Sermons*, 2:377-78. (On the Trinity) As anyone who has ever read large portions of Wesley's works knows, the Methodist leader was not above sarcasm as evidenced by his use of the phrase "merciful John Calvin" in the same paragraph in which the fate of Servetus was discussed. Cf. 2:378.
2. Ibid.
3. Ibid.
4. Ibid., 2:383. For a thorough and penetrating treatment of the doctrine of the trinity, especially in terms of its creedal expressions Cf. J. Kenneth Grider, "The Holy Trinity: the Triune God," in *A Contemporary Wesleyan Theology*, ed. Charles Carter 2 Vols. (Grand Rapids, Michigan: Francis Asbury Press, 1983) 1:375-408.
5. Outler, *Sermons*, 2:384.
6. Ibid., 2:385. Outler indicates that the phrase "Three-One God" was found in Samuel's *Life of Christ*. Cf. note # 35.

> But I know not how anyone can be a Christian believer till he hath (as St. John speaks) 'the witness in himself'; till 'the Spirit of God witnesses with his spirit that he is a child of God' — that is, in effect, till God the Holy Ghost witnesses that God the Father has accepted him through the merits of God the Son — and having this witness he honours the Son and the blessed Spirit 'even as he honours the Father.'[1]

For Wesley, then, the threeness and the oneness of God must be affirmed simultaneously, without contradiction, and — almost but not quite — without comment.

B. The Filioque Clause

There were many differences between the Eastern and Western churches — doctrinal, political, and ecclesiastical — when they finally divided in 1054. One of the chief points of contention concerned the matter of the procession of the Holy Spirit as revealed in Scripture and as displayed in the early ecumenical creeds. The original Nicene creed, for instance, read: "And [I believe] in the Holy Ghost, the Lord and Giver of Life: who proceedeth from the Father..."[2] In time, however, the West saw fit to add the phrase "and from the Son" (the Latin is "filioque") to indicate the dual procession of the Spirit. The East, on the other hand, maintained that the Holy Spirit proceeded *from* the Father and *through* the Son.

Though at first glance, it appears as if this is simply an arcane theological point, actually some remarkable theology emerges out of a consideration of these two positions. Wesley for his part, being the good Anglican that he was, basically affirmed the position of the West. In his commentary on John 15:26, for example, he first of all notes that "the Spirit's coming and being sent by our Lord from the Father to testify of him [Christ)] are personal characters [sic], and plainly distinguish him from the Father and the Son."[3] In other words, though Wesley did not insist on the language of "person" in exploring the distinctiveness of each of the Three, he himself felt quite comfortable with and utilized this vocabulary. The Holy Spirit *is* a person just like the Father and Son are persons. Moreover, that the Holy Spirit proceeds from the Son, as well as from the Father, "may be fairly argued," Wesley writes, "from his being called *the Spirit of Christ*, 1 Pet. i, 11; and from his being here said to be sent by Christ from the Father."[4] Indeed, to argue otherwise, to fail to see the procession of the Spirit from both the

---

1. Ibid.
2. Philip Schaff, ed., *The Creeds of Christendom* 3 vols. (Grand Rapids, Michigan: Baker Book House, 1983), 2:59.
3. Wesley, *N.T. Notes*, p. 259. Bracketed material is mine.
4. Ibid. Sometimes the ascription of personality to God is seen as an instance of anthropomorphism — of ascribing human characteristics and traits to the Divine Being. But actually the process is quite the reverse: God is the true person and we as His creatures come to an understanding of the dignity of our own personhood only through the knowledge and love of God. For another example of Wesley's assent to the filioque clause, see his letter to Mrs. Cook on 3 November 1789 in John Telford, ed., *The Letters of John Wesley, A.M.* 8 vols. (London: The Epworth Press, 1931), 8:183.

Father and the Son would unnecessarily separate the Son from the Spirit with the result that the unity and harmony of the Godhead would be marred. Wesley's position then was not simply a rallying point for his own theological tradition, but represented his best judgment concerning some vital and difficult theological matters.

It should also be noted at this point that the Trinitarian issue and the question of the filioque clause have been considered not really as ends in themselves — though they are interesting subjects in their own right — but as a means to come to some understanding of Wesley's doctrine of the Holy Spirit. And this approach has, in fact, been informative.

In summary, on the one hand, Wesley emphasized the unity of the Spirit with the other persons of the Godhead especially in terms of essence, knowledge, will, and testimony. And on the other hand, he underscored the particularity of the Holy Spirit, that the Spirit is not to be confused with either the Father or the Son, but is to be seen in relation to and proceeding from both. Thus, Wesley affirmed the fact of the unity and the diversity of the Godhead simultaneously, but without explaining just how this can be so. Moreover, though all of this material has revealed facets of the Spirit's person and nature, the person of the Holy Spirit is perhaps best understood in terms of His work. Indeed, much of what Wesley has to say about the character of the Holy Spirit emerges from a discussion of the Spirit's ministry.

II. The Work of the Holy Spirit

In the chapter on Christology, a distinction was made between the non-mediatorial and the mediatorial activity of the Son: the former term was used to describe Christ's work in creation and in His continuing governance of the world; the latter to depict His role in redemption. Though Wesley does clearly treat the Spirit's role in creation (commentary on Genesis 1:2) and in governing and preserving the cosmos, much of this material is found outside the parameters of his sermons. Let it, therefore, be sufficient to note, as was done in the preceding chapter, but this time in contrast to T. W. Pillow and other scholars like him, that, for Wesley, the work of the members of the Trinity *cannot* be accurately described along strictly functional lines where creation is assigned to the Father, redemption to the Son, and sanctification to the Holy Spirit.[1] To be sure the principal activity of the Spirit as found in Wesley's homilies concerns the work of sanctification *and* redemption. Once again, "The work of redemption," Wesley contends, "[is] the work of the whole Trinity."[2] There is no exclusivity of roles here.

1. Thomas Wright Pillow, "John Wesley's Doctrine of the Trinity," *The Cumberland Seminarian* 24 (Spring 1986): 8. Pillow cites Wesley's commentary on Rev. 16:13 in support of his view, but actually Wesley's remarks in this context do not specifically indicate a functional ordering, and his comments elsewhere (see note # 21) belie such an interpretation. Cf. Wesley, *N.T. Notes*, p. 711-12.
2. Wesley, *N.T. Notes*, p. 581.

Continuing this line of thought, the real significance of the doctrine of the Holy Spirit for Wesley, as Starkey aptly points out, "is seen in his practical emphasis upon the Holy Spirit as the agent or 'administrator' of redemption ... as the bearer of the redemptive effects of the historical atonement."[1] And the accuracy of this view is demonstrated by the language contained in Wesley's *Farther Appeal* where the Methodist leader affirms that "it is certain all true faith, and the whole work of redemption, every good thought, word, and work, is altogether by the operation of the Spirit of God."[2] Therefore every person, in order to believe unto salvation, "must receive the Holy Ghost."[3] Moreover, Colin Williams, for his part, notes that although one of the Spirit's offices is "working in the world" — like the Son's non-mediatorial activity — "his main office is his work in believers."[4] To be sure, the Spirit's redemptive work is so considerable that Cushman claims it is the "first principle of Wesley's experimental divinity."[5]

A. Prevenient Grace (Preparer)

The Christocentric nature of the work of the Holy Spirit is revealed in His application of the benefits of the death of Christ to humanity.[6] Thus, the atonement of Christ, completed at Calvary, is the foundation for all the grace — prevenient, convincing, and sanctifying — which God showers on the world, but it is the Holy Spirit who conveys this boon to humanity by His very presence. And with respect to prevenient grace in particular, our present topic, the benefits conveyed are four.[7]

First of all, keeping in line with his doctrine of original sin, Wesley denied that human beings possess natural free will.[8] Nevertheless, he avoided the deterministic implications (elimination of moral responsibility etc.) of this denial by affirming that a certain measure of free will was supernaturally restored to all people by the Holy Spirit, based upon the work of Christ. In his treatise, *Predestination Calmly Considered*, written in 1752, Wesley states:

> **But I do not carry free-will so far: (I mean, not in moral things;) Natural free-will, in the present state of mankind, I do not understand: I only assert, that there is a measure of free will supernaturally restored to every man, together with that supernatural light which 'enlightens every man that cometh into the world.'[9]**

1. Lycurgus M. Starkey, Jr., *The Work of the Holy Spirit: A Study in Wesleyan Theology* (Nashville: Abingdon Press, 1962), p.26.
2. Thomas Jackson, ed., *The Works of John Wesley*, 14 vols. (Grand Rapids, Michigan: Baker Book House, 1978), 8:49.
3. Ibid.
4. Colin Williams, *John Wesley's Theology Today* (Nashville: Abingdon Press, 1960), p. 98.
5. Robert E. Cushman, *John Wesley's Experimental Divinity* (Nashville: Kingswood Books, 1989), p. 43.
6. Williams, *Theology Today*, p. 98-99.
7. For a thorough discussion of these benefits Cf. Charles Allen Rogers, "The Concept of Prevenient Grace in the Theology of John Wesley" (Ph.D. dissertation, Duke University, 1967), p. 196.
8. Jackson, *Wesley's Works*, 10:229.
9. Ibid., 10:230.

Second, just as Wesley appealed to John 1:9 — his favorite verse to explore the reality of prevenient grace — to argue for a partial restoration of free will, so too he appealed to this portion of Scripture to indicate that humanity has not been left in the natural state, devoid of all grace and therefore knowing nothing of God, but that all people have at least some knowledge of God and His attributes, however clouded or scant this knowledge may be as revealed in the following excerpt:

> **For what is to be known of God — Those great principles which are indispensably necessary to be known, 'is manifest in them; for God hath showed it to them' — By the light which enlightens every man that cometh into the world.[1]**

Third, the Spirit of Christ, a biblical and Wesleyan synonym for the Holy Spirit,[2] is also involved in mitigating some of the most damaging effects of the Fall by illuminating the minds of humanity, that is, by providing men and women with some knowledge of general moral principles, of right and wrong, as expressed in the law of God itself. On this head Wesley writes:

> **But it was not long before man rebelled against God, and by breaking this glorious law well nigh effaced it out of his heart; ... And yet God did not despise the work of his own hands; but being reconciled to man through the Son of his love, he in some measure re-inscribed the law on the heart of his dark, sinful creature.[3]**

And last, in his sermon *On Conscience* which was produced in 1788, Wesley argues that although in one sense conscience may be viewed as natural, since this faculty appears to be universal, yet, properly speaking, "it is not natural; but a supernatural gift of God, above all his natural endowments."[4] More to the point, Wesley maintains in this same sermon that "it is his Spirit who giveth thee an inward check, who causeth thee to feel uneasy, when thou walkest in any instance contrary to the light which *he* hath given thee.[5] In other words, the Spirit not only re-inscribes, in some measure, the law of God upon human hearts, but He also gives the conscience pause when the disparity between the moral law and human thought and action is great.

The gracious ministry of the Holy Spirit in each of these four areas, His application of the benefits of Christ's atonement, has two important consequences: First, these gifts of grace are universal and are not restricted to Christian believers. For instance, with respect to conscience in particular, Wesley writes: "Something of this is found in every human heart, passing sentence concerning good and evil not only in all Christians, but in all Mahometans, all pagans, yea

---

1. John Wesley, *N.T. Notes*, p. 363.
2. Cf. 1 Peter 1:11 and Wesley's commentary on John 15:26 where he specifically identifies the Spirit of Christ with the Holy Spirit.
3. Outler, *Sermons*, 2:7. (Original, Nature, Properties, and Use of the Law)
4. Ibid., 3:105. (On Conscience)
5. Ibid.

the vilest of savages."[1] Likewise, some glimmer of the knowledge of God and His attributes is found in all who bear a human face, not as a result of any natural capacity, but as a result of the rich and unmerited favor of God.[2] Thus, the Holy Spirit has *already* acted in a broad way even before humanity is fully aware of this. And such initial activity is one facet of precisely what is meant by the notion of "prevenience."

Beyond this, the Oxford leader even went so far as to maintain that the fruits of prevenient grace "imply some tendency toward life, some degree of salvation, the beginning of a deliverance from a blind, unfeeling heart, quite insensible of God and the things of God."[3] And so when Wesley looked beyond the walls of his own church and tradition, he saw not total darkness, as some modern Barthians are apt to see, but a measure of light, due to the healing, illuminating, and preparatory activity of the Spirit of Christ.

The second major consequence of the Spirit's prior work is an anthropological one and concerns the basic moral and spiritual posture of people. To use a maxim drawn from Wesley's sermons, "God worketh in you; therefore you can work.... God worketh in you; therefore you must work."[4] Here, the initiating operations of the Holy Spirit as manifested in prevenient (and other) grace removes "all imagination of merit from man,"[5] while at the same time it increases human ability and, consequently, human responsibility as well. This means, of course, that Wesley's understanding of grace, different in so many respects from that of the continental Reformers, issues in a thoroughgoing synergism, but clearly avoids both Pelagianism and Semi-pelagianism because the *initium fidei* (the first move in the process of salvation) is clearly from God. But precisely because God has previously acted and continues to do so, humanity must not sit on its hands, so to speak, but must improve the considerable grace of God already given.[6] Wesley cautions:

> **Even St. Augustine, who is generally supposed to favour the contrary doctrine, makes that just remark, 'he that made us without ourselves, will not save us without ourselves.' He will not save us unless we 'save ourselves from this untoward generation'; unless we ourselves 'fight the good fight of faith, and lay hold on eternal life'; unless we 'agonize to enter in at the strait gate,' 'deny ourselves, and take up our cross daily,' and labour, by every possible means, to 'make our own calling and election sure.'[7]**

1. Ibid., 4:163. (Heavenly Treasure in Earthen Vessels)
2. For more material on the question of the relation between special and general revelation understood against the backdrop of Wesley's notion of prevenient grace Cf. Starkey, *The Work of the Holy Spirit*, p. 151.
3. Outler, *Sermons*, 3:203-04. (On Working Out Our Own Salvation)
4. Ibid., 3:206,208.
5. Ibid., 3:202.
6. Ibid., 3:208.
7. Ibid., 3:208-09.

Thus, remarkably enough, the imperative mood has a place at every stage along the way in Wesley's order of salvation, for "there is no man, unless he has quenched the Spirit, that is wholly void of the grace of God."[1]

B. Convincing Grace (Convincer and Illuminator)

As noted earlier in passing, the Holy Spirit is intimately involved in the operations of conscience. "In order to the very existence of a good conscience," Wesley writes, "as well as to the continuance of it, the continued influence of the Spirit of God is absolutely needful."[2] And this anointing of the Spirit, referred to by Wesley in his sermon *On Conscience*, is necessary for a number of reasons: First, the Spirit teaches us the meaning of God's Word which, at times, is not so readily apparent to sinfully diseased hearts; illumination and instruction are therefore required. Second, the Spirit makes us aware of our own lives and dispositions, "bringing all our thoughts, words, and actions to remembrance."[3] And finally, the good graces of the Holy Spirit are requisite in order to perceive the agreement of our lives with "the commandments of God."[4]

As expected, the Spirit plays a leading role in the process of repentance: convicting, illuminating, and teaching. In addition, the intelligence of the Spirit — it is He who knows our true spiritual state without illusion — is nicely contrasted by Wesley with the dullness, spiritually speaking, of humanity. In fact, both Charles and John referred to unrepentant sinners as sleepers — as slow and insensible, ignorantly and mistakenly optimistic about their true condition in the sight of a Holy God. Charles, for instance, remarks in his homily *Awake, Thou That Sleepest*:

> **"Full of all diseases as he is, he fancies himself in perfect health. Fast bound in misery and iron, he dreams that he is happy and at liberty. He says, 'Peace, peace,' while the devil as 'a strong man armed' is in full possession of his soul."[5]**

And the older brother, for his part, struck the same chord in his sermon, *The Spirit of Bondage and of Adoption* where he writes:

> **"By some awful providence, or by his Word applied with the demonstration of his Spirit, God touches the heart of him that lay**

---

1. Ibid., 3:207. Lindström, argues that in the last resort Wesley's doctrine of prevenient grace is based upon his conception of God. "Such free will harmonizes better to Wesley's mind with God's wisdom, justice, and mercy than the reprobation which he says is the alternative." Cf. Harald Lindström, *Wesley and Sanctification* (Grand Rapids, Michigan: Francis Asbury Press), p. 46.
2. Outler, *Sermons*, 3:486. (On Conscience)
3. Ibid. For more material on the Spirit's role in repentance see my earlier book, *Wesley On Salvation* p. 27-31.
4. Ibid.
5. Ibid., 1:143. (Awake, Thou That Sleepest)

asleep in darkness and in the shadow of death. He is terribly shaken out of his sleep."[1]

Again, the Holy Spirit "teacheth [us] all things,"[2] opens "the eyes of our understanding,"[3] and enlightens us "with all such knowledge as is requisite to our pleasing God."[4] In other words, conviction and illumination go hand in hand.

However, in Wesley's theology, the Spirit's work of conviction is not exhausted in bringing the sinner to repentance. Thus, once a person does truly repent and is justified, a further work awaits, namely, the conviction not of actual sins but of inbred sin — the painful recognition that the carnal nature, with all its lusts, yet remains in the life of the believer. And this second repentance, which is displayed in Wesley's sermon *The Repentance of Believers*, is both similar to and different from the repentance previous to justification. It is similar in that it entails self-knowledge, the realization that all is not well in the heart of the believer, that sin in some form is still in fact present. However, it is different from the former repentance — which Wesley calls legal as opposed to evangelical repentance[5] — in that it is a full conviction of the carnal nature, of the original sin which "remains, but does not reign."[6] Here too in this later work the Spirit's convincing and illuminating graces are present. All, then, is not complete in one grand stoke, "till it shall please our Lord to speak to our hearts again, to 'speak the second time, 'Be clean.'"[7]

C. Justification (Comforter)

Justification, according to Wesley, is not — as is often mistakenly supposed — the "being made actually just and righteous."[8] Indeed, such cleansing and renewal is more aptly termed sanctification which, though it occurs simultaneously with justification, must be logically (and theologically) distinguished from

---

1. Ibid., 1:255. (The Spirit of Bondage and of Adoption) And notice that Wesley uses quite dramatic language on this subject of conviction of sin as revealed in his following comments: "But the moment the Spirit of the Almighty strikes the heart of him that was till then without God in the world, it breaks the hardness of his heart, and creates all things new. The Sun of Righteousness appears, and shines upon his soul, showing him the light of the Glory of God in the face of Jesus Christ." Cf. Ibid., 4:172. (Living without God).

2. Ibid., 4:123. (On a Single Eye)

3. Ibid., 2:427. (God's Love to Fallen Man)

4. Ibid., 2:410-411. (On the Fall of Man)

5. Wesley, *N.T. Notes*, p. 15. Wesley's full comments on this distinction are revealed in the following: "Repentance is of two sorts; that which is termed legal, and that which is styled evangelical repentance. The former (which is the same that is spoken of here) is a thorough conviction of sin. The latter is a change of heart (and consequently of life) from all sin to all holiness."

6. Ibid., 1:327. (On Sin in Believers)

7. Ibid., 1:346. (The Repentance of Believers) Emphasis is mine.

8. Ibid., 1:187. (Justification by Faith) Observe that the logical though not temporal distinction which Wesley makes between justification and sanctification contradicts the teaching of the Council of Trent which in its deliberations (Sixth Session) on the matter stated: "This disposition, or preparation, is followed by Justification itself, which is not remission of sins merely, but also the sanctification and renewal of the inward man ..." Cf. Schaff, *Creeds*, 2:94.

it. "The one implies," the Oxford don cautions, "what God *does for us* through his Son; the other what he *works in us* by his Spirit."[1] Simply put, justification is pardon, the forgiveness of sins; sanctification, on the other hand, involves the actual impartation of righteousness, what Wesley often calls "holiness."

It would be a mistake, however, to conclude from this distinction, as Williams correctly points out, either that the Spirit is not involved in justification or that Christ does not play a role in the new birth and sanctification.[2] The distinction is simply not that discrete. In fact, "pardon is applied to the soul," Wesley declares, "by a Divine faith, wrought by the Holy Ghost..."[3] That is, the sinner is convinced by the Spirit that "Christ loved me, and gave himself for me,"[4] thereby making the death of Christ a present benefit. And it is this faith, the Methodist leader reasons, "by which he is justified, or pardoned, the moment he receives it."[5]

Clearly, Wesley was well aware that the Spirit, so mysterious and subtle, does not work in the same manner with everyone, and therefore no set form of the experience of justification by faith should be held up as normative. In fact, in 1785, in a pertinent letter to Mary Cooke who was troubled over this very issue the one time Georgia missionary counseled:

> **There is an irreconcilable variability in the operations of the Holy Spirit on the souls of men, more especially as to the manner of justification. Many find Him rushing upon them like a torrent, while they experience**

> The o'erwhelming power of saving grace.

> **This has been the experience of many; perhaps of more in this late visitation than in any other age since the times of the Apostles. But in others He works in a very different way:**

> He deigns His influence to infuse,
> Sweet, refreshing, as the silent dews.[6]

Once again, what is of consequence for Wesley is not so much the manner of this experience, but the *fact* of it, the realization of "the love of a pardoning God ... shed abroad in our hearts by the Holy Ghost which is given unto us."[7] This

---

1. Ibid.

2. Williams, *Theology Today*, p. 100.

3. Wesley, *N.T. Notes*, p. 371.

4. Jackson, *Wesley's Works*, 8:276. Compare the *pro me* language here with Wesley's account of his Aldersgate experience. Once this is done, it should be clear that 24 May 1738 was the time when the Oxford leader exercised a saving, justifying faith, a faith that went far beyond mere intellectualization. Cf. W. Reginald Ward and Richard P. Heitzenrater, eds., *The Works of John Wesley* Vol. 18 *Journals and Diaries* I (Nashville: Abingdon Press, 1988), p. 249-250.

5. Ibid.

6. Telford, *Letters*, 7:298.

7. Outler, *Sermons*, 3:336. (Family Religion)

means, then, that the atonement of Christ, and the forgiveness which is based upon it, must not remain mere historical curiosities, but must become present realities.

D. The New Birth (Purifier and Liberator)

The distinction between justification and sanctification, the "for us"/"in us" vocabulary noted earlier in the sermon *Justification by Faith*, surfaced again in two of Wesley's later homilies. In his piece, *The Great Privilege of Those that are Born of God* (1748), for example, Wesley describes the work of sanctification as something which God does *in us* so that "our inmost souls are changed."[1] To be born of God, therefore, to be renewed in heart and life, is not "barely being baptized, or any outward change whatever; but a vast inward change; a change wrought in the soul by the operation of the Holy Ghost."[2] Likewise, in his sermon *The New Birth*, produced in 1760, Wesley not only continues this theme but indicates that the new birth is absolutely necessary in order to be holy. He elaborates:

> **Now this holiness can have no existence till we are renewed in the image of our mind. It cannot commence in the soul till that change be wrought, till by the power of the highest overshadowing us we are brought from darkness to light.**[3]

The Spirit's activity, then, in the new birth — or what can be referred to as initial sanctification — entails a true transformation, a vital cleansing of the heart, so that believers are not just positionally holy (relative change) but actually are holy (real change). In other words, the life of God, the mind of Christ with all its affections and tempers, has been implanted in the soul in some measure by the presence of the Holy Spirit.

However, this cleansing and purifying ministry of the Holy Spirit is only one aspect of His work in this area; liberation and empowerment are graces conferred as well. Accordingly, those who have found favor in the sight of God, one of Wesley's favorite ways of describing grace, not only have their eyes opened "to see a loving, gracious God,"[4] but they also are truly liberated: free from "both the guilt and power of sin."[5] Moreover, "where the Spirit of the Lord is," Wesley affirms, "there is liberty,"[6] not from the law of God or from holiness, of course, which would reflect an antinomian understanding, but from "guilt, fear ... and sin."[7] Here, then, the harshest of all slaveries, the cruelest of all bondages, is at

1. Ibid., 1:432. (The Great Privilege of those that are Born of God)
2. Ibid.
3. Ibid., 2:194-95. (The New Birth) For additional references to the sanctifying work of the Holy Spirit in Wesley's sermons Cf. 1:262-63. (The Spirit of Bondage and of Adoption); 3:200. (Working Out Our Own Salvation); 4:398, 406. (Hypocrisy in Oxford).
4. Ibid., 1:260. (The Spirit of Bondage and of Adoption)
5. Ibid., 1:261.
6. Ibid., 1:262.
7. Ibid. Wesley also defined Christian liberty in terms of the freedom necessary to keep the commandments of God. In his *Plain Account of Christian Perfection*, for example, he writes: "Whatever God has forbidden, he avoids; whatever God has enjoined, he does. He runs the way of God's commandments, now He hath set his heart at liberty." Cf. Jackson, *Wesley's Works*, 11:372.

and end. To be sure, one is liberated and empowered precisely in order to love and to participate thereby in a remarkably and qualitatively different kind of life. All this, and more, is brought about by the ever-quickening Spirit. Reason, natural ability, and gentility are simply not enough.

E. The Gifts and Fruit of the Spirit (Fortifier)

Just as rays of light inevitably stream from the sun, so too do various gifts and fruit pour forth from the believer's life in the Spirit. In terms of the spiritual gifts, in particular, which grace the Christian life, Wesley made a distinction between the extraordinary and the ordinary. The former included such things as "gifts of healing, of working miracles, of prophecy, of discerning spirits, the speaking with divers kinds of tongues, and the interpretation of tongues"(1 Cor 12:9-10).[1] And the latter embraced "convincing speech, persuasion, knowledge, faith, [and] easy elocution..."[2]

Though in the early history of the church there was keen interest in the extraordinary gifts of the Spirit, most notably among the Corinthians and the Montanists, these endowments do not appear to have been the major focus of John Wesley. In fact, in his sermon, *The More Excellent Way*, this Anglican cleric contends, "It does not appear that these extraordinary gifts of the Holy Ghost were common in the church for more than two or three centuries."[3] What was the problem here? In one word, Constantine. Accurate or not, Wesley attributes the decline and virtual elimination of the extraordinary gifts to this Roman Emperor "who called himself a Christian, and from a vain imagination of promoting the Christian cause thereby heaped riches, and power, and honour, upon the Christians in general; but in particular upon the Christian clergy."[4] And Wesley adds to this indictment, making his meaning on this topic very clear: "From this time they [the extraordinary gifts] almost totally ceased; very few instances of the kind were found.[5]

In addition, Wesley's reserve concerning the extraordinary gifts was also expressed in his comments to Joseph Butler, Bishop of Bristol, who rebuked the

---

1. Ibid., 1:160. (Scriptural Christianity)

2. Howard A. Snyder with Daniel V. Runyon, *The Divided Flame* (Grand Rapids, Michigan: Francis Asbury Press, 1986), p. 58. And Cf. Outler, *Sermons*, 3:264. (The More Excellent Way)

3. Outler, *Sermons*, 3:263. (The More Excellent Way)

4. Ibid.

5. Ibid. Bracketed material is mine. In his sermon, *Of Former Times*, Wesley writes what perhaps is his most stinging indictment of Constantine as revealed in the following: "Constantine's calling himself a Christian, and pouring in that flood of wealth and power on the Christian church, the clergy in particular — was productive of more evil to the church than all the ten persecutions put together....From the time that the church and state, the kingdoms of Christ and of the world, were so strangely and unnaturally blended together, Christianity and heathenism were so thoroughly incorporated with each other that they will hardly ever be divided till Christ comes to reign upon earth. So that instead of fancying that the glory of the new Jerusalem covered the earth at that period, we have terrible proof that it was then, and has ever since been, covered with the smoke of the bottomless pit." Ibid., 3:450 Other references to Constantine and his malign influence on the church include: 2:461, 2:462, 2:464, 2:501, 2:529, 3:263, 3:264, 3:470, and 4:77.

leader of the Methodists for his alleged enthusiasm: "Sir, the pretending to extraordinary revelations and gifts of the Holy Ghost is a horrid thing — a very horrid thing."[1] An accusation to which Wesley replied: "I pretend to no extraordinary revelations, or gifts of the Holy Ghost: none but what every Christian may receive and ought to expect and pray for."[2] Indeed, Wesley much preferred to talk about the fruit of the Spirit rather than the gifts. "Without busying ourselves then in curious, needless inquires touching the *extraordinary* gifts, the Oxonian warns, "let us take a nearer view of these his *ordinary fruits*, which we are assured will remain throughout all ages."[3] Just what are these fruits? Building on Galatians 5:22 as his guide, Wesley expounds upon the spiritual resources of the early church:

> It was to give them (what none can deny to be essential to all Christians in all ages) 'the mind which was in Christ', those holy 'fruits of the Spirit' which whosoever hath not 'is none of his'; to fill them with 'love, joy, peace, long-suffering, gentleness, goodness'; to endue them with faith ... with meekness and temperance'; to enable them to 'crucify the flesh with its affections and lusts', its passions and desires;[4]

Moreover, just as Wesley affirmed that there was a diversity of gifts, but the same Spirit (1 Cor 12:4) so too did he maintain that love, itself, was "the root of all the rest"[5] of the fruit. Consequently, joy, peace, gentleness, goodness and all the other fruits were viewed by Wesley as the active and effective flowering of the "love of God shed abroad in our hearts by the Holy Ghost given unto us."(Rom 5:5. KJV) Notice here that, once again, the stress is on a real change in the life of the believer. This gracious work, so mysterious and hidden, begins in the recesses of the human heart as "the Holy Spirit actually works love and these other tempers in those that are led by him."[6] But love, of course, cannot be hidden, and it is soon revealed quite publicly in the thoughts, words, acts of mercy, etc., of those who walk not after the flesh, but after the Holy Spirit of God.

F. Assurance (Comforter)

Wesley's doctrine of assurance has often been misunderstood simply because many interpreters fail to take into account that the Methodist leader's views in this area underwent significant development and change as he backed away from some of the erroneous notions mediated to him by the Moravians. For instance,

1. Nehemiah Curnock, *The Journal of the Rev. John Wesley, A.M.*, 8 vols. (London: The Epworth Press, 1938), 2:257n.
2. Ibid.
3. Outler, *Sermons*, 1:161. (Scriptural Christianity)
4. Ibid., 1:160. The fruits of the Holy Spirit, resident in the human heart, were underscored by Wesley in a number of ways. In a real sense, these fruits (love, joy, peace, etc.,) can be identified with all those "holy tempers" which the Methodist leader insisted on for the promotion of vital Christianity, as indicated in his sermon *On Zeal*. Cf. Outler, *Sermons*, 3:313
5. Wesley, *N.T. Notes*, p. 485.
6. Outler, *Sermons*, 3:77. (On Perfection)

while he was in Georgia, Wesley at times confused the assurance which pertains to a child of God with that which properly belongs to one more mature in faith. For instance, in his journal account on board the *Samuel* on 29 January 1738 Wesley asserts:

> The faith I want is 'a sure trust and confidence in God, that, through the merits of Christ, my sins are forgiven, and I reconciled to the favor of God' ... I want that faith which none can have without knowing that he hath it; For whosoever hath it, is 'freed from sin', 'the *whole* body of sin is destroyed' in him: He is freed from fear, 'having peace with God through Christ, and rejoicing in hope of the glory of God.'[1]

Likewise, in his sermon *Free Grace*, written in 1739, Wesley mistakenly contends that the assurance of faith common to all believers "excludes all kind of doubt and fear concerning their future perseverance;..."[2] But such notions could hardly remain viable in the face of significant evidence to the contrary.[3] In fact, as early as October of 1738, that is, even before the sermon *Free Grace* was produced, Wesley's own spiritual experience, as revealed in his *Journal*, was already beginning to belie the Moravian teaching as revealed in the following:

> I have not that joy in the Holy Ghost; no settled, lasting joy. Nor have I such a peace as excludes the possibility either of fear or doubt....Yet, upon the whole, although I have not yet that joy in the Holy Ghost, nor the full assurance of faith, much less am I, in the full sense of the words, 'in Christ a new creature'; I nevertheless trust that I have a measure of faith, and am 'accepted in the Beloved;'[4]

However, it would take Wesley several years to work out the proper nuances and implications, to show that there are degrees of faith, and to argue articulately that full assurance is a spiritual development which requires a further work of grace. All is not received in one grand stoke.

A second set of issues, not to be confused logically with the first, concerns the question of the believer's consciousness of the Spirit's direct witness (assurance) that he or she is a child of God. In other words, this question does not involve the

---

1. Ward and Heitzenrater, *Journals* 1:215-216.
2. Outler, *Sermons*, 3:550. (Free Grace) Notice in Starkey's scheme which follows that full assurance is not necessarily identified with entire sanctification as is often supposed:

These degrees of assurance are three and are generally designated as:

(1) The clear assurance of faith, that is, faith mixed with doubts and fears and preached as 'the common privilege of all Christians.'

(2) The full assurance of faith consists of a full, abiding conviction of pardon, undimmed by doubts and fears.

(3) The full assurance of hope means a full conviction of 'being with God in glory.'

It is the last (# 3 above) which Starkey identifies with the distinction "fathers in Christ" (1 John 2:12 ff.) Cf. Starkey, *Work*, p. 68 -69.

3. Richard P. Heitzenrater, *Mirror and Memory* (Nashville: Kingswood Books, 1989), p. 140. Bracketed material is mine.
4. Williams, *Theology Today*, p. 112.

matter of full assurance, of freedom from doubt and fear, though it does raise the issue, once again, of degrees of faith. Simply put, can a person exercise justifying faith and not enjoy the assurance which results from a direct witness of the Spirit? Initially, Wesley appears to say, "No." Thus, in a letter to Melville Horne, written in the latter part of his career, Wesley recounts his earlier teaching on assurance with some dismay:

> When fifty years ago my brother Charles and I, in the simplicity of our hearts, told the good people of England that unless they knew their sins were forgiven, they were under the wrath and curse of God. I marvel, Melville, they did not stone us! The Methodists, I hope, know better now; we preach assurance as we always did, as a common privilege of the children of God; but we do not enforce it, under the pain of damnation, denounced on all who enjoy it not.[1]

What Wesley, however, did in the interim, at least by the Methodist Conference of 1747, was to separate the issues of justifying faith and assurance (a sense of pardon) so that he now no longer condemned those whom God has not condemned. Accordingly, in an important letter to his brother Charles in that same year, John made a number of distinctions which were to remain throughout his career:

> By justifying faith I mean that faith which whosoever hath is not under the wrath and the curse of God. By a sense of pardon I mean a distinct, explicit assurance that my sins are forgiven.

> I allow: (1) that there is such an explicit assurance; (2), that it is the common privilege of real Christians; (3), that it is the proper Christian faith, which purifieth the heart and overcometh the world....(4) But I cannot allow that justifying faith is such an assurance, or necessarily connected therewith.[2]

Notice in the last item just cited (#4 above) that in separating justification and assurance, Wesley was free to argue that one may in fact be justified, and yet be unaware of the witness of the Spirit. Moreover, Wesley underscored this same point in his correspondence to Mr. Tompson in February 1756: "Can a man who has not a clear assurance that his sins are forgiven be in a state of justification? I believe there are some instances of it."[3] However, it was not until much later that Wesley indicated *the reason* for this exception. In a letter to Dr. Rutherforth in 1768, he elaborates:

1. Edward H. Sugden, ed., *Wesley's Standard Sermons*, 2 vols. (London: The Epworth Press, 1921), 1:82n
2. Frank Baker, ed., *The Works of John Wesley, The Letters* (New York: Oxford University Press, 1982), 26:254-55. I have added "(4)" (just the number itself) to make the argument easier to understand and discuss.
3. Telford, *Letters*, 3:163. Nevertheless, not even this significant exception undermined Wesley's strong association of justification and assurance. Indeed, a month later, in March 1756, Wesley wrote to Richard Tompson: "My belief in general is this — that every Christian believer has a divine conviction of his reconciliation with God." Cf. Telford, *Letters*, 3:174.

> I believe a consciousness of being in the favour of God (which I do
> not term plerophory, or full assurance, since it is frequently weakened,
> nay perhaps interrupted, by returns of doubt or fear) is the common
> privilege of Christians fearing God and working righteousness.
> Yet I do not affirm there are no exceptions to this general rule. Pos-
> sibly some may be in the favour of God, and yet go mourning all the
> day long. But I believe this is usually owing either to disorder of Body
> or ignorance of the gospel promises.[1]

In other words, Wesley's seasoned teaching on this score is that assurance, in
most instances, accompanies justification by faith. There are, of course, exceptions to this association, but they are, after all, *exceptions*. In fact, the later Wesley so strongly identified justification with a measure of assurance that he wrote
in his sermon *On the Trinity* in 1775, apparently forgetting, at least for the
moment, the exempt cases:

> But I know not how *anyone* can be a Christian believer till 'he hath'
> (as St. John speaks) 'the witness in himself'; till 'the Spirit of God wit-
> nesses with his spirit that he is a child of God" — that is, in effect, till
> God the Holy Ghost witnesses that God the Father has accepted him
> through the merits of God the Son — and having this witness he hon-
> ours the Son and the blessed Spirit 'even as he honours the Father.'[2]

It should also be noted, thirdly, that the distinction of a servant of God from
a child of God is yet another matter and does not directly pertain to the question
of assurance presently being discussed. For Wesley nowhere in his writings
maintained that the Holy Spirit witnesses to a servant of God that he or she is a
child of God. The contradiction entailed is simply insurmountable. Indeed, there
can be little comfort and assurance in a spiritual state which is characterized by
continual anxiety and fear. And yet the servants of God, even though they are
marked by a "spirit of bondage unto fear,"[3] — what Wesley calls the legal state
— nevertheless have a measure of faith (so the question of degrees of faith is
appropriate here) and they, therefore, are not to be condemned. But again, why
are they not to be troubled? Is it because they have "the proper voice of a child
of God"?[4] No, it is because Wesley knew that "unless the servants of God halt
by the way, they will receive the adoption of sons. They will receive the faith of
the children of God by his revealing his only-begotten Son in their hearts."[5] In
other words, the servants of God are already involved in the process of salvation;
they are *en route* so to speak. Consequently, a positive rather than a negative
work is called for: they should be encouraged to improve the rich grace of God,

---

1. Ibid., 5:358. This may reflect Wesley's own condition in 1738. That is, perhaps Wesley experienced justification and regeneration sometime in 1738 prior to Aldersgate, and his assurance on
May 24th therefore "completed" the process. Though a conversionist view can argue in this fashion,
it would seem that 1738 would have to be the *terminus a quo* simply because before this time Wesley, by his own admittance, confused the nature of justification and sanctification.

2. Outler, *Sermons*, 2:385. (On the Trinity) Emphasis is mine.

3. Ibid., 4:35 (On the Discoveries of Faith)

4. Ibid., 4:35-36.

5. Ibid., 3:497-98. (On Faith)

and not discouraged, until they receive their adoption as sons and daughters of the Most High.

Though much attention in this present section has been paid to the witness of the Spirit, actually, in his doctrine of assurance, Wesley postulated two witnesses, not just one: that of our own spirit and that of the Holy Spirit. The first testimony is indirect and proceeds largely by reason: that is, the proper estimation of one's spiritual condition is reached in light of the appropriate evidences of the fruit of the Spirit, the marks of the children of God (faith, hope, and love), keeping the commandments of God, and conscience.[1] And in his sermon, *The Witness of the Spirit, I* the Methodist leader indicates in a syllogistic fashion just how the appropriate deduction is made:

> Yet all this is no other than rational evidence: the 'witness of our spirit', our reason or understanding. It all resolves into this: those who have these marks, they are the children of God. But we have these marks: therefore we are the children of God.[2]

The witness of the Holy Spirit, however, is needed over and above this witness of our own spirit, for some very important reasons. First, as expressed in a letter to Samuel Furley in 1766, Wesley declares that without this second witness there is the danger that "we should get back again unawares into justification by works."[3] Put another way, our own works and conscience are simply not sufficient to provide the kind of peace and assurance necessary to live the Christian life with all its problems and challenges. Second, as Wesley relates in his second installment on this subject, *The Witness of the Spirit, II*, "there is a danger lest our religion degenerate into mere formality [or legalism]; lest, 'having a form of godliness', we neglect if not 'deny, the power of it.'[4] And last, the Spirit's testimony that we are both forgiven and the children of God is, as was noted above, the privilege of all Christians. Why, then, neglect such an important testimony?

Moreover, it is clear that Wesley sees the two witnesses in concert, in harmony with one another. Thus, on the one hand, the direct witness is in a real sense the cause of the fruit of the Spirit, the indirect witness. And, on the other hand, the witness of the Spirit itself cannot remain if the fruit are lacking. Wesley explains:

> The testimony now under consideration is given by the Spirit of God to and with our spirit. He is the person testifying. What he testifies to us is 'that we are the children of God.' The immediate result of this testimony is the 'fruit of the Spirit'; namely, 'love, joy, peace; longsuffering, gentleness, goodness.' And without these the testimony itself cannot continue.[5]

1. Ibid., 1:270-74. (The Witness of the Spirit,I)
2. Ibid., 1:272.
3. Telford, *Letters*, 5:8.
4. Outler, *Sermons*, 1:285. (The Witness of the Spirit,II) Bracketed material is mine.
5. Ibid.

The relation offered here, therefore, is dialectical. Both testimonies, then, are necessary ingredients for Wesley's doctrine of assurance. No one witness can stand alone.[1]

G. Entire Sanctification

The role of the Holy Spirit in entire sanctification entails three basic movements: first, conviction of the sin which yet remains; second, purifying the heart and filling it with love; and third, witnessing to and assuring the believer that the work is done. Concerning the first movement, Wesley makes a distinction between a repentance which is necessary at the beginning of the Christian life (which was referred to earlier as legal repentance) and a repentance "which [is] requisite after we have believed the gospel" (evangelical repentance).[2] And it is this latter repentance, Wesley points out, which is fully as necessary in order to our continuance and growth in grace as the former repentance was "to our entering the kingdom of God."[3] But observe, as noted earlier, that this "evangelical" repentance of which Wesley writes is *both* similar to and different from legal repentance. Again, it is similar in the sense that there is self-knowledge, conviction of sin, and a painful, though therapeutic, realization of our utter helplessness apart from the grace of God.[4] It is different in that evangelical repentance involves not a conviction of actual sin — for the child of God is freed from both the guilt and power of sin[5] — but a conviction of inbred sin.

Second, after the Holy Spirit applies the Word of God to believers convicting them of all the sin which remains, their hearts are subsequently purified by faith such that the "evil root, the carnal mind, is destroyed."[6] Here, negatively speaking, the pollution of the heart with all its unholy tempers is washed away. And, positively speaking, the love of God and neighbor is implanted in the soul to reign without a rival. Moreover, in his sermon, *The Repentance of Believers* Wesley not only calls for this *second* work of grace to complete the healing of believers, but also affirms that this work is, in part, instantaneous. He elaborates:

> **Though we watch and pray ever so much, we cannot wholly cleanse either our hearts or hands. Most sure we cannot, till it shall please our Lord to speak to our hearts again, to speak the second time, 'Be clean,'. And then only 'the leprosy is cleansed.' Then only the evil root, the carnal mind, is destroyed, and inbred sin subsists no more. But if there be no such second change, if there be no instantaneous deliverance after justification, if there be none but a gradual work of God (that**

---

1. See more earlier book, *Wesley On Salvation*, pp. 78-83., for more information on the witness of our own spirit.

2. Outler, *Sermons*, 1:336 (The Repentance of Believers) Bracketed material is mine.

3. Ibid., 1:336.

4. Ibid., 1:336-345.

5. Ibid., 1:328. (On Sin in Believers) Starkey notes that, for Wesley, the change entailed in the new birth is so radical that life is "lived in terms of a completely new orientation and perspective." Cf. Starkey, *Work*, p. 52-53.

6. Outler, *Sermons*, 1:346. (The Repentance of Believers)

there is a gradual work none denies) then we must be content, as well as we can, to remain full of sin till death.[1]

Third, the parallelism or similarity present with respect to the Spirit's work in conviction of actual and inbred sin is also mirrored in the Spirit's ministry of assurance concerning the new birth and Christian perfection. Observe the "parallel" language Wesley employs in his *Plain Account of Christian Perfection* which demonstrates the remarkable correspondence between the Spirit's work in regeneration and in entire sanctification: "None therefore ought to believe that the work is done," Wesley declares "till there is added the testimony of the Spirit, witnessing his entire sanctification, *as clearly as* his justification."[2] And continuing this line of thought, the Methodist leader writes:

> **But how do you know, that you are sanctified, saved from your inbred corruption?**
> **I can know it *no otherwise* than I know that I am justified. Hereby know we that we are of God, in either sense, by the Spirit that he hath given us.**[3]

As the reader might expect, the witness of the Spirit to entire sanctification is also in some sense different from the witness to justification and regeneration. "As, when we were justified, the Spirit bore witness with our spirit, that our sins were forgiven;" Wesley notes, "so, when we were sanctified he bore witness, that they were taken away."[4] Indeed, it is this blending of both similarity and difference, evident here and elsewhere, which constitutes the Wesleyan soteriological fingerprint and which does much in this instance to illuminate the Spirit's function in Christian perfection.

1. The Question of a Specialized Vocabulary

Though much of the material in Wesley's sermons on the question of the Holy Spirit's agency in entire sanctification revolves around the issues of assurance, did he ever employ a specialized vocabulary, namely Pentecostal terminology, to describe the Spirit's work in this area? In other words, did Wesley, as some writers claim, equate the "baptism of the Holy Spirit" with entire sanctification in an exclusive way? To answer this important question, the primary evidence must first of all be explored.

It appears, at the outset, that Wesley employed three basic phrases to display the work of the Holy Spirit in the life of the believer: (1) "receiving the Holy Ghost"; (2) "filled with the Holy Ghost"; and (3) "baptized with the Holy Ghost." With respect to the first phrase, "receiving the Holy Ghost," Wesley specifically

---

1. Ibid. It is obvious from this material that the language of "secondness" was not created either by nineteenth-century Methodists or by the Holiness movement; instead, it represents most accurately Wesley's own thinking on this subject.
2. Jackson, *Wesley's Works*, 11:402. Emphasis is mine.
3. Ibid., 11:420. Emphasis is mine.
4. Ibid.

denied that it is appropriate only for those who have attained Christian perfection. Accordingly, in a letter to Joseph Benson in 1770 he cautions:

> If they like to call this [being perfected in love] 'receiving the Holy Ghost,' they may: only the phrase in that sense is not scriptural and not quite proper; *for they all 'received the Holy Ghost' when they were justified.* God then 'sent forth the Spirit of His Son into their hearts, crying, Abba, Father.'[1]

Likewise, Wesley utilized the second phrase "filled with the Holy Ghost" in an interchangeable way: sometimes in terms of the new birth and at other times in terms of Christian perfection. He, therefore, did not restrict it to a second work of grace. Speaking of Christians in general in his *Farther Appeal*, he affirms:

> "Indeed I do not mean, that Christians now receive the Holy Ghost in order to work miracles; but they do doubtless now 'receive;' yea, are 'filled with, the Holy Ghost,' in order to be filled with the fruits of that blessed Spirit.[2]

Again, in his sermon *Scriptural Christianity* preached at Oxford University in 1744, Wesley "expressed the view," as Arnett candidly points out (even though it is detrimental to his view), "that every Christian should be Spirit-filled."[3] And Arnett continues: "the intimation is that anyone who is not Spirit-filled is not a Christian."[4] Observe in the quotation which follows Wesley's choice of words as he preached them before an Oxford audience:

> It was therefore for a more excellent purpose than this that they were all filled with the Holy Ghost....It was to give them (what none can deny to be essential to all Christians in all ages) 'the mind which was in Christ,' those holy fruits of the Spirit which whosoever hath not 'is none of his' to fill them with 'love, joy, peace, long-suffering, gentleness, goodness'; to endue them with faith...[5]

Moreover, in his sermon *The First-fruits of the Spirit*, written two years later, Wesley uses the phrase "filled with the Holy Ghost" to refer to all Christians, anyone who is in Christ. "They who are of Christ, who abide in him..." he notes, "These are they who indeed 'walk after the Spirit.' Being filled with faith and with the Holy Ghost."[6] There is no restrictive use here.

---

1. Telford, *Letters*, 5:215. Bracketed material and emphasis are mine.

2. Jackson, *Wesley's Works*, 8:107.

3. William Arnett, "The Role of the Holy Spirit in Entire Sanctification in the Writings of John Wesley," *Wesleyan Theological Journal* Vol. 14, No. 2 (Fall 1979): 23. In his candor, Arnett cites this material even though he takes a different position on the matter — one which links entire sanctification with Pentecostal language.

4. Ibid.

5. Outler, *Sermons*, 1:160. (Scriptural Christianity)

6. Ibid., 1:236-37. (The First-fruits of the Spirit) Again, Arnett realizes that this passage is problematic for his position and observes: "Later in the sermon Wesley points out that these 'children of God' still have 'the corruption of nature,' or 'inward sin,' remaining in them.. The problem is, of course, how a Christian can be filled with the Holy Spirit and yet have 'inward sin' remaining. Presumably, for Wesley, they were not entirely sanctified." Cf. Arnett, "The Role of the Holy Spirit," p. 23.

Nevertheless, in fairness and for accuracy, it must also be indicated that Wesley did, at times, associate the language of "filled with the Holy Ghost" with those who were perfected in love. Thus, in a subsequent letter to Joseph Benson in 1771, the Oxonian declares: "A babe in Christ has the witness sometimes. A young man has it continually. I believe one that is perfected in love, or filled with the Holy Ghost, may be properly termed a father."[1] However, this passage, and others like it, in no way undermines the present position being offered: that Wesley utilized this vocabulary to speak of entire sanctification is allowed; that he limited his language to such usage is not.

Beyond these considerations, one might at least expect that Wesley intimately identified the third phrase, "baptize with the Holy Ghost" with entire sanctification. Yet here too, the reader is in for a surprise. Commenting on Acts 1:5 (Ye shall be baptized with the Holy Ghost. KJV) Wesley notes: "And so are all true believers, to the end of the world."[2] Ever cautious in his concern over the gifts and graces of the children of God, Wesley was well aware that the ministry of the Spirit is richly enjoyed by those who are justified by the blood of Christ — a spiritual state which need not be minimized for the sake of another. The baptism of the Holy Spirit and Christian perfection, then, might have been strongly linked in later Methodism, but clearly not in the writings of the father of Methodism himself.

Nevertheless, in the face of such considerable evidence, some scholars continue to put forth a contrary position. A favorite way of accomplishing this, and one taken by George Turner, is to point out that Wesley "endorsed Fletcher's last 'check' in which Fletcher equates Christian perfection with the baptism of the Holy Spirit."[3] And Oswalt, for his part, suggests that "Wesley himself, with his almost intuitive feel for the wholeness of biblical teaching, [was] responsible for Charles' and Fletcher's thought."[4] However, Wesley's thought should not be confused with Fletcher's (or his brother's). And the former's endorsement of the *Checks* does not indicate that he approved of every line or phrase of the latter's work. One has only to recall the Calvinistic controversies of the 1770's to realize the significance of this last point. Remember that the Hill brothers charged Wesley with inconsistency due to some of the teachings expressed in his *Christian Library*. However, in his defense, Wesley simply distinguished his thought from what he had reprinted. The same caveat applies in this present context as well.

But all of this raises an ever larger issue: how are Wesley's texts being read by his theological and spiritual heirs; more particularly, how are they being read by contemporary American Methodists? For one thing, it is very likely that Arnett,

---

1. Telford, *Letters*, 5:229.
2. Wesley, *N.T. Notes*, p. 393.
3. George Allen Turner, "The Baptism of the Holy Spirit in the Wesleyan Tradition," *The Wesleyan Theological Journal* Vol. 14 No. 1. (Spring 1979): 67.
4. John N. Oswalt, "John Wesley and the Old Testament Concept of the Holy Spirit," *Religion in Life* 48 (Autumn 1979): 284.

Turner, and Oswalt, and those who follow in their train, are interpreting the Wesleyan material on entire sanctification chiefly from an ecclesiastical and traditional context. In fact, Donald Dayton has explored this historical shift in interpretation — from a literary context to a ecclesiastical one — in an important piece written in 1978. In it, he tracks the slow and subtle development whereby the holiness movement essentially capitulated, at least in this area, to Pentecostal constructions. "In America the Pentecostal formulation took root and grew," Dayton writes, "especially after the Civil War, to become the dominant holiness formulation by the end of the century."[1] And again, in a courageous move, this leading Wesleyan scholar goes on to criticize his own movement:

> But the adoption of this new way of explicating entire sanctification failed to resolve the fundamental tensions that had been present from the beginning. The fact remained that from the doctrine of Christian Perfection as it had been articulated classically by Wesley there were few real crossovers to the Pentecostal accounts and vocabulary.[2]

Beyond these historical considerations — and more importantly from my perspective — a literary analysis of Wesley's language in this area reveals that he did not, as is mistakenly supposed, employ a unique Pentecostal terminology to describe the Spirit's role in entire sanctification. Whether the Methodist leader was describing conviction of sin, cleansing, or assurance, he employed roughly the *same* vocabulary to elucidate the admittedly quite different works of regeneration, on the one hand, and entire sanctification on the other. Recall Wesley's "parallel" language cited earlier:

> *"Exactly as* we are justified by faith, so are we sanctified by faith."[3]

> "None therefore ought to believe that the work is done, till there is added the testimony of the Spirit, witnessing his entire sanctification, *as clearly as* his justification."[4]

> "But how do you know, that you are sanctified, saved from your inbred corruption? I can know it *no otherwise* than I know that I am justified."[5]

Moreover, what differences will emerge between the Spirit's role in justification and in entire sanctification — and they are considerable — are reflected not so much in Wesley's language itself (although they are present here as well), but in the referents of that language, that is, in the specific *context*, the theological setting in the *ordo salutis*, in which that language reverberates. Thus, the different role of the Holy Spirit in witnessing to a believer's entire sanctification needs to be understood not only in terms of the Spirit's witness to justification,

---

1. Donald Dayton, "The Doctrine of the Baptism of the Holy Spirit: Its Emergence and Significance," *The Wesleyan Theological Journal* Vol. 13 (Spring 1978): 121.
2. Ibid., p. 120.
3. Outler, *Sermons*, 2:163. (The Scripture Way of Salvation)
4. Jackson, *Wesley's Works*, 11:402.
5. Ibid., 11:420. Emphasis is mine.

but also in terms of the soteriological distance, the growth in grace, experienced by believers since their justification.   As already noted, Wesley affirmed that "when we were justified, the Spirit bore witness with our spirit, that our sins were forgiven; so, when we were sanctified, he bore witness, that they were taken away."[1] The hermeneutical clues, then, for a proper interpretation of Wesley's texts need to be gathered not from an American Methodist tradition, but from Wesley's own order of salvation — clues which will take into account both the similarities and the differences entailed. Only in this way will Wesley's doctrine of the Holy Spirit, or any other doctrine for that matter, be correctly understood.[2]

1. Ibid.
2. In taking this position, the present writer in no way diminishes the importance of entire sanctification as an instantaneous event that is preceded and followed by spiritual growth, which cleanses the heart of inbred sin, and which fills it with love. The danger with the "Pentecostal" position, on the other hand, is that it runs the risk of underestimating the value of regeneration, of depreciating the glorious state of the children of God who are free from both the guilt and power of sin and who have the Holy Spirit very much in their lives. For more on Wesley's parallel language see my earlier book, *Wesley on Salvation*, p. 131-37.

CHAPTER FOUR

THE DOCTRINE OF THE CHURCH
"I believe in ... the holy catholic Church, the communion of saints..."

When the secondary sources on Wesley's ecclesiology are consulted, a confusing picture often emerges. For instance, Luke Tyerman, a nineteenth-century scholar, maintained that the real purpose of Wesley's Georgia mission was to rid him of "his high church nonsense."[1] But some contemporary scholars, like Burtner and Chiles, affirm with equal force that John Wesley "was first and last a churchman."[2] That Wesley has been read so differently in this area by a number of scholars suggests at the outset the importance of this topic in two key respects: First, Wesley's doctrine of the church was and remains a controversial one. Therefore, whatever interpretations are offered may actually be more descriptive of the ecclesiastical or theological setting from which they arise than from any eighteenth century one. Second, the disparity in views indicates perhaps that Wesley's own estimation of the church in terms of its nature and function was much more complex than some earlier treatments have imagined. With these two cautions in mind, this present work will attempt to explore Wesley's ecclesiology as it surfaced in his sermons, a task complicated by the fact that Wesley's thought emerged in the context of a burgeoning revival which was, at times, at odds with its parent church.

I. The Catholic or Universal Church

It comes as something of a surprise, given the significance of this topic, to learn that Wesley did not produce a sermon specifically devoted to the question of the church until 1785.[3] Of course, the Methodist leader had written certain "ecclesiastical" pieces much earlier, such as *The Principles of a Methodist* (1742), the sermon *Catholic Spirit* (1750), and the *Nature, Design, and General*

---

1. Luke Tyerman, *The Life and Times of Rev. John Wesley, M.A.*, 3 vols. (New York: Burt Franklin, 1872) 1:168.

2. Robert W. Burtner and Robert E. Chiles, *John Wesley's Theology: A Collection From His Works* (Nashville: Abingdon Press, 1982), p. 253.

3. Albert C. Outler, ed., *The Works of John Wesley, The Sermons* 4 vols. (Nashville: Abingdon Press, 1984), 3:45. (Of the Church)

Rules of the United Societies (1743), as well as some important letters, but none of this material defined the church as clearly and succinctly as did the sermon *Of the Church*. For instance, in this late homily, Wesley seeks to articulate the nature of the Body of Christ in a number of ways: first of all, by eliminating, on the one hand, the mistaken notion, present even in his own age, that the church is a building, and by affirming, on the other hand, that the church is an organism composed of living members whose head is Christ. Not surprisingly, people, not things, are the principal focus throughout this piece.

Second, Wesley, knowing Greek as he did, attaches some significance to the Pauline phrase της κλησεως ης εκληθητε which serves as the text for this homily (Ephesians 4:1-6). And though Outler casts some doubt on the lexical relationship between this particular phrase and the term *ecclesia*,[1] Wesley's basic point remains: the church constitutes those "whom God [has] 'called out' [ek kaleo] of the world."[2]

But just how are those who are called out to be considered: as a house church or as a city church; as a national church or as the universal church? In other words, what grouping, what level of generality, best describes the ecclesia? Again, in his sermon *Of the Church*, Wesley acknowledges that all these levels are present in the Bible, from the smallest to the largest, from the statement of Jesus found in Matthew 18:20, "For where two or three are gathered in my name, there am I in the midst of them,"(RSV) to Paul's depiction of the church universal for which Christ died as recorded in Acts 20:28, "... take care for the church of God which he obtained with the blood of his own Son." And though all these kinds of churches are affirmed by the Oxford don, only two, the universal church and the national church, receive any considerable treatment in his sermons.

To be sure, Wesley's attention in *Of the Church* moves immediately to the catholic or universal church, since this is the level of generality St. Paul most probably had in mind as he wrote Ephesians 4:1ff. Along these lines, Wesley describes the universal church by noting that it is one body which embraces Christians not only from one particular city or nation, but it also includes "all the persons upon the face of the earth who answer the character here given."[3] And these members, so distinct and diverse in many ways, are united not only as a body, but also in the Spirit, "who animates all these, all the living members of the church of God."[4] The faithful community, then, drawn together in this fashion, is united in love, in purpose, and also in will. Moreover, with this one Spirit there is likewise one hope, not a hope that is fixed on any earthly object or temporal thing, but one that grasps the eternal, the unseen. Believers know that "to die is not to be lost: their prospect extends beyond the grave."[5]

1. Ibid., 3:47 n. #4.

2. Ibid. Bracketed material is mine.

3. Ibid., 3:48.

4. Ibid. In his *NT Notes* Wesley writes the following commentary on Ephesians 4:4: *"There is one body* — The universal Church, all believers throughout the world, *one Spirit, one Lord, one God, and Father* — The ever-blessed Trinity, *one hope,* — Of heaven." Cf. John Wesley, *Explanatory Notes Upon the New Testament* (Salem, Ohio: Schmul Publishers), p. 496.

5. Outler, *Sermons*, 3:49.

Perhaps the most obvious characteristic of the church universal is that it has one Lord, Jesus Christ. Quite naturally, Eastern Orthodoxy, Roman Catholicism, and Protestantism, though distinct in many respects, all affirm the preeminence of Christ as the redeemer of humanity. In this sense, then, all communions which bear the name Christian have one Lord, and on this point Wesley notes:

> **There is one Lord who has now dominion over them, who has set up his kingdom in their hearts, and reigns over all those that are partakers of this hope. To obey him, to run the way of his commandments, is their glory and joy.**[1]

Observe in this passage just cited that the Methodist leader maintains that the concept of Lord in this instance entails three major ideas: a) a kingdom which is established in human hearts (always an evangelical emphasis); b) a ruler who exercises dominion in this kingdom; and c) subjects who obey. Note also that this understanding of Lordship is in stark contrast to the self-sufficiency suggested by Wesley's own enlightened age. In short, the church is not under its own law or reason (autonomy), but is under the law of another (heteronomy), Jesus Christ.

Having one Lord, the church also has one faith which is not suitably described as a dry, speculative assent to doctrinal propositions, nor is it merely the belief that there is a God, for even the heathens believe as much.[2] Instead, it is to use Wesley's own words, "the faith of St. Thomas, teaching him to say with holy boldness, 'My Lord and my God.'"[3] It is that faith whose object is Christ and which derives its power and conviction from the grace of God; it is that trust which engages not only the intellect, but the affections as well.

And finally, the universal church is marked by one baptism and by one God and Father of all. By the former phrase, that is, one baptism, Wesley does not have in mind one particular form of this sacrament to the exclusion of others — although he apparently once did.[4] On the contrary, he simply notes that baptism is an outward sign (however it is performed) of "all that inward and spiritual grace which he [Christ] is continually bestowing on the church."[5] Again, it is a precious means whereby "faith and hope are given to those that diligently seek him."[6] Moreover, by the latter phrase, one God and Father of all, Wesley once more underscores the importance of the Spirit, in this particular case the Spirit of

---

1. Ibid.
2. Ibid. Though Wesley does not specifically use the word "Deist" in this context, he may very well have had this group in mind as he wrote this material since some of the major tenets of this "enlightened" faith are expressed here.
3. Ibid.
4. While he was in Georgia, in May 1736, Wesley balked at baptizing the child of Mr. Parker, the second Bailiff of Savannah, simply because the Bailiff's wife would not allow the child to be dipped. For a detailed account of this incident, which by the way is a good example of what Tyerman has called Wesley's "high church nonsense," Cf. W. Reginald Ward and Richard P. Heitzenrater, eds., *The Works of John Wesley* Vol. 18 *Journals and Diaries* I (Nashville: Abingdon Press, 1988), p. 157.
5. Outler, *Sermons*, 3:49. (Of the Church) Bracketed material is mine.
6. Ibid.

adoption, "which crieth in their hearts, Abba, Father; [and] which witnesseth continually with their spirits that they are the children of God;..."[1]

So then, bringing all these attributes together, the church is characterized by its oneness in terms of body, Spirit, hope, Lord, faith, baptism, and God. Wesley puts it this way: "The catholic or universal church is all the persons in the universe whom God hath so called out of the world as to entitle them to the preceding character."[2]   However, the English evangelical is not content to leave it at this, and so in the latter part of this same sermon he appeals to the language of the Apostles' Creed, specifically the phrase "the holy catholic church," to emphasize that the church is not only one, but it is also holy, set apart. He writes:

> How many wonderful reasons have been found out for giving it this appellation! One learned man informs us, 'The church is called holy because Christ the head of it is holy.' Another eminent author affirms, 'It is so called because all its ordinances are designed to promote holiness'; and yet another, 'Because our Lord *intended* that all the members of the church should be holy.'[3]

Interestingly, it has been claimed that Wesley's reckoning here is an oversimplification of a complex issue.[4]   Granted, Wesley may not have accurately portrayed the sentiments of such traditional authorities as Cyprian, Augustine, and others in his comments noted above, but can his major point, that the church is holy, be challenged or clouded? Not really. In fact, in this very sermon Wesley argues that "no common swearer, no sabbath-breaker, no drunkard, no whoremonger, no thief, no liar, none that live in outward sin ... can be a member of his [Christ's] church."[5]   Indeed, so concerned was Wesley with the holiness of the church that even as late as 1785, the date of this present piece, he goes on to make the distinction between real members, on the one hand, and by implication, nominal members, on the other, in his comment: "In the meantime let all those who are real members of the church see that they walk holy and unblamable in all things."[6]   And elsewhere, in *The Reformation of Manners*, the Oxonian affirms that the church is a body of people united in order: "first, to save each his own soul, then to assist each other in working out their salvation, and afterwards,... to save all men from present and future misery."[7]

1. Ibid., 3:50. Bracketed material is mine. In his sermon, *The Spirit of Bondage and of Adoption*, Wesley not only makes a distinction between the natural, legal, and evangelical states, but also underscores the role of the Spirit of adoption in the last state. Indeed, the implications of this association are highly instructive for the assessment and interpretation of Wesley's often-made distinction between nominal and real Christianity. Cf. Outler, *Sermons*, 1:260-63.

2. Ibid.

3. Ibid., 3:55.

4. Ibid., 3:55. n.#54.

5. Ibid., 3:56. Bracketed material is mine. The Nicene creed confessed "one holy catholic and apostolic church." Cf. Philip Schaff, ed., *The Creeds of Christendom* 3 vols. (Grand Rapids, Michigan: Baker Book House, 1983), 2:59.

6. Ibid. Though Wesley does not always utilize traditional authority with precision, one is struck by the numerous biblical references, accurately cited, in his treatment of the holiness of the church. Cf. Outler, *Sermons*, 3:55-57.

7. Ibid., 2:302. (The Reformation of Manners)

II. The Early Church

Wesley, like so many Christian writers before him, marked the beginning of the church universal with Pentecost when "all the members thereof [were] 'filled with the Holy Ghost.'"[1] However, the first specific use of the word church, he points out, does not occur until Acts 5:10, a passage which relates the fear which fell upon the ancient community because of the deaths of Ananias and Sapphira. Moreover, as he comments on these passages in his *N T Notes*, Wesley describes the New Testament church in a brief but pungent manner: "It is a company of men, called by the Gospel, grafted into Christ by baptism, animated by love, united by all kind of fellowship, and disciplined by the death of Ananias and Sapphira."[2]

Though Wesley was in agreement with his Anglican peers concerning the origin of the church, he distinguished himself from some of them, at least in part, by claiming that the corruption of the ecclesia had taken place much earlier than had been supposed. And though Wesley himself, as an Anglican priest, often looked favorably upon the ante-Nicene church, as did his peers, his sermons offer a more balanced and mature picture of his estimation of the spiritual life of this era. In his *Wisdom of God's Counsels*, for instance, the Methodist leader declares that no sooner did the church begin than it began to fall.[3] In other words, the Apostolic age was not one grand success story, nor was it utterly innocent, but was already plagued by what Wesley in his sermon *On Attending the Church Service* calls "the mystery of iniquity."[4] In this homily he writes:

> **Soon after the pouring out of the Holy Ghost on the day of Pentecost, in the infancy of the Christian church, there was indeed a glorious change .... But how short a time did this continue! How soon did 'the fine gold become dim'!**[5]

In a similar fashion, the second and third centuries receive a negative judgment at Wesley's hands. Of the former age, he declares that "undoubtedly it grew worse and worse";[6] and of the latter, he notes that Cyprian himself, great churchman that he was, held that "such abominations even then prevailed over all orders of men."[7] However, what makes Wesley's judgments of the early church

1. Ibid., 2:554. (The Wisdom of God's Counsels) Bracketed material is mine. And note that Wesley maintains that *all* the members of the church were filled with the Holy Ghost. In other words, Pentecostal language, here and elsewhere (see Chapter Three, The Doctrine of the Holy Spirit), was not reserved for the entirely sanctified.

2. John Wesley, *Explanatory Notes Upon the New Testament* (Salem, Ohio: Schmul Publishers), p. 287.

3. Outler, *Sermons* 2:555. (The Wisdom of God's Counsels) It should also be noted that even when Wesley praises the primitive Fathers as he does, for example, in his letter to Dr. Conyers Middleton in 1749, he does so primarily because they faithfully *reflect* "true, genuine Christianity, and direct us to the strongest evidence of the Christian doctrine." Cf. John Telford, ed., *The Letters of John Wesley, A.M.* 8 vols. (London: The Epworth Press, 1931), 2:387.

4. Ibid., 3:469. (On Attending the Church Service)

5. Ibid.

6. Ibid., 2:461. (The Mystery of Iniquity)

7. Ibid., 3:450-51. (Of Former Times)

even more remarkable and distinctive is that the story, so to speak, is told with a truly new voice; that is, some of the heretofore "heretics" emerge as "saints" (Montanus and Pelagius) while some of the "saints" (Constantine) emerge as "heretics." Such transvaluation is reflected in Wesley's sermon *The Wisdom of God's Counsels* in which he reasons that Montanus may well have been one of the holiest persons in the second century,[1] and that the real "sin" of Pelagius was neither more nor less than "holding that Christians may by the grace of God (not without it; that I take to be a mere slander) 'go on to perfection.'"[2]

Of Constantine, the fourth century emperor, Wesley has little good to say in his sermons or elsewhere, and he declares that the corruption which had been creeping into the church during the second and third centuries now "poured in upon [it] with a full tide,"[3] once this leader called himself a Christian. In fact, in his sermons, the negative references to Constantine are so numerous that they must surely offer some clues to Wesley's doctrine of the church. More to the point, three major charges, accurate or not, are laid at the feet of this ruler: First, and most importantly, Wesley contends that Constantine struck a "grand blow" at the very root of the Christian faith, at the "whole essence of true religion" by — oddly enough — actually favoring it.[4] Second, this detrimental work was accomplished, in part, by suffocating "humble, gentle, patient love"[5] in a sea of wealth, honor and power. In his sermon, *Of Former Times*, for example, Wesley exclaims:

> **Constantine's calling himself a Christian, and pouring in that flood of wealth and power on the Christian church, the clergy in particular — was productive of more evil to the church than all the ten persecutions put together.**[6]

And last, Wesley asserts that the extraordinary gifts of the Holy Spirit were seldom mentioned after "that fatal period when the Emperor Constantine called himself a Christian."[7] With these gifts gone, Christians once again "turned heathens," the Oxford don writes, "and had only a dead form [of religion] left."[8] Here then was the real beginning of nominal Christianity, the start of a faith

---

1. Ibid., 2:555. (The Wisdom of God's Counsels)
2. Ibid., 2:556. Wynkoop contends that Pelagius and Augustine were each attempting to preserve valid truths. Pelagius was concerned about preserving human dignity and moral responsibility; Augustine, the absolute sovereignty of God and the absolute need for His grace. However, it is difficult for the historian to determine precisely what Pelagius taught, since some of the best evidence for his teaching is based on the writings of Augustine, his chief theological opponent. Cf. Mildred Bangs Wynkoop, *Foundations of Wesleyan Arminian Theology* (Kansas City, Missouri: Beacon Hill Press, 1967.), p. 33.
3. Outler, *Sermons*, 3:470. (On Attending the Church Service) Bracketed material is mine.
4. Ibid., 2:462-63. (The Mystery of Iniquity)
5. Ibid., 2:462.
6. Ibid., 3:450. (Of Former Times) For additional references to Wesley's claim that Constantine flooded the church in riches, honor, and power Cf. Outler, *Sermons*, 2:501. (The New Creation); 2:529. (The Signs of the Times); and 4:77. (Prophets and Priests).
7. Ibid., 3:263. (The More Excellent Way)
8. Ibid., 3:264.

which was no longer clearly animated by the Spirit, but by the will and power of humanity. And such has been "the deplorable state of the Christian church," Wesley adds, "from the time of Constantine till the Reformation."[1]

But Constantine is not the only culprit in this story; Wesley has disparaging remarks for monasticism as well. Thus, in his homilies, this institution, though highly praised by others, appears as one that actually contributes to the general spiritual decline of the church. Such a strong judgment may indeed come as a surprise to some; nevertheless, it is amply borne out in the primary material. In his sermon *On Attending the Church Service*, for instance, Wesley maintains:

> **Some of these retired into the desert, and lived altogether alone; others built themselves houses, afterwards termed 'convents,' and only secluded themselves from the rest of the world. But what was the fruit of this separation? The same that might easily be foreseen. It increased and confirmed in an astonishing degree the total corruption of the church.[2]**

Moreover, the precise reasons for rejecting both anchoretic (solitary) and cenobitic (communal) monasticism as the staples of spiritual life are displayed in an another piece in which Wesley states:

> **Whenever there was a great work of God in any particular city or nation, the subjects of that work soon said to their neighbors, 'stand by yourselves, for we are holier than you! As soon as ever they separated themselves, either they retired into deserts, or they built religious houses; or at least formed parties, into which none was admitted but such as subscribed both to their judgment and practice. But with the Methodists it is quite otherwise. They are not a sect or party.[3]**

In a real sense, the Constantinian church and monasticism are singled out for rebuke by Wesley most probably because, in his mind at least, they represented two extremes, two improper solutions to the relation between church and world. The one, in heaping wealth, honor, and power on the community of faith, produced a church which was compromised and dominated by the world; it lost, in other words, the distinctiveness of its witness. The other, in its exaggerated quest for exclusivity and seclusion, eventually became irrelevant to the world, and ran the risk, at least in some instances, of spiritual narcissism.[4] Wesley's understanding of the church, however, which will be outlined below, held both of these poles in tension: the church is in the world, ever active in service to others, but the church is not of the world; it is holy because its Lord is holy.

1. Ibid., 2:464. (The Mystery of Iniquity)

2. Ibid., 3:474. (On Attending the Church Service)

3. Ibid., 4:80. (Prophets and Priests) For a more favorable judgment on monasticism Cf. Owen Chadwick, *Western Asceticism* (1958); L. Bouyer, *The Spirituality of the New Testament and the Fathers* (1963); and M.D. Knowles, *Christian Monasticism* (1969).

4. The practitioners of anchoretic monasticism sometimes went to extremes in their ascetic practices. Symeon Stylites, for instance, unbalanced as he was, tried to achieve holiness by sitting on the top of a pole for thirty-six years. Cf. Philip Schaff, *History of the Christian Church* 8 vols. (Grand Rapids, Michigan: Wm. B. Eerdmans Publishing Co., 1910), 3:191 ff.

III. The Church of England

Wesley's account of the state of the church in the Middle Ages is even less promising than that of the early church. Thus, in his *Wisdom of God's Counsels* he traces the fourteen hundred years (counting from the first century) which led up to the Protestant Reformation, and concludes that the church was "corrupted more and more, as all history shows, till scarce any either of the power or form of religion was left."[1] Observe that Wesley's historiography expressed in this context is typically Protestant in two key ways: First, the decline of the church, which begins in Apostolic times, is viewed as progressive and therefore is judged to be at its lowest point precisely during the Middle Ages. Second, the Reformation of the sixteenth century is seen as a reversal, at least in part, of this general decline. With these points in mind, Wesley's assessment of the great national churches — many of them products of the Reformation — may now be considered.

As one might expect, Wesley's definition of the Church of England contains two major components: a "Catholic" one and a "Protestant" one. With respect to the former, Wesley builds on his understanding of the Christian community cited earlier. Thus, the Anglican Church is that part of the universal church — characterized by one body, faith, Lord etc. — whose members inhabit the land of England.[2] However, since the catholicity, the unity of the Western church, was disrupted during the sixteenth century, many Protestant leaders, especially those who had a hand in the construction of the Augsburg Confession, attempted to distinguish their communions from that of Rome in what was to become a standard Protestant definition of the church:

> "They [adherents of the Augsburg Confession] teach that the one Holy Church will remain for ever. Now this Church is the congregation of the saints, in which the Gospel is rightly taught and the sacraments rightly administered."[3]

This "additional" definition soon found its way across the Channel and appeared as Article XIX in the Anglican *Thirty-Nine Articles* and in Wesley's *Sunday Service*, composed in the latter half of the eighteenth century, as Article XIII which reads, in part: "The visible Church of Christ is a Congregation of faithful men, in the [sic] which the pure Word of God is preached and the Sacraments duly administered..."[4] This, then, constitutes Wesley's second major definition of the church and supplements, but does not contradict, the one already encountered.

Few people, whether scholars of lay persons, can doubt the rich, deep, and abiding respect which John Wesley had for the Church of England: He was an ordained Anglican priest and an Oxonian; he served his church as one of its mis-

---

1. Outler, *Sermons*, 2:555. (The Wisdom of God's Counsels)
2. Ibid., 3:52. (Of the Church)
3. Henry Bettenson, ed., *Documents of the Christian Church* (New York: Oxford University Press, 1963), p. 210.
4. John Wesley, ed., *John Wesley's Sunday Service of the Methodists in North America* (Nashville: The United Methodist Publishing House, 1984), p. 310.

sionaries; he revered Cranmer's Homilies, especially as they helped him to understand the vital doctrine of justification by faith; he cherished the polity and sacramental life of this communion as revealed in *The Book of Common Prayer*; and he was indebted to such English reformers as Cranmer, Jewel, and Hooker for much of his ecclesiology.[1] Nevertheless, John Wesley was, by his own admission, unwilling to defend in a thoroughgoing manner the accuracy of the so called "Protestant" definition cited above. "I dare not exclude from the church catholic all those congregations," he cautions, "in which any unscriptural doctrines which cannot be affirmed to be the pure Word of God are sometimes, yea, frequently preached."[2] This tolerant attitude, however, valuable as it was, must not be mistaken for indifference. For though Wesley realized that members of the body of Christ can and do exist even where unscriptural doctrines are proclaimed, he remained unwilling to cut the cord completely between the preaching of the Word of God on the one hand, and the suitability of the church on the other. "I lay this down as an undoubted truth," he affirms," the more the doctrine of any Church agrees with the Scripture, the more readily ought it to be received."[3] In fact, this last point became the basis for Wesley's preference of his own Anglican church as revealed in the following comments:

> **Having had an opportunity of seeing several of the Churches abroad, and having deeply considered the several sorts of Dissenters at home, I am fully convinced that our own Church, with all her blemishes, is nearer the scriptural plan than any other in Europe.[4]**

A. Preaching the Pure Word of God

Although many Protestant bodies prided themselves on the soundness of their preaching, their use of the vernacular, and the elevation of the pulpit above the table (or altar), it would be naive to assume that only the pure Word of God was delivered in these congregations on Sunday mornings. Indeed, the difference between homiletical ideal and actual reality was sometimes great. And though Anglicanism, for example, could certainly cherish the cadence, beauty, and grace of Cranmer's *Homilies* — which were more doctrinal and literary productions than anything else — it must also be remembered that these very sermons, especially during the sixteenth century, were often read *verbatim* from the pulpit due to low level of education of some of the parish clergy.[5]

1. Albert C. Outler, ed., *John Wesley* (New York: Oxford University Press, 1964), p. 306.

2. Outler, *Sermons*, 3:52. (Of the Church)

3. Thomas Jackson, ed., *The Works of John Wesley*, 14 vols. (Grand Rapids, Michigan: Baker Book House, 1978), 10:133. Wesley's tolerance in this area probably grew out of his realization that Christian faith is "not barely a speculative, rational thing, a cold, lifeless assent, a train of ideas in the head; but also a disposition of the heart." Cf. Outler, *Sermons*, 1:120. (Salvation by Faith), and 1:419. (The Marks of the New Birth).

4. Ibid., 13:146. In addition, Wesley also claims: "Now it is a known principle of the Church of England, that nothing is to be received as an article of faith, which is not read in the Holy Scripture, or to be inferred therefrom by just and plain consequence." Cf. Jackson, *Wesley's Works,* 10:134.

5. John R. H. Moorman, *A History of the Church in England* (Wilton, Connecticut: Morehouse-Barlow Co., Inc., 1963), p. 219.

Moreover, in the eighteenth century, though the education of priests had improved, especially through the efforts of such people like Bishop Gibson, parish sermons were sometimes judged deficient in other respects — especially by John Wesley and his followers. And here the Methodist leader placed the blame not so much on the church itself or its doctrine as on its priests. But this time the deficiency was viewed not really as an intellectual one, but as a moral and spiritual one. In Wesley's judgment, many of his contemporary clerics neither lived according to, nor properly preached, the gospel. Thus, in an early manuscript sermon, *On Corrupting the Word of God*, the young Wesley addresses this important topic and indicates that such failure in the pulpit comes from a number of sources: First, the preacher sometimes errors in declaring the Word by "mixing it either with the heresies of others or the fancies of his own brain,"[1] or secondly, "by mixing it with false interpretations,"[2] or lastly, by either adding to it or taking away from it.[3]

Much later in his career, in 1782, Wesley dealt with this problem once again in his piece, *On Hearing Ministers who Oppose the Truth*. And here the "moral argument" is much more clearly expressed. It seems that many of the contemporary Methodists under his care complained that they had difficulty listening to the preaching of some Anglican clerics who flatly denied some of the truths cherished and espoused by Wesley. In response to this troubled situation, especially as it concerned the Society at Baildon, Wesley laid the matter before the Conference where it was unanimously agreed that if a minister preached the absolute decrees or ridiculed the doctrine of Christian Perfection, then the Methodist people "should quietly and silently go out of the church, yet attend it again the next opportunity."[4] And in a similar vein in that same year, Wesley addressed the matter of preaching politics from the pulpit and concluded that it was "our main business to preach 'repentance towards God, and faith in our Lord Jesus Christ.'"[5] Christianity, in other words, was not to be confused with, nor reduced to, a political ideology.

B. The Sacraments Duly Administered

It is highly appropriate that a discussion of Wesley's view of the sacraments be reserved until now. This is not to suggest, however, that the Methodist leader did not appreciate the vital and necessary role that the sacraments played in the early and medieval church, for he clearly did. Nevertheless, Wesley's thoughts on the sacraments belong under this heading simply because in many respects they presuppose Protestant distinctions and emphases, and are, therefore, for the most part, unintelligible without them.

---

1. Outler, *Sermons*, 4:247. (On Corrupting the Word of God)
2. Ibid.
3. Ibid.
4. Rupert E. Davies, *The Works of John Wesley*, Vol 9 *The Methodist Societies: History, Nature, and Design* (Nashville: Abingdon Press, 1989), p. 520.
5. Jackson, *Wesley's Works*, 11:154-55.

Not surprisingly, then, when Wesley addresses the question of the number of the sacraments in his sermons, he lists only two: baptism and the Lord's Supper. And his judgment of those additional sacraments, five in number, traditionally affirmed by Roman Catholicism, is expressed in his *Sunday Service* which states:

> Those five commonly called Sacraments; that is to say, Confirmation, Penance, Orders, Matrimony, and extreme Unction, are not to be counted for Sacraments of the Gospel, being such as have grown, partly of the corrupt following of the Apostles, partly are states of life allowed in the Scriptures: but yet have not the like nature of Baptism and the Lord's Supper, because they have not any visible Sign or Ceremony ordained of God.[1]

That is, Confirmation, Penance, and the like are excluded because they lack one of the necessary ingredients of a sacrament; namely, the sign. But a sign in and of itself does not sufficiently define a sacrament according to Wesley; there must also be inward grace, otherwise mere formalism or an *opus operatum* view will result. And so these two components together, sign and inward grace, none to the exclusion of the other, basically constitute what Wesley has in mind by the term sacrament. And in his sermon, *The Means of Grace*, for example, he writes: "a sacrament is 'an outward *sign* of *inward grace*, and a *means* whereby we receive the same."[2]

Continuing this line of thought, that sacraments are means of grace indicates that they are "the ordinary channels whereby he [God] might convey to men preventing, justifying, or sanctifying grace."[3] In other words, the sacraments are the conduits, the vehicles, through which the many and rich blessings of the Most High are communicated to the faithful community. And the chief of these instituted means, though only one is a sacrament by definition, are prayer, searching the Scriptures, and receiving the Lord's Supper.[4]

1. Baptism

Wesley's mature views on the sacrament of baptism are revealing and suggest both a "catholic" emphasis and an "evangelical" one. For instance, concerning the former, Wesley recounts his spiritual biography just prior to Aldersgate in the following words: "I believe till I was about ten years old I had not sinned away that 'washing of the Holy Ghost' which was given me in baptism."[5] In other words, if the phrase "washing of the Holy Ghost" here is to be equated with the new birth, a likely conclusion, then it reveals that even after Aldersgate, John Wesley retained a sacramental or catholic view of the new birth by associating it

---

1. Wesley, *Sunday Service*, p. 311.
2. Outler, *Sermons*, 1:381. (The Means of Grace) Emphasis is mine.
3. Ibid. Bracketed material is mine.
4. Ibid. See also Outler's note # 24 in which he indicates that Wesley did not, for whatever reason, list baptism under the chief means of grace.
5. Ward and Heitzenrater, *Journals and Diaries*, 18:242-43.

with baptism at least in some instances. And this factor will explain, first of all, his continuing support of the practice of infant baptism where the relation between the sign and the thing signified (inward grace) was deemed to be exact. "It is certain," Wesley notes, "our Church supposes that all who are baptized in their infancy are at the same time born again."[1] And elsewhere in his sermon *Catholic Spirit*, produced in 1750, he adds: "I believe infants ought to be baptized, and that this may be done either by dipping or sprinkling. If you are otherwise persuaded, be so still, and follow your own persuasion."[2]

Nevertheless, it should also be noted that even though Wesley upheld the appropriateness of infant baptism, its soteriological significance was diminished somewhat by his notion of prevenient grace. Accordingly, in a letter to John Mason in 1776 he points out: "Therefore no infant ever was or ever will be 'sent to hell for the guilt of Adam's sin, 'seeing it is canceled by the righteousness of Christ as soon as they are sent into the world."[3]

Second, Wesley, as one of the principal leaders of the Evangelical Revival in the eighteenth century, was well aware that the relation between sign and inward grace, though exact as it pertained to infants, was not always so with respect to adults. Thus, in his sermon *The New Birth,* he asserts that regeneration does not always accompany baptism; they do not always go together. "A man may possibly be born of water, and yet not be 'born of the Spirit.'"[4] Yet another way in which the two elements are not so closely associated is when adults, either through sins of omission or commission, forfeit the grace of God which they once so bountifully received. The Oxford don cautions:

> Say not then in your heart, I *was once* baptized; therefore I am *now* a child of God. Alas, that consequence will by no means hold. How many are the baptized gluttons and drunkards, the baptized liars and common swearers, the baptized railers and evil-speakers, the baptized whoremongers, thieves, extortioners! What think you? Are these now the children of God?[5]

In addition, to counsel these unfortunates that there is no new birth but in baptism, that they can no longer be renewed and cleansed, is cruel counsel indeed; it is, says Wesley, "to seal [them] all under damnation, to consign [them] to hell, without any help, without any hope."[6]

---

1. Outler, *Sermons*, 2:197. (The New Birth) For an extensive treatment of the subject of baptism and the Lord's supper Cf. Ole E. Borgen, *John Wesley on the Sacraments* (Grand Rapids: Zondervan\Francis Asbury Press, 1972).

2. Ibid., 2:90. (Catholic Spirit)

3. John Telford, ed., *The Letters of John Wesley, A.M.* 8 vols. (London: The Epworth Press, 1931), 6:239-40.

4. Outler, *Sermons*, 2:197. (The New Birth)

5. Ibid., 1:428-29. (The Marks of the New Birth)

6. Ibid., 1:429. Bracketed material is mine. Of the association of regeneration and baptism, Borgen writes: "All of which goes to prove that the new birth and Baptism do not *always* go together; which also implies that they go together *most of the time.* Several passages in the *Notes upon the New Testament* express the same." Cf. Borgen, *Sacraments*, p. 155.

So then, to the sacramental view of baptism, noted earlier, Wesley added an evangelical one which was expressed in terms of both the reception of grace and in terms of real, vital change. Simply put, those born of God should bear the proper fruit. And Wesley's evangelical emphasis is perhaps most evident in a mid-career sermon in which he stresses that the thing signified in baptism should be "a death unto sin, and a new birth unto righteousness."[1] Real, actual, transformation at its most personal level is Wesley's constant theme and interest.

2. The Lord's Supper

It is apparent from Wesley's many writings that his view of the Lord's Supper was expressed in a Protestant vocabulary. First of all, Wesley, like Luther who preceded him, denied that the Lord's Supper (or Mass) is a sacrifice since such a view would detract from the "infinite value of Christ's sacrifice,"[2] at Golgotha — a sacrifice which needs no repetition. Christ "needeth not daily, as those High Priests, to offer sacrifice," Wesley writes, "for this he did once, when he offered up himself."[3]

Second, the doctrine of transubstantiation, which was formally articulated at the Fourth Lateran Council in 1215 by the Roman Catholic Church, was rejected by the Methodist leader in his consideration of the role of the two key signs in this sacrament. Consequently, in Wesley's view, the bread is not literally the body of Christ, but "signifies or represents" the body.[4] Commenting on Luke 22:19 ("This is my body") the one time Oxford fellow explains:

As he just now celebrated the paschal supper, which was called the passover, so in like figurative language, he calls this bread his body. And this circumstance of itself was sufficient to prevent any mistake, as if this bread was his real body, any more than the paschal lamb was really the passover.[5]

Likewise, wine after the consecration remains wine; it is not, therefore, literally the blood of Christ, nor has it been transformed. Rather, it is the *seal* of the new covenant and the "*sign* of that blood which was shed to confirm it."[6] Again, to use Wesley's own words, it is a "perpetual sign and memorial of [Christ's] blood, as shed for establishing the new covenant."[7] Simply put, the elements as signs point to a reality beyond themselves.

But Wesley's views on this sacrament can also be distinguished from those of the continental Reformers. Luther, for example, in his *Babylonian Captivity of the Church*, maintained that the body and blood of Christ are *really present* in the

---

1. Outler, *Sermons*, 2:196-97. (The New Birth)
2. Jackson, *Wesley's Works*, 10:120.
3. Ibid.
4. Wesley, *N.T. Notes*, p. 87.
5. Ibid., p. 200.
6. Ibid., p. 200. Emphasis is mine.
7. Ibid., p. 131.

untransformed bread and wine.[1] Thus, on the one hand, contrary to the Enthusiasts, Luther affirmed that the elements contain within them the actual body and blood of Christ, and at one point to underscore this teaching he even quipped: "Before I would drink mere wine with the Enthusiasts, I would rather have pure blood with the Pope."[2] However, on the other hand, contrary to Rome, the German reformer declared that the realities of bread and wine remain. Luther's view then is somewhat of a balance between some quite divergent conceptions, and it has been referred to as consubstantiation. Nevertheless, it was similarly rejected by Wesley in his own determination that "no corporeal, carnal, material, substantial or localized presence of Christ in the sacrament can be accepted."[3] Christ's presence, though real, must be otherwise expressed.

In light of these differences with Luther, some Methodist scholars have claimed that Wesley's assessment of the Lord's Supper was remarkably similar to that of John Calvin largely because not only did both leaders stress that Christ is corporally present only in heaven, but also because both underscored a strong spiritual presence in this sacrament.[4] Ole Borgen in his book *John Wesley on the Sacraments* assesses this judgment and writes:

> **[Those who] have claimed Wesley for the Calvinistic and Reformed camp, must resign themselves to the fact that Wesley will not fully satisfy this side either. Although there is a large degree of agreement with Calvin here, still, the latter will stress the importance of the presence of Christ's body in terms of 'power and strength' mediated through the Holy Spirit, while Wesley will emphasize the presence of Christ in his divinity.[5]**

This means, of course, that Wesley's conception of the "Real Presence" in the Lord's Supper excluded even the slightest hint of a physical, bodily presence. Christ is present in the sacrament, to be sure, but in terms of a "'Dynamic' or 'Living Presence.'"[6] In other words, Christ is actually in the sacrament in the sense that He is working through this means of grace, to heal, transform and restore. But, once again, He is not localized in the elements.

In Wesley's view, then, the Lord's Supper is preeminently a means of grace, an objective expression of the bounty and favor of God towards humanity.

---

1. Paul Althaus, *The Theology of Martin Luther* (Philadelphia: Fortress Press, 1966), p. 376. Luther also rejected the idea of transubstantiation in his *Babylonian Captivity of the Church* in which he writes: "Since it is not necessary, therefore, to assume a transubstantiation effected by divine power, it must be regarded as a figment of the human mind, for it rests neither on the Scriptures nor on reason, as we shall see." Cf. Abdel Ross Wentz, ed., *Luther's Works*, Vol. 26. *Word and Sacrament II* (Philadelphia: Fortress Press, 1959), p. 31 ff.

2. Ibid., p. 376.

3. Borgen, *Sacraments*, p. 65. Borgen maintains "that instead of indulging in metaphysical speculations concerning Christ's human and glorified body, he [Wesley] is more concerned with the unity of the Godhead: Father, Son and Holy Spirit are one God. God is a Spirit and, therefore, the only way Christ can be present with us is as Spirit." Cf. Ibid., p. 65-66.

4. Ibid., p. 67.

5. Ibid., p. 67.

6. Ibid., p. 69.

Unlike baptism, which is an initiatory rite, the Lord's Supper is suited for life's journey, for assistance along the way, as one is continually transformed into the likeness of Christ. And in his sermon, *The Means of Grace* Wesley points out:

> **Is not the eating of that bread, and the drinking of that cup, the outward, visible means whereby God conveys into our souls all that spiritual grace that righteousness, and peace and joy in the Holy Ghost, which were purchased by the body of Christ once broken and the blood of Christ once shed for us? Let all, therefore, who truly desire the grace of God, eat of that bread and drink of that cup.**[1]

Wesley's last phrase just cited, "Let all, therefore, who truly desire the grace of God ..." is revealing and distinguishes his position in one important respect from that of John Calvin. All people, whether justified or not, whether a member of the Church of England or not, were welcomed at the Lord's table by the Methodist leader, provided they were heartily sorry for their sins. Why? Because the Lord's Supper was ordained by God to be "a means of conveying to men either preventing, or justifying, or sanctifying grace, *according to their several necessities.*"[2] This means, then, that Wesley viewed the Lord's Supper not simply as a confirming ordinance, but also as a converting ordinance, open to humble, contrite sinners. On this head, the Oxonian reasons:

> **But experience shows the gross falsehood of that assertion that the Lord's Supper is not a converting ordinance. Ye are the witnesses. For many now present know, the very beginning of your conversion to God (perhaps, in some, the first deep conviction) was wrought at the Lord's Supper. Now, one single instance of this kind overthrows the whole assertion.**[3]

John Calvin might have unduly "fenced the table"; John Wesley, on the other hand, did not.

With these last points in mind, the reader can now understand why Wesley stressed the duty (and privilege) of constant communion in an important sermon written in 1787. First, it is a plain command of Christ (Do this in remembrance of me), and second the benefits to be received are so great — the forgiveness of our sins and the strengthening of our souls — that it would be unfortunate if they were not continually received.[4] In a real sense, the Lord's Supper, as a means of grace, represents an accommodation to our physical being; it is nothing less than the gospel itself expressed in a concrete and tangible form.

---

1. Outler, *Sermons*, 1:389-90. (The Means of Grace)

2. Nehemiah Curnock, *The Journal of the Rev. John Wesley, A.M.*, 8 vols. (London: The Epworth Press, 1938), 2:361.

3. Ibid.

4. Outler, *Sermons*, 3:428-29. (The Duty of Constant Communion) It should also be noted that the sacraments, for Wesley, have an objective force to them such that the grace of God is communicated through them even though the priest who administers them may be wicked. In other words, Wesley, in agreement with the early church, rejected the Donatist position that the moral or spiritual state of the priest affects the efficacy of the sacrament. Cf. Outler, *Sermons*, 3:477. (On Attending the Church Service).

IV. Methodism

As the Church of England, with its rich sacramental life, was a child of the Reformation, so Methodism was a child of the Church of England. But of the precise origin of Methodism within this historic communion, there is something of a debate, and Heitzenrater claims, for instance, that it is much too simplistic to argue that Methodism began in November, 1729, when John Wesley returned to reside in Oxford.[1] However, bracketing out some of the more technical questions for a moment, the year 1729, generally speaking, is the one that most often emerges in Wesley's recollections. It is found, for instance, in the sermon On God's Vineyard, written in 1787,[2] as well as in an earlier piece, A Short History of the People Called Methodists, in which the elderly Oxonian reminisces and delineates a three-fold rise of Methodism:

> ... the first rise of Methodism (so called) was in November 1729, when four of us met together at Oxford; the second was at Savannah, in April 1736, when twenty or thirty persons met at my house; the last was at London, on this day, when forty or fifty of us agreed to meet together every Wednesday evening, in order to a free conversation, begun and ended with singing and prayer.[3]

At any rate, what is important for the task at hand is neither the exact date of the rise of Methodism, nor speculation concerning the name itself,[4] but the nature of this movement as a clue to Wesley's ecclesiology. Along these lines, Davies suggests that early Methodism should be conceived under the rubric of a "society" in order to be properly understood. Interestingly, this British scholar appeals to the language of Troeltsch, of a century earlier, and argues that Methodism in its infancy represented a third category of Christian communion which fell somewhere between a church and sect.[5] He elaborates:

> A 'society acknowledges the truths proclaimed by the universal church and has no wish to separate from it, but claims to cultivate, by means of sacrament and fellowship, the type of inward holiness, which too great an objectivity can easily neglect and of which the church needs constantly to be reminded.[6]

If this designation of Davies is accurate, then it means that the relationship of the Methodist societies to the Anglican church was perhaps a dialectical one — offering both affirmation and protest simultaneously. Thus, on the one hand,

---

1. Richard P. Heitzenrater, *Mirror and Memory: Reflections on Early Methodism* (Nashville: Kingswood Books, 1989), p. 69.

2. Outler, *Sermons*, 3:503. (On God's Vineyard)

3. Davies, *The Methodist Societies*, 9:430.

4. For an interesting account of the possible origins of the name "Methodist" Cf. Heitzenrater, *Mirror and Memory*, p. 13ff. And note also in his sermon, *On Laying the Foundation of the New Chapel*, Wesley writes: "The regularity of their behaviour gave occasion to a young gentleman of the college to say, 'I think we have got a new set of *Methodists* — alluding to a set of physicians who began to flourish at Rome about the time of Nero, and continued for several ages." Cf. Outler, *Sermons*, 3:581.

5. Davies, *The Methodist Societies*, 9:3.

6. Ibid., 9:3.

Wesley could in a rather self-conscious way look to Methodism as representing the best of Anglicanism as in his sermon *On God's Vineyard.*[1] And, likewise, in his homily, *On Laying the Foundation of the New Chapel,* he could compare this movement quite favorably not only with the primitive church — which we've come to expect — but once again with the Church of England:

> **Methodism, so called, is the old religion, the religion of the Bible, the religion of the primitive church, *the religion of the Church of England.* This 'old religion' ... is no other than love; the love of God and of all mankind; the loving God with all our heart, and soul, and strength, as having first loved us ...**[2]

So understood, Methodism was not so much a protest against the Anglican church as a call for its enrichment — an invitation to live out its highest ideals, teachings, and creeds. In fact, Methodism was spawned at Oxford by some earnest and sincere young people who sought in every way to take their Anglicanism seriously and not for granted.

But, on the other hand, the Methodist societies which were created to support the church could also challenge it in a thoroughgoing way, especially in terms of their use of the laity, and in their criticism, on occasion, of the Anglican clergy. Accordingly, Albert Outler points out that these societies, at times, served the established church "even against the good will of her leaders [as] a distinctive adaptation of the pietistic patterns of the 'religious societies.'"[3] Here, the more forceful protest of Spener's *ecclesiola in ecclesia* of a century earlier comes to mind.[4]

Moreover, given the relatively independent status of the Methodist societies (but always under Wesley's tight control), the tensions between Anglicanism and Methodism were inevitable and were later aggravated when Wesley, being the proficient administrator that he was, not only developed a burgeoning infrastructure to support the British revival, but also employed such practices as lay preaching, extempore prayer, field preaching, and the violation of parish boundaries — all of which irritated many of the regular and more-settled Anglican clergy.[5] Judged from Wesley's perspective, the Methodist classes, bands, and select societies were necessary in order to spread scriptural holiness across the land. Judged from the Anglican clergy's perspective, however, these groups loomed so large at times as to threaten the good order of the church itself. And it is precisely at this point that the rudiments of Wesley's protest against the eighteenth-

---

1. Outler, *Sermons,* 3:503ff. (On God's Vineyard)

2. Outler, *Sermons,* 3:585. (On Laying the Foundation of the New Chapel) Emphasis is mine.

3. Outler, *John Wesley,* p. 307. Bracketed material is mine.

4. Howard Snyder, "Pietism, Moravianism, and Methodism as Renewal Movements" (Ph.D. dissertation, University of Notre Dame, 1983), p. 261. Snyder offers seven frameworks to explore the structure of renewal movements, ranging from *ecclesiola in ecclesia* to Catholic/Anabaptist typology. See p. 11 ff. Moreover, Snyder contends that although Wesley did not explicitly draw on the Pietist *ecclesiola* model, he in fact viewed Methodism as an *ecclesiola*; that is, the Methodist leader's views seem to presuppose some kind of *ecclesiola* conception. Cf. p. 261.

5. Frank Baker, *John Wesley and the Church of England* (Nashville: Abingdon Press, 1970), p. 88 ff.

century Church of England begin to emerge. However, Wesley's most strident and telling remarks, his deepest criticisms of his own church, emerge out of his consideration of the nature and goals of ministry, and the role of ecclesiastical order in support of that ministry.

V. Methodist Ministry and Anglican Etiquette

Convinced that preacher - evangelist was a different order of ministry than pastor - priest, and that the former could be filled by competent lay people, Wesley began to employ "assistants" who were directly responsible to him in order to further the Methodist revival. Basically, this order of ministry was comprised of those preachers who were appointed to administer the societies and the other preachers within the circuits. Lay people could qualify for this largely administrative role by evidencing a close walk with God, by understanding and loving discipline, and "By loving the Church of England, and resolving not to separate from it."[1] In 1747, a differentiation was made between those assistants who traveled and those who served only in one place, and thus arose the distinction between traveling and local preachers which is a part of Methodism even today.

However, it was not long after Wesley began to employ his assistants that a hue and cry arose among the Anglican clergy concerning this irregular practice. Two chief objections emerged: The first concerned the unordained status of these ministers, and the second entailed their supposed ignorance. With respect to the former charge, Wesley thought that he had strong Scriptural support for the distinction between an extraordinary prophetic role which could be filled by lay people and an ordinary priestly one which was reserved for the ordained. In his *Explanatory Notes Upon the New Testament*, he remarked with respect to Ephesians, chapter four, verse eleven:

> **A prophet testifies of things to come: an evangelist of things past: and that chiefly by preaching the Gospel before or after any of the apostles. All these were extraordinary officers: the ordinary were, some pastors—Watching over their several flocks, and some teachers—Whether of the same, or a lower order, to assist them as might require.[2]**

Moreover, when John Toppin, the curate of Allendale in Northumberland, took umbrage with lay preaching and questioned in 1752, "whether any orthodox members of Christ's church ever took upon them the public office of preaching without episcopal ordination, and in what century,"[3] Wesley referred him to the Bible and replied: "Yes, very many, after the persecution of Stephen in the very first century, as you may read in the eighth chapter of the Acts."[4]

---

1. Jackson, *Wesley's Works*, 8:319.
2. Wesley, *N.T. Notes*, p. 496.
3. Frank Baker, ed., *The Works of John Wesley: The Letters* 2 vols. (Nashville: Abingdon Press, 1982), 26:495.
4. Ibid.

By employing lay ministers who were allowed to preach, but who were not permitted to administer the sacraments, John Wesley believed that the Methodist movement remained well within the ecclesiastical setting of the Church of England.   In his mind, at least, the repudiation of lay administration of the sacraments, and Methodism's connection with the Anglican Church were inextricably tied.   John feared, like his brother Charles, that if his preachers insisted on administering the sacraments without being ordained, then Methodism would soon emerge as an independent movement, incapable of reforming the larger Church.   Ordination, therefore, became the watershed in early Methodism between those who could administer and those who could not. In a certain sense, ordination was the fence or barrier wrapped around the ecclesiastical structure of primitive Methodism in order to keep it within the bounds of the Anglican church.

Though Wesley respected the right and privilege of the Anglican clergy to administer the sacraments, this does not mean that he always respected these clerics themselves or their ministries.   Once again the relation to the mother church is one of ambivalence. To be sure, throughout his lengthy career Wesley had seen an ordained, educated clergy operating under the auspices of the Church of England, some of whom were spiritually dead, while still others were outright wicked.[1] They neither preached the doctrines contained in the Anglican Articles, nor did they practice holiness, and yet they had all the formal trappings of ministry. To make certain that this kind of minister did not emerge within the Methodist movement Wesley exercised discipline. For example, in a "Letter to the Evangelical Clergy" in 1764 he specified a number of essential doctrines such as original sin, justification by faith, and holiness of heart and life to which all clergy who were associated with him should assent. Clearly, this was not an attempt on the part of Wesley to stifle theological discussion or to suppress various opinions and interpretations, for the same irenic spirit that characterized his sermon *The Catholic Spirit* was present in this letter as well. But, on the other hand, Wesley simply did not wish to see the Methodist movement fall into a latitudinarianism that would dilute the heart of the gospel and with it Methodism's very reason for being. And upon reflecting as to just what is a Gospel Minister Wesley wrote:

> **Who then is such? Who is a Gospel Minister, in the full, scriptural sense of the word? He, and he alone, of whatever denomination, that does declare the whole counsel of God; that does preach the whole gospel, even justification and sanctification, preparatory to glory....those only are, in the full sense, Gospel Ministers who proclaim the 'great salvation;' that is, salvation from all (both inward and outward) sin, into "all the mind that was in Christ Jesus;...[2]**

Beyond a consideration of who may suitably engage in ministry, Wesley's evangelical thrust is also apparent as he reflected upon the task of ministry itself.

1. Telford, *Letters*, 4:303.
2. Jackson, *Works*, 1o:456

At the first Methodist conference, for example, Wesley declared that the major purpose for convening was "To consider how we should proceed to save our own souls and those that heard us."[1] And in the deliberations of this same conference it was asked, "What is the office of a Christian Minister?" To which it was replied, "[It is] to watch over souls, as he that must give an account."[2] Without doubt, Wesley never departed from this evangelical conception of the ministerial task, nor was he embarrassed by the language of "saving souls." In fact, such language can be found in most any period of his ministry. In a letter to his brother, Charles, in 1772, for example, John reflected back upon the time when they both had taken priests' orders and noted that their principal task of ministry, then as now, was "to save souls."[3]

But just what did it mean to save souls according to Wesley? It was not a work of the by and by, concerned only with the afterlife, nor was it an impractical affair. Instead, it was the arduous and present work to rescue people from the death of sin, and to reclaim them for life with God. Moreover, Wesley expressed this most important task both positively and negatively. Positively, to save a soul was to lead it to the gospel through which the love of God and neighbor could be reestablished in the heart through faith. Negatively, it entailed the breaking of the yoke of sin, freedom from its power and its guilt, and from all that stifled the ability to love.[4] Indeed, Wesley knew full well both that the greatest of all bondages was bondage to sin and that the greatest of all liberties was the freedom to walk in the love of God blameless. To this task, and to this task preeminently, he committed his ministers as evidenced in his *Farther Appeal*:

> To 'seek and save that which is lost;' to bring souls from Satan to God; to instruct the ignorant; to reclaim the wicked; to convince the gainsayer; to direct their feet in the way of peace, and then keep them therein; to follow them step by step, lest they turn out of the way, and advise them in their doubts and temptations; to lift up them that fall; to refresh them that are faint; and to comfort the weak-hearted; to administer various helps, as the variety of occasions re-quire, according to their several necessities: These are parts of our office...[5]

So emphatic was Wesley on this score that he boldly asserted elsewhere that true evangelical ministers were those who saved souls from death,[6] and that if they failed to do so, then, whatever else they might be, they were no ministers of Christ.[7]

---

1. Ibid., 13:248.
2. Ibid., 8:309.
3. Telford, *Letters*, 5:316. And in his sermon, *The Wisdom of God's Counsels*, Wesley maintains that the early Methodists sought "no honour, no profit, no pleasure, no ease, but merely to save souls." Cf. Outler, *Sermons*, 2:558-59.
4. See "The Great Privilege of those that are Born of God" in Outler, *Works*, 1:431ff.
5. Jackson, *Works*, 8:177-78.
6. Telford, *Letters*, 2:149.
7. Ibid.

VI. Some Concluding Observations

When Wesley realized that he had failed to arouse sufficient support within his own church, he undertook the task of developing the instruments of ministry necessary to sustain the awakening that was sweeping across the British Isles. Thus, in a pungent letter to Nicholas Norton in 1756, the leader of the Methodist revival revealed that he tolerated lay preaching — as noted earlier — because of the "absolute necessity for it,"[1] and declared that were it not for this instrument of ministry, "thousands of souls would perish everlastingly."[2] In other words, Wesley, as an energetic evangelist, simply refused to stand by and watch the spiritual harvest of England rot on the ground for want of laborers. Taking the offensive, and in a pragmatic mood, he urged his detractors to consider the goal of ecclesiastical order at all. "Is it not to bring souls from the power of Satan to God,"[3] he queried. "Order then," he continued, "is so far valuable as it answers these ends; and if it answers them not, it is nothing worth."[4]

In light of the preceding, it can be argued that many of the strains between Methodism and Anglicanism — though certainly not all — were due, in part, to the former's emphasis of the ends or goals of ministry and the latter's stress on the proper, traditional forms of such service. In other words, here was a clash between soteriology on the one hand, and church order on the other. More to the point, here was the rise of an "evangelical order within [a] national church."[5] "The Wesleyan accent," as Outler points out, "is the insistence that the church is *best defined in action*, in her witness and mission, rather than by her form of polity."[6]

Caught in the middle between ecclesiastical etiquette and the burden to preach the gospel as widely as possible, Wesley performed a balancing act for many years. But when finally forced to decide — and Wesley was after all very reluctant to do this — he preferred to save souls, even by what seemed to others to be very unorthodox means, over obedience to what he had come to believe was an all-too-human ecclesiastical order. His conception of ministry, therefore, was functional, goal-oriented (teleological), and frankly evangelical. In fact, at several points in his career, Wesley was even bold enough to believe that his own Methodist movement was reversing the "mystery of iniquity," which had plagued the church throughout the ages,[7] that Methodism was "only the beginning of a

---

1. Ibid., 3:186 Henry D. Rack in his book Reasonable Enthusiast: *John Wesley and the Rise of Methodism* (Philadelphia: Trinity Press International, 1989) considers the question "Who was the first 'Methodist' lay preacher? and then chronicles the ever-larger role that lay preachers played throughout the Evangelical Revival. See p. 210 ff.

2. Ibid.

3. Baker, *The Works of John Wesley*, 26:206.

4. Ibid.

5. Outler, *John Wesley*, p. 384 Bracketed material is mine.

6. Ibid., p. 307. Emphasis is mine.

7. Ibid., 2:490, 495. (The General Spread of the Gospel)

far greater work — the dawn of 'the latter day glory,'"[1] and that its fruits would ultimately reach "from sea to sea."[2] "Give me one hundred preachers who fear nothing but sin and desire nothing but God,"[3] he thundered in his later years, "and I care not a straw whether they be clergymen of laymen, such alone will shade the gates of hell and set up the kingdom of heaven on earth."[4]

1. Ibid., 2:493. Wesley was not alone in his sentiments here. For instance, Jonathan Edwards in his *Faithful Narrative* — a work, by the way, which Wesley eagerly read — considered the revival in Northampton, Massachusetts, an ocean away, to be an anticipation of "the latter day glory" as well. Indeed, the Evangelical Revival of the 18th century was, in a real sense, a transatlantic phenomenon. Cf. Jonathan Edwards, *A Faithful Narrative of the Surprising Work of God* (Grand Rapids, Michigan: Baker Book House, Reprinted 1979).

2. Ibid., 3:452-53. (Of Former Times)

3. Telford, *Letters*, 6:272.

4. Ibid.

CHAPTER FIVE

THE DOCTRINE OF HUMANITY
"I believe in the forgiveness of sins..."

As Leslie Stevenson has argued so well in his recent book, *Seven Theories of Human Nature*, different conceptions of human nature, whether they arise from Christianity, Marxism, or Freudianism, inevitably entail different diagnoses of, and prescriptions for, the human predicament.[1] Anthropology, in other words, is an important consideration in any given world-view; it colors (and is colored by) our most fundamental conceptions of reality. And in the area of theology, in particular, our present concern, the doctrine of humanity has great consequence for our understanding of creation, the person of Jesus Christ, and the doctrine of salvation, to name a few. Moreover, if John Wesley's theological interests were indeed largely practical and soteriological (as I have argued earlier in *Wesley on Salvation*), then his doctrine of humanity should prove to be an excellent window on the overall contours of his theological thinking.

I. Humanity as Body and Spirit

In his second sermon entitled, *What is Man?*, produced in 1788 (the first was written in 1787), Wesley follows the body/mind dualism of Descartes put forth a century earlier. Thus, concerning the first aspect of the body, the Cartesian *res extensa*, Wesley observes in a way reminiscent of Empedocles that it is composed of four basic elements: earth, air, fire, and water.[2] And these elements, the Anglican priest continues, are properly proportioned and mixed together to form the greater unity. However, not only do these four roots cast light on the nature of the body, indicating its basic composition, but they also help to explain the various functions of the body's many organs. Wesley explains:

> **Let me consider this yet a little farther. Is not the primary use of the lungs to administer fire to the body, which is continually extracted from the air by that curious fire-pump? By inspiration it takes in the**

1. Leslie Stevenson, *Seven Theories of Human Nature* (New York: Oxford University Press, 1987), p. 4.

2. Albert C. Outler, ed., *The Works of John Wesley: Sermons*, 4 vols. (Nashville: Abingdon Press, 1984), 4:20. (What is Man?, 1788)

air, water, and fire together. In its numerous cells (commonly called air-vessels) it detaches the fire from the air and water. This then mixes with the blood...[1]

But what is especially interesting in this context is neither Wesley's speculation concerning the elements which make up the body, nor his understanding of its organs — both of which are primitive — but rather his tendency on occasion to attribute many of the basic limitations of human beings to the body itself. Thus, in the earlier sermon *What is Man?* he affirms that human beings are restricted in terms of both space and time. Concerning space, or what Wesley calls magnitude, an individual is lost in comparison with all the inhabitants of the earth.[2] And concerning time, human life runs its course most often by "threescore years and ten."[3] But notice, more importantly, the lessons which Wesley draws from all this. It appears that he highlights these limitations precisely in order to place human existence in proper perspective and to allow his readers to draw the appropriate moral and spiritual conclusions: namely, that since human existence is precarious due to the ever-present possibility of physical death, the wise person will fear God and act accordingly.[4]

But a person is not simply a body; he or she is also what Wesley calls a "soul" — a self-moving, thinking principle (res cogitans).[5] And although Wesley affirms that in the present state of existence the human soul cannot be considered apart from the body, the two being intimately connected, yet the death of the body will not involve the death of the soul. Simply put, the essence of a person, what is often identified as the "I" or the "self," will continue to exist even when the body dies. "I cannot but believe this self-moving, thinking principle, with all its passions and affections," Wesley writes, "will continue to exist although the body be mouldered into dust."[6] However, the independence of the soul is only an interim state, according to the Methodist leader, for the unity of body and soul will be restored at the resurrection (more on this in the last chapter).

II. Humanity Created in the Image of God

The excellency and immortality of the soul suggest that it and not the body constitutes what is meant by the image of God. Not surprisingly, Wesley in his

---

1. Ibid., 4:20-21.
2. Ibid., 3:456 (What is Man?, 1787)
3. Ibid., 3:458.
4. Ibid., 1:104-05. (Preface)
5. Ibid., 4:23. (What is Man? 1788) Parenthetical material is mine. It is interesting to note that Wesley's speculations as to where thinking is located in the body followed Descartes' discussion of a similar matter to some degree. Thus, Wesley thought that thinking might be located in the pineal gland, while the French philosopher viewed this area of the brain as the possible site for the body-mind interaction. Cf. Outler, *Sermons*, 4:22. (What is Man? 1788) and *Meditations*, translated by Haldane and Ross, in *The Philosophical Works of Descartes* (Cambridge University Press, 1931), Vol. I, pp. 192 and 196.
6. Ibid.

sermon *What is Man?* specifically identifies the *imago dei* with the soul or with what at other times he calls the "spirit of man."[1] He writes:

... David does not appear to have taken at all into his account, namely, that the body is not the man; that man is not only a house of clay, but an immortal spirit; a spirit made in the image of God, an incorruptible picture of the God of glory; a spirit that is of infinitely more value than the whole earth.[2]

Observe in the remainder of this sermon that Wesley uses the terms "spirit" and "soul" interchangeably and as counterpoints to the term "body." His anthropology, therefore, as noted earlier, is and remains basically dualistic. Tripartite conceptions of humanity, on the other hand, distinguish not only the body from the soul, as Wesley does, but also the soul from the spirit. Note, however, that the question of anthropological dualism, the body/soul distinction, should not be confused with the way in which the soul itself is created in the image of God. On this latter topic, Wesley explains in his sermon *The New Birth*, that humanity is created in the image of God under three aspects: namely, the natural, political, and moral images.[3] This means, then, that the soul (of Wesley's body/soul dualism) is created in the image of God in a threefold way.

The first aspect of the *imago dei*, the natural image, reveals that humanity was created a spirit, as God is a spirit, and was endued with understanding, which, "if not the essence, seems to be the most essential property of a spirit."[4] Beyond this, Wesley indicates that the natural image entails not only understanding but also a "will, with various affections,"[5] and "liberty."[6] And these same three ingredients of the natural image (understanding, will, and liberty) are found in several of Wesley's homilies ranging from *The New Birth* to *On Divine Providence*.[7] But what few Wesleyan scholars have observed in earlier discussions of the natural image is that "every spirit in the universe," as Wesley aptly points out, "is endued with understanding, and in consequence with a will and with a measure of liberty;..."[8] In other words, the entire animal kingdom participates in the natural image of God in however limited a fashion. Humanity does not hold exclusive rights here. In fact, in his sermon, *The General Deliverance*, produced in 1781, Wesley notes that the original state of the brute creation was char-

1. Ibid., 3:460. (What is Man?, 1787).
2. Ibid.
3. Ibid., 2:188. (The New Birth) Moreover, commenting on 1 Thessalonians 5:23, Wesley again underscores a dualistic conception of humanity and repudiates a tripartite view as revealed in his following thoughts: "To explain this a little farther; of the three here mentioned [spirit, soul, and body], only the two last are natural, constituent parts of man.... That man cannot possibly consist of three parts appears hence. The soul is either matter or not matter; there is no medium. But if it is matter, it is part of the body; if not matter, it coincides with the spirit." Cf. John Wesley, *Explanatory Notes Upon the New Testament* (Salem, Ohio: Schmul Publishers), p. 532. Bracketed material is mine.
4. Outler, *Sermons*, 2:474. (The End of Christ's Coming)
5. Ibid.
6. Ibid., 2:475. (The End of Christ's Coming)
7. Ibid., 2:188. (The New Birth) and 2:540-41. (On Divine Providence)
8. Ibid., 2:475. (The End of Christ's Coming)

acterized by an innate principle of self-motion, a degree of understanding, a will including various passions, and liberty — all the ingredients which have just been noted in terms of humanity.[1] Just what does distinguish human beings from the rest of the animal kingdom will be detailed shortly.

The second aspect of the *imago dei* is the so-called political image. In defining and explaining the nature of this aspect, Wesley appeals to the language of Genesis and notes that humanity was given "dominion over the fish of the sea, and over the fowl of the air, and over every living thing that moveth upon the earth."[2] Describing the order and government established in creation, Wesley writes, "Man was God's viceregent upon earth, the prince and governor of this lower world;"[3] This means, interestingly enough, that although God is the Governor *par excellence*, the Supreme Being has not claimed exclusive prerogatives here, but has graciously allowed humanity to share in this rule and to exercise an authority over the lower creation. Here humanity is distinguished in certain respects from the rest of creation and a hierarchy of sorts is established. God as Governor does not rule in isolation, but governs through His appointed viceregents.

But humanity's position within the created order can also be viewed another way, not so much in terms of rule and authority, but in terms of the mediation of divine, bountiful grace. Humanity, according to Wesley, is the great conduit, the chosen channel, of God's blessings for the rest of creation, and is therefore in some sense responsible for the general state of the animal realm.[4] And in describing the original nature of this relationship of humanity and beast Wesley observes:

> As all the blessings of God in paradise flowed through man to the inferior creatures; as man was the great channel of communication between the Creator and the whole brute creation; so when man made himself incapable of transmitting those blessings, that communication was necessarily cut off.[5]

Moreover, it should also be noted that God has not only chosen to bless the lower creation through human beings, "but it is generally his pleasure," Wesley acknowledges, "... to help man by man."[6] The grace of God then often bears a human face.

---

1. Ibid., 2:440. (The General Deliverance) The implications of Wesley's views here are significant and would suggest that humanity should not treat the animal kingdom in a merely instrumental way. For this eighteenth century leader, it is evident that all living creatures come from the hand of God and they therefore should be treated accordingly. Animals are not mere machines, as Descartes postulated, but instead are living spirits. Cf. Outler, *Sermons*, 2:437ff.

2. Ibid. 2:440.

3. Ibid.

4. Ibid.

5. Ibid. 2:442.

6. Ibid., 3:349. (On the Education of Children) Though seldom appreciated, this sermon displays the basic contours of Wesley's soteriological synergism (grace-assisted divine/human cooperation). But notice that Wesley makes a distinction between reward and glory in this homily, a distinction which keeps his doctrine of salvation free from any notion of merit: "He honours men to be, in this sense, 'workers together with him'. By this means the reward is ours, while the glory redounds to him." Ibid.

The third and last aspect of the *imago dei* is the moral image. And when Wesley describes the nature of this image in his sermons he often appeals to the language of Ephesians 4:24, more specifically to the phrase, "righteousness and true holiness." This exact phrase, for example, is repeated in the sermons: The *New Birth*,[1] *On the Fall of Man*,[2] *The End of Christ's Coming*,[3] and *On Perfection*.[4] And it is obviously Wesley's favorite way of portraying the moral image of God. But just what does this phrase mean? What after all is meant by "righteousness and true holiness"? Some clues can be gathered from Wesley's comments on this subject in his sermon, *The New Birth* where he states:

> So God created man in his own image ... but chiefly in his *moral image*, which, according to the Apostle, is 'righteousness and true holiness'. In this image of God was man made. 'God is love:' accordingly man at his creation was full of love, which was the sole principle of all his tempers, thoughts, words, and actions. God is full of justice, mercy, and truth: so was man as he came from the hands of his Creator. God is spotless purity: and so man was in the beginning pure from every sinful blot.[5]

Notice in the quotation just cited that "righteousness and true holiness," the moral image of God, is described in terms of love, justice, mercy, truth, and purity — all those "holy tempers" that Wesley desired to be richly established in his heart even as a young man.[6] Observe also that Wesley maintains that the moral image is the chief image with respect to the other two. Put another way, because humanity is created in righteousness and true holiness, it can participate in a rich moral and spiritual life in a way that other animals cannot. And though even beasts have understanding (natural image), as Wesley freely admits,[7] they are not creatures capable of God. The moral image, therefore, probably describes most accurately and succinctly what for Wesley was *the* human-defining characteristic.

In light of the preceding, it should be evident that Wesley argues for the essential goodness of the created order at its inception. And such views are expressed not only in his *O T Notes* on the book of Genesis, but also in his sermon, *God's Approbation of His Works*. However, the goodness of humanity, though the first

---

1. Ibid., 2:188. (The New Birth)
2. Ibid., 2:411. (On the Fall of Man)
3. Ibid., 2:475. (The End of Christ's Coming)
4. Ibid., 3:75. (On Perfection)
5. Ibid., 2:188. (The New Birth) The importance of the moral image of God for Wesley is revealed in his life-long pursuit of the holy life which basically began in 1725 (roughly speaking) with his reading of the triumvirate of A Kempis, Taylor, and Law. And the sermons, *The Circumcision of the Heart* (1733), *Christian Perfection* (1741), *The Scripture Way of Salvation* (1765), and *The More Excellent Way* (1787), mark important points along the way. Moreover, Wesley closely associates salvation with the restoration of the moral image of God in many of these pieces.
6. One of the best places to view Wesley's understanding of the relation between love, holy tempers, and works of piety and mercy —in other words between internal and external religion — is in his sermon, *On Zeal*. Cf. Outler, *Sermons*, 3:313.
7. Outler, *Sermons*, 2:441. (The General Deliverance)

chord struck in Wesley's anthropology, is certainly not its principal theme, as will be clear from the following discussion.

III. Humanity as Fallen

A. The Adamic Fall

When Wesley asks the question, "How came evil into the world?" as he does in his sermon, *The End of Christ's Coming*, he answers this query initially in terms of Lucifer, that fallen angel often identified with the figure of Isaiah 14:12 ff.[1] However, elsewhere in this same sermon, he also traces the origin of evil to the devil,[2] and then later on to Satan.[3] Apparently, the Methodist leader makes little distinction between these names; all seem to refer to the same source of evil.

Following a well-established church tradition that goes back at least as far as Gregory the Great,[4] Wesley conceives the essence of Lucifer's sin in terms of pride. "Lucifer ... of the first, if not the first archangel was self-tempted to think too highly of himself," Wesley notes, "He freely yielded to the temptation, and gave way first to pride, then to self-will."[5] So understood, satanic evil appears to be starkly irrational since it lacks a prior cause; it simply emerges in the context of both goodness and freedom as their perversions. However, when Wesley considers the fall of humanity itself, he distinguishes it in some important respects from that of Lucifer: the former succumbed to the temptation of an active, external power of evil; the latter fell in the face of an entirely good creation. "The devil," Wesley remarks, was "self-tempted."[6] Humanity was not.

Such a difference in terms of the source and origin of evil leads, secondly, to a different estimation of the essence or root of evil in each instance. For example, in the case of the devil the *ordo depravatio* as displayed in the sermon *The End of Christ's Coming* is as follows:

Self-Temptation —> Pride —> Self-Will —> Evil Affections

But with respect to humanity the following order pertains:

External Temptation —> Unbelief —> Pride —> Self-Will —> Evil Affections

Consequently, when Wesley describes the fall of Eve in this same sermon he maintains that Satan, as an external foil, mingled truth with falsehood so that "unbelief begot pride ... it begot self-will."[7] Elsewhere, in his sermon *On the*

---

1. For an excellent treatment of diabology, which takes the approach of the history of ideas, Cf. Jeffrey Burton Russell, *Lucifer: The Devil in the Middle Ages* (Ithica: Cornell University Press, 1984)

2. Outler, *Sermons*, 2:476. (The End of Christ's Coming)

3. Ibid., 2:477.

4. Matthew Baasten, *Pride According to Gregory the Great: A Study of the Moralia* (New York: Edwin Mellon Press, 1986)

5. Outler, *Sermons*, 2:476. (The End of Christ's Coming)

6. Ibid.

7. Ibid., 2:477.

Fall of Man, the Oxford don again underscores unbelief as the primal factor and exclaims: "Here sin began, namely, unbelief. 'The woman was deceived,' says the Apostle. She believed a lie: she gave more credit to the word of the devil than to the word of God."[1] For Wesley, then, the nature of human sin, its irreducible essence, is not pride, as is sometimes mistakenly supposed,[2] but unbelief. A lack of faith in God is the true foundation for the *subsequent* evils of pride and self-will. In other words, out of alienation and unbelief, pride and self-will inevitably flow. That this assessment is correct is also borne out in Wesley's further comments as he considers the solution to the problem of human wickedness: "As Satan began his work in Eve by tainting her with unbelief, so the Son of God begins his work in man by enabling us to believe in him."[3]

Though Wesley in following the Genesis accounts attributes the beginning of human evil to Eve, he nevertheless appears to place the greater blame on Adam who sinned in a manner different from his mate. Thus, the English evangelist contends that Eve was deceived, tricked so to speak, but that Adam was not. The man, in contrast to the woman, sinned in a self-conscious and deliberate fashion, "with his eyes open."[4] That is, he committed inward idolatry, by loving the creature more than the Creator.[5] And to illustrate this tension between reason on the one hand and affection on the other, the peculiar problem of Adam (and perhaps of Wesley as well), Wesley paraphrases a few lines drawn from Milton's *Paradise Lost*:

> Not by stronger reason moved,
> But fondly overcome with female charms.[6]

At any rate, the descent of Adam into evil, however understood, produced a number of detrimental effects according to Wesley. First of all, by his rebellion, Adam destroyed himself and lost the favor of God in which he was originally cre-

---

1. Ibid., 2:402-03. (On the Fall of Man)

2. Cannon contends that the nature of sin in Wesleyan thought is the same as it is in Augustine, Luther, and Calvin's thought: namely, spiritual pride. However, this is not quite accurate at least in terms of Wesley's mature view on this subject. And even Cannon himself notes elsewhere in his book that, according to Wesley, sin in its beginning is unbelief (Adam and Eve story) and not pride. What Cannon has probably done, then, is to set up a distinction in Wesley's thought that appears to be unfounded: that is, for Adam original sin consists in unbelief, but for his spiritual descendants it is pride. However, it is much more descriptive of Wesley's view, especially as reflected in his later sermons, to note that unbelief is the foundation in both instances. Observe also that in Wesley's sermon *Original Sin* he begins by noting that by nature we are *atheists* (highlighting unbelief) and he then discusses pride, self-will, and love of the world etc. Cf. William Ragsdale Cannon, *The Theology of John Wesley* (Nashville: Abingdon Press, 1946), p. 192-93; and Outler, *Sermons*, 2:178-79.

3. Outler, *Sermons*, 2:480-81. (The End of Christ's Coming)

4. Ibid., 2:403. (On the Fall of Man)

5. Ibid.

6. Ibid., note # 11. It is interesting to note that the tension of obedience to God/the love of woman is one that surfaced on occasion in Wesley's *Journal*. For example, on 14 February 1337, Wesley told Sophy Hopkey he was resolved that if he married at all, he would not do it until after he ministered to the Indians. Cf. Nehemiah Curnock, *The Journal of the Rev. John Wesley, A.M.*, 8 vols. (London: The Epworth Press, 1938), 1:318.

ated.[1] No longer did God look upon humanity with approval; no longer did men and women enjoy the rich blessings of the Most High in an uninterrupted fashion. And with this loss of favor, went also the loss of grace, leaving humanity in a truly accursed state.

Second, the fall of Adam entailed the loss of the image of God. But in order to understand Wesley's teaching here it is perhaps best to organize the discussion under the same three aspects of natural, political, and moral images outlined above. Thus, concerning the natural image, Wesley relates in an early manuscript sermon, *The Image of God*, that it was greatly marred, but not utterly obliterated by the fall. Adam's *understanding*, for instance, though still in place, was now confused and often in error. "It mistook falsehood for truth, and truth for falsehood. Error succeeded and increased ignorance."[2] In like fashion, *the will* of Adam was corrupted, overrun with such devilish passions as grief, anger, hatred, fear, and shame,[3] but it too was not destroyed. The will indeed remained, but in a perverted form. And lastly, *liberty*, fell away along with virtue; "instead of an indulgent master it was under a merciless tyrant."[4]

In a similar fashion, the political image was greatly obscured. That gentle chain let down from heaven — or to view it from the opposite direction — that slow ascent of beings culminating in humanity had been badly shaken and disrupted by the fall. Instead of humanity constituting a blessing to the rest of creation, through the mediation of graces and benefits from God, it was now a curse. "By his apostasy from God," Wesley declares, "he [Adam] threw not only himself, but likewise the whole creation, which was intimately connected with him, into disorder, misery, death."[5] And elsewhere, in his sermon, *The New Creation* Wesley affirms that the whole animated creation, from leviathan to the smallest mite, was made "subject to such 'vanity' as the inanimate creatures could not be."[6]

Since Wesley postulates that the moral image is the principal image in that it is a reflection of the very righteousness and holiness of God, one would naturally expect the greatest disruption here. And this is precisely what is found. For example, whereas Wesley noted that the natural and political images were polluted or lost in part, he affirmed, on the other hand, that the moral image was *totally* lost. In his sermon, *The End of Christ's Coming* Wesley elaborates:

> **The life of God was extinguished in his soul. The glory departed from him. He lost the whole moral image of God, righteousness and**

1. Outler, *Sermons*, 2:452. (The Mystery of Iniquity)
2. Ibid., 4:298. (The Image of God)
3. Ibid.
4. Ibid.
5. Ibid., 2:399. (God's Approbation of His Works) For a contemporary assessment of Wesley's doctrine of the fall of Adam and its implications for both the race and the animal kingdom Cf. Charles W. Carter, "Man, the Crown of Divine Creation," in *A Contemporary Wesleyan Theology*, 2 vols. ed. Charles W. Carter (Grand Rapids, Michigan: Francis Asbury Press, 1983), 1:220ff.
6. Outler, *Sermons*, 2:508. (The New Creation)

true holiness. He was unholy; he was unhappy; he was full of sin, full of guilt and tormenting fears.[1]

Having lost the moral image of God, Adam sunk partly into "the image of the devil"[2] in pride, malice, and in other evil dispositions, and partly into "the image of the brute,[3] having fallen under the power of brutal passions and degrading appetites. In addition, Wesley declares that from the devil the spirit of independence, self-will, and pride, "quickly infused themselves into the hearts of our first parents in paradise."[4]   The *imago diaboli* now replaced the *imago dei*, and a rule of darkness replaced one of light. In short, Adam and Eve were unhappy precisely because they were unholy; their hearts were overrun with vile, tormenting affections; their innocence was lost.

But the effects of the fall of Adam were not only spiritual; they were physical as well. According to Wesley, originally, the body had been created immortal, but obviously not immutable. Indeed, once the fruit of the knowledge of good and evil was tasted, "the sentence of death passed on that body, which before was impassive and immortal."[5] And with death, "pain, sickness, and a whole train of uneasy as well as unholy passions and tempers"[6] descended upon humanity as well. In his treatise on original sin, Wesley states:

> They [Christians] suppose farther, that through temptations of which we cannot possibly judge, he [Adam] did fall from that state; and that hereby he brought pain, labour, and sorrow on himself and all his posterity; together with death, not only temporal, but spiritual, and eternal.[7]

The passage just cited, however, poses a problem: not, of course, in terms of the issue of physical death, but with respect to spiritual death. For example, in his sermon *Justification by Faith*, the Methodist leader contends that the soul of Adam died, and was alienated from God after it had sinned; it was "separate from whom the soul has no more life than the body has when separate from the soul."[8] But can the soul really die according to Wesley? And if so, what becomes of his preference for the doctrine of the immortality of the soul referred to earlier?

Help in answering these questions can be found in an early manuscript sermon, *The Image of God*, which Outler claims was in fact Wesley's first "univer-

1. Ibid., 2:477. (The End of Christ's Coming)
2. Ibid., 2:423. (God's Love to Fallen Man)
3. Ibid.
4. Ibid., 4:154. (The Deceitfulness of the Human Heart)
5. Ibid., 4:297. (The Image of God). It seems that the notion of mutability is necessary to clarify Wesley's thought here, for if something is truly immortal, it is *never* capable of dying. This problem, however, is solved by arguing that Adam was created immortal, though mutable. In other words, the immortality of the body could indeed be lost through sin.
6. Ibid., 2:423. (God's Love to Fallen Man)
7. Thomas Jackson, ed., *The Works of John Wesley*, 14 vols. (Grand Rapids, Michigan: Baker Book House, 1978), 9:291.
8. Outler, *Sermons*, 1:185. (Justification by Faith)

sity sermon."[1] In this piece, the Oxonian argues that because of the fall of Adam the body became mortal, and that "the soul felt a like change through all her powers, except only that she could not die."[2] Admittedly, this is a sermon which, for whatever reason, Wesley chose not to publish. However, if the ideas contained in this homily are brought to bear on the later sermon, *Justification by Faith*, produced in 1746, it appears that the "death" of the soul recounted in each instance must be understood in a metaphorical sense: that is, the soul is dead in the sense that it is alienated from the life of God; nevertheless, it continues to exist. That this interpretation is accurate is demonstrated by an appeal to a late sermon of Wesley's, *On Eternity*, in which he maintains striking continuity with this earlier thought. "Their bodies indeed are 'crushed before the moth,'" he reasons, "but their souls will never die. God made them, as an ancient writer speaks, to be 'pictures of his own eternity'."[3] Once again, the immortality of the soul is affirmed.

B. The Doctrine of Original Sin

Following what Lindström has referred to as Calvinist federalism,[4] Wesley maintains that the sin of Adam did not merely affect himself, but was imputed to all of humanity. All men and women, therefore, sinned in Adam in the sense that he was their representative, their federal head. All, therefore, are guilty; none remain unspotted. And something of Wesley's reasoning on this head is revealed in his following comments:

> My reason for believing he was so [a federal head or representative], in some sense, is this: Christ was the representative of mankind, when God 'laid on him the iniquities of us all' ... But Adam was a type or figure of Christ; therefore, he was also, in some sense, our representative.[5]

If Wesley balked at the phrase "the imputation of the righteousness of Christ" by restricting it basically to the issues of justification and forgiveness — as he does in his sermon *The Righteousness of Faith* — thereby cutting off the possibility for antinomian interpretations, he on the other hand showed little pause in using the parallel phrase "the imputation of Adam's sin" even when it had real moral and spiritual implications.[6] Thus, for example, at the first Methodist con-

1. Ibid., 4:290. (The Image of God)
2. Ibid., 4:298.
3. Ibid., 2:361. (On Eternity) Wesley also argues in this sermon that all spirits are clothed with immortality. In other words, the essence or heart of even the animals will, in some sense, continue to exist. Cf. 2:361.
4. Harald Lindström , *Wesley and Sanctification* (Wilmore, Kentucky: Francis Asbury Publishing Co.), p.29.
5. Jackson, *Wesley's Works*, 9:332. Bracketed material is mine.
6. In his sermon, *On the Wedding Garment*, Wesley typically will not permit the phrase "the righteousness of Christ" to stand alone. Thus, in this piece he writes: "The righteousness of Christ is, doubtless, necessary for any soul that enters into glory. But so is personal holiness." Cf. Outler, *Sermons*, 4:144. For more on this topic see Wesley's tract, *A Blow at the Root; or, Christ Stabbed in the House of His Friends* in Jackson, *Wesley's Works*, 10:364-69.

ference held in 1744, those assembled, Wesley among them, answered the question "In what sense is Adam's sin imputed to all mankind,"[1] in the following manner:

> In Adam all die; that is, (1) Our bodies then became mortal (2) Our souls died; that is, were disunited from God and hence, (3) We are all born with a sinful devilish nature. By reason whereof, (4) We are children of wrath, liable to death eternal.[2]

This legacy, then, transmitted by Adam to his heirs is physical (# 1 above), moral, and spiritual (# 2,3,4, above). To be sure, it will be profitable to trace this malignant inheritance — though Wesley does not know exactly how it is communicated[3] — in each of its principal veins. Concerning the physical aspects, for instance, Wesley expounds upon the important passage of Romans 5:12 in his sermon, *The General Deliverance*. In this piece, he notes that because of Adam's sin, "death passed upon all men."[4] And he adds: "And not on man only, but on those creatures, also that did not sin after the similitude of Adam's transgression."[5] In fact, one of the principal aims in the Oxford don's sermon, *Upon Our Lord's Sermon on the Mount, Discourse Eighth*, written many years earlier, is to personalize this Adamic legacy of death and to affirm that all men and women are rightful heirs. Notice Wesley's choice of language in this homily:

> But there is at hand a greater trouble than all these. *Thou* art to die. *Thou* art to sink into dust; to return to the ground from which thou wast taken, to mix with common clay. *Thy* body is to go to the earth as it was, while thy spirit returns to God that gave it.[6]

Furthermore, with death, a "whole army of evils," such as pain, sickness, and ignorance, "broke in upon rebel man and all other creatures, and overspread the face of the earth."[7] Death was sown within the very fabric of human existence, "in the very principles of our nature."[8]

In order to gain a greater appreciation of the impact that Wesley's teaching on original sin had in the eighteenth century, especially in terms of its spiritual dimensions, our next concern, it is important to know something of the intellectual temper of these times. Broadly speaking, the eighteenth century (in conjunction with the seventeenth) is often referred to as the "Age of Reason"; more particularly, as "the Enlightenment." As such, it was an age in which reason and

1. Jackson, *Wesley's Works*, 8:277.

2. Ibid.

3. Concerning the transmission of original sin, Wesley writes: "And if you ask me, how, in what determinate manner, sin is propagated; how it is transmitted from father to son: I answer plainly, I cannot tell;" Cf. Jackson, *Wesley's Works*, 9:335.

4. Outler, *Sermons*, 2:444. (The General Deliverance)

5. Ibid.

6. Ibid., 1:624. (Upon Our Lord's Sermon on the Mount Discourse the Eighth)

7. Ibid. 2:398. (God's Approbation of His Works)

8. Ibid. 2:408. (On the Fall of Man) Wesley observes in this same sermon that "God has indeed provided for the execution of his own decree in the very principles of our nature." (2:407). See also, *Heavenly Treasure in Earthen Vessels* in Outler, *Sermons*, 4:161.

human competency ascended, and ecclesiastical and Scriptural authority, on the other hand, declined. On the continent, for instance, Rousseau developed the thesis in his *Emile* that church and doctrine had together forged an artificial and institutional overlay which obscured the essential goodness of humanity. Elsewhere, closer to home in the British Isles, John Toland argued *against* special revelation and *for* natural religion in his *Christianity Not Mysterious* and Matthew Tindal did much the same in his *Christianity as Old as the Creation*, a work which eventually became known as "the Bible of Deism." Moreover, in 1740 Dr. John Taylor, a dissenting minister in Norwich,[1] published *The Scripture Doctrine of Original Sin: Proposed to Free and Candid Examination* in which original sin was deemed a fiction. And it was with respect to this last work in particular that John Wesley decided to pick up his pen.

Apparently, the Methodist leader was greatly troubled over Taylor's work, since, in response to it, he published the longest treatise that he ever wrote, a treatise even larger than his famous *A Plain Account of Christian Perfection*.[2] In fact, *The Doctrine of Original Sin: According to Scripture, Reason, and Experience*, written in 1757, totaled more than five hundred pages. Two years later, in 1759, realizing that its length would most likely prevent a wide reading, Wesley summarized the leading ideas of this treatise and published them in the more manageable and popular sermon form.

As expected, the opening passages of the sermon *Original Sin* move quickly to the salient moral and spiritual issues and offer an assessment of the general religious climate. In this homily, Wesley observes:

> **Nor have heathens alone, men who were guided in their researches by little more than the dim light of reason, ... spoke as magnificently concerning the nature of man, as if it were all innocence and perfection. Accounts of this kind have particularly abounded in the present century; and perhaps in no part of the world more than in our own country. Here not a few persons of strong understanding, as well as extensive learning, have employed their utmost abilities to show what they termed 'the fair side of human nature.'[3]**

"But in the meantime," Wesley asks, "what must we do with our Bibles?"[4] Here then is a genuine parting of the ways. The one view, championed by Toland, Taylor, and Tindal, holds that men and women are marked by many vices, but that the good outbalances the evil. The other view, offered by Wesley and the Methodists, contends that people are conceived in sin and that every person has, to use Wesley's own words, "a carnal mind which is enmity against God."[5] The one denies the import of the doctrine of original sin; the other affirms it.

So impressed was Wesley with the significance of the doctrine of original sin that he considered it the fundamental difference between Christianity and hea-

1. Ibid., 2:170. (Original Sin)
2. Ibid., 2:171.
3. Ibid., 2:172.
4. Ibid., 2:173.
5. Ibid., 2:183.

thenism.[1] Accordingly, he declares in his sermon *Original Sin* that all who deny this vital doctrine, for whatever reason and with whatever justifications, "are but heathens still."[2] And elsewhere, in this same sermon, he regards the question (and others like it), "Is man by nature filled with all manner of evil?," as a virtual shibboleth to distinguish Scriptural Christianity from paganism.[3] No doubt, Wesley's concern, expressed in this context, grew out of his strong soteriological interests. In other words, if the problem (original sin) were repudiated or soft-pedaled — as it was by Deism and rational religion — then perhaps the solution (the new birth) would be lost or misunderstood as well. And that this last point is no mere conjecture is demonstrated by an appeal to Wesley's homily, *The New Birth*, where he writes: "This then is the foundation of the new birth — the *entire corruption* of our nature." [4]

Since Adam lost the moral image, and the natural and political ones were greatly marred, this is the fruit, argues Wesley, which was passed along to his descendants; this is their inheritance. Considered apart from the grace of God, then, the spiritual condition of humanity is suitably described as dark and bleak. And again in his sermon *Original Sin*, Wesley employs what can only be described as "negative superlatives" to display the general moral and spiritual abyss into which humanity has descended. He remarks:

> **Is man by nature filled with all manner of evil? Is he void of all good? Is he wholly fallen? Is his soul totally corrupted? Or, to come back to the text, is 'every imagination of the thoughts of his heart evil continually'? Allow this, and you are so far a Christian. Deny it, and you are but a heathen still.[5]**

In a similar way, the language of total depravity, which the champions of reason were loath to recognize, can be found in several other pieces by Wesley. In *The Way to the Kingdom*, for instance, it is expressed in the comments: "thou are corrupted in every power, in every faculty of thy soul, that thou art totally corrupted in every one of these, all the foundations being out of course."[6] And in the piece *The Deceitfulness of the Human Heart* it appears in the observation that "every imagination of the thought of man's heart is evil, only evil, and that continually."[7] Moreover, in the *NT Notes* it surfaces as "entire depravity and corruption."[8]

1. Ibid., 2:182.

2. Ibid., 2:183. Notice that the language used by Wesley in this sermon to describe the carnal nature, such terms as "total corruption," "empty of all good," "filled with all manner of evil," and the like, reveal the basis for his criticism of such classical pagan anthropologies as those of Horace, and Seneca. Cf. Burton Raffel, trans., *The Essential Horace: Odes, Epodes, Satires and Epistles* (New York: North Point Publishing Co.) and Seneca, *Moral Essays*, 3 vols. (Cambridge, Massachusetts: Harvard University Press), Vol 1.

3. Ibid.

4. Ibid., 2:190. (The New Birth) Emphasis is mine.

5. Ibid., 2:183-84. (Original Sin)

6. Ibid., 1:225. (The Way to the Kingdom)

7. Ibid., 4:154-55. (The Deceitfulness of the Human Heart)

8. John Wesley, *Explanatory Notes Upon the New Testament* (Salem, Ohio: Schmul Publishers), p.377

The language just cited is of course reminiscent of that used by the continental Reformers, Luther and Calvin, in their descriptions of original sin. For his part, Luther in his *Lectures on Romans* argues that original sin involves "the loss of all uprightness ... it is a proneness toward evil; the loathing of the good."[1] And such emphases are also maintained by the German reformer in his treatise *The Bondage of the Will*, a polemical work written in opposition to some of the teachings of Erasmus. Likewise, Calvin declares in his *Institutes* that "Paul removes all doubt when he teaches that corruption subsists not in one part only, but that none of the soul remains pure or untouched by that mortal disease."[2]

While at first glance it appears that there is great similarity between Wesley's doctrine of original sin and that of the continental Reformers — and Wesley thought as much — since all emphasize the universality of condemnation and the inability of humanity apart from God to do anything to rectify this situation, upon closer examination, however, there are important differences to be noted largely due to different conceptions of grace. It must be borne in mind, for instance, that when Wesley uses the vocabulary of total depravity, he is referring to what he calls "the natural man," that is, to a person who is without the grace of God. But does such a person actually exist? Not according to Wesley, for in the sermon *On Working Out Our Own Salvation*, he writes:

> **For allowing that all souls of men are dead in sin by nature, this excuses none, seeing there is no man that is in a state of mere nature; there is no man, unless he has quenched the Spirit, that is wholly void of the grace of God. No man living is entirely destitute of what is vulgarly called "natural conscience." But this is not natural; it is more properly termed "preventing grace." Every man has a greater or less measure of this, which waiteth not for the call of man.**[3]

Along these same lines, Umphrey Lee in his book *John Wesley and Modern Religion* correctly maintains that for Wesley the "natural man" is a logical abstraction which does not correspond to actual men and women. "In this world," he notes, "man exists as a natural man *plus* the prevenient grace of God."[4] And this last issue of prevenient grace, important as it is, must neither be ignored nor min-

---

1. Martin Luther, *Luther's Works*, ed. Hilton C. Oswald, Vol. 25: *Lectures on Romans* (Saint Louis: Concordia Publishing House), p. 167-68.

2. John Calvin, *Institutes of the Christian Religion*, ed. John T. McNeill 2 Vols. (Philadelphia: The Westminster Press), 1:253.

3. Outler, *Sermons*, 3:207. (On Working Out Our Own Salvation)

4. Umphrey Lee, *John Wesley and Modern Religion* (Nashville: Cokesbury Press, 1936), p. 124-25. Emphasis is mine. And it should also be noted that Wesley used the phrases "natural man" and "natural state" in two distinct senses. This has led to much confusion in Wesley Studies among those scholars who have failed to appreciate the difference. On the one hand, in the sermon *Original Sin*, the natural state is depicted as exclusive of the grace of God. But as has been indicated above, such a person does not exist, for there are no people without divine prevenient grace. On the other hand, the phrases "natural man" and "natural state" which appear in the sermons *Awake, Thou That Sleepest*, produced by Charles in 1742, and *The Spirit of Bondage and of Adoption* produced by John in 1746, correspond to real flesh and blood individuals, not to theoretical constructs. See my earlier book, *Wesley on Salvation* (Francis Asbury Press, 1989), p. 24-25.

imized if Wesley's doctrine of sin and his anthropology are to be properly understood.[1]

So then, interpreters of Wesley's doctrine of original sin must bear in mind that the language of total depravity — and it is clearly there — pertains only to Adam in his fallenness and to the remainder of humanity *considered apart from the grace of God*. However, this is not to suggest that the principal expressions of original sin as found in Wesley's homilies are therefore no longer in some sense descriptive of actual, real men and women, for they clearly are. The major difference, though, and it's an important one, is that human evil must always be understood against the backdrop of divine, preventing grace. "There is no man," Wesley cautions, "unless he has quenched the Spirit, that is wholly void of the grace of God."[2] All is not darkness.

With these caveats in mind, a proper assessment can now be made in terms of the spiritual legacy which Adam and Eve have bequeathed to their heirs. And Wesley explores this topic under the four major — and by now familiar — heads: atheism (unbelief), pride, self-will and love of the world. In other words, these four elementary ingredients of human evil, when considered together, constitute the essence (with a few subdivisions) of what the Methodist leader means by the concept original sin or the carnal nature — especially in terms of its present implications. Thus not only are atheism, pride, self-will, and love of the world listed in the sermon *Original Sin* as expected, but Wesley also enumerates these same four items in his piece, *The Deceitfulness of the Human Heart*, written many years later in 1790. In it he writes:

> **It would be endless to enumerate all the species of wickedness, whether in thought, word, or action, that now overspread the earth, in every nation and city and family. They all *centre* [sic] in this *atheism*, or idolatry: *pride*, ... and *self-will*, ... Add to this *seeking happiness out of God*.[3]**

And again in this same sermon, Wesley refers to the unholy four as "the inward root, the enmity against God."[4] However, an interesting change takes place if one observes how Wesley describes the carnal nature in the sermon *The Repentance of Believers*. In the first section of this piece, he simply lists pride, self-will, and love of the world, perhaps to underscore the point that he is, after all, writing to *believers*. Nevertheless in the latter part of this work, he affirms

---

1. Charles Allen Rogers, "The Concept of Prevenient Grace in the Theology of John Wesley" (Ph.D. dissertation, Duke University, 1967), p.196 ff.

2. Outler, *Sermons*, 3:207. (On Working Out Our Own Salvation)

3. Ibid. 4:154. (The Deceitfulness of the Human Heart) Emphasis is mine. Wesley's phrase "seeking happiness out of God" is equivalent to the phrase "the love of the world" since under the former topic he lists the same items (the desire of the flesh, the desire of the eye, and the pride of life) that he lists under the latter. Compare *The Deceitfulness of the Human Heart* 4:154 ff., and *Original Sin* 2:179 ff.

4. Ibid., 4: 155. Notice, however, that Wesley refers to the fourth element, "seeking happiness out of God," as idolatry.

that even Christian believers have a "general proneness to *depart from God*"[1] —
a tendency which can otherwise be referred to as unbelief or atheism.

Furthermore, when Wesley fills out and specifies the evil of humanity, he
often does so in terms of the last category of "the love of the world" under which
he lists three main symptoms: the desire of the flesh, the desire of the eyes, and
the pride of life.[2] Writing on the first, the desire of the flesh, Wesley exposes the
pretense often used by people of good breeding that in the area of the gratifica-
tion of the senses they are much more refined than the common lot and are well
above the beasts. However, as the Oxford don cogently argues, not even reason
can prevent men and women from being dragged to and fro by their sensual
appetites which more or less exercise dominion over them.[3] And to make his
points even more emphatic Wesley engages in a bit of dry and seldom-used
humor, for in this sermon he observes: "The man, with all his good breeding and
other accomplishments, has no pre-eminence over the goat. Nay, it is much to be
doubted whether the beast has not the pre-eminence over him!"[4]

Of the desire of the eye, Wesley has in mind the pleasures of the imagination,
seeking and gaining "great, or beautiful, or uncommon objects."[5] And he per-
ceptively delineates the psychological dynamics entailed in desiring some
object, in deriving pleasure from obtaining it, and in eventually becoming dis-
satisfied once the novelty of the thing has worn off. And thus the cycle begins
afresh; boredom sets in only to be broken up by new desire. And the more this
"inbred thirst ... is indulged," Wesley cautions, "the more it increases."[6]

The last symptom of the disease of the love of the world is the pride of life —
a pride which is not noble, but ignoble; which desires the praise and honor which
comes from humanity, but not that which comes from God. Such pride ever
seeks the applause of the crowd and is determined above all to have a good rep-
utation among society. Indeed, Wesley notes that among "men of refined and
improved understanding ... Not to regard what men think of us is the mark of a
wicked and abandoned mind."[7] And he adds: "they [Christians as well as hea-
thens] account it the sign of a virtuous mind to seek the praise of men, and of a
vicious one to be content with 'the honour which cometh of God only.'"[8]

Beyond this delineation of evil, Wesley appeals to the distinction between
original and actual sin to illustrate once again the difference between "general"
sin on the one hand, and "particular" sins on the other, sin as a state of being and
sin as an act. So understood, actual sin proceeds from original sin; evil works

---

1. Ibid., 1: 345. (Repentance of Believers)
2. Ibid., 2:180-82. (Original Sin)
3. Ibid., 2:180.
4. Ibid. For another example of Wesley's wit Cf. *The General Deliverance* Outler, *Sermons*, 2:450.
5. Ibid., 2:181.
6. Ibid.
7. Ibid. 2:182. In addition, Wesley notes concerning those who greatly value the opinion of their
peers: "So that to go calm and unmoved 'through honour and dishonour, through evil report and good
report, is with them a sign of one that is indeed 'not fit to live; away with such a fellow from the
earth." Ibid.
8. Ibid.

issue from an evil heart.[1] The inclination to iniquity, in other words, so mysterious and hidden, eventually manifests itself quite publicly in human activity. Wesley explains:

> From this infection of our nature (call it original sin, or what you please) spring many, if not all, actual sins. And this St. James (i. 14) plainly intimates.... Another proof that actual sins spring from original, is, 'out of the heart proceed evil thoughts, murders, adulteries, fornications, thefts, false witness, blasphemies.'[2]

Nevertheless, it would be a mistake to conclude, as Lindström correctly points out, that this transition from one form of sin to the other is inevitable. No, "if man takes advantage of God's grace, he can conquer the inclination to evil."[3] Therefore, original sin, the carnal nature, does not by necessity lead to actual sin — a teaching which does not undermine in the least the universality of human participation in sin. More to the point, that men and women eventually act out of their sinful natures, thereby abusing their grace-restored-freedom, Wesley affirms; however, that they do so by necessity or coercion is denied. Thus, the prevenient grace of God not only mitigates in some measure the inheritance which is received from Adam, but it also renders men and women responsible in the sight of God for any spiritual descent from inbred sin to actual sin. Indeed to argue otherwise is to move in the direction of a determinism (with its corollaries of a diminished responsibility and possible antinomianism) which Wesley as an Arminian clearly rejected.

C. The Ultimate Consequences of the Fall

It should be evident by now that the fall along with its results (transmission of original sin etc.) paint a dark, pessimistic, and unenviable view of humanity. And if God is really omniscient, as Wesley claims, and foresaw all this evil, why then did He permit it? In other words, here the question of theodicy breaks out afresh — a question which Wesley faced head on earlier in his career and also later in a couple of his more important sermons. In his piece, *God's Love to Fallen Man*, for example, he highlights the very omniscience of God itself as the clue to this dilemma and suggests that the allowance of evil is really only a problem when a short-sighted perspective is maintained. Wesley reasons:

> He [God] saw that to permit the fall of the first man was far best for mankind in general; that abundantly more good than evil would accrue to the posterity of Adam by his fall; that if 'sin abounded' thereby over all the earth, yet 'grace would much more abound';[4]

In addition, Wesley indicates in this same sermon how God is able to bring great good out of the evil of the fall in two key ways: first, humanity now has the

1. Jackson, *Wesley's Works*, 9:275.
2. Ibid., 9:274.
3. Harald Lindström , *Wesley and Sanctification* (Wilmore, Kentucky: Francis Asbury Press Publishing Co.), p. 37
4. Outler, *Sermons*, 2:424. (God's Love to Fallen Man)

capability of attaining more happiness and holiness on earth than if Adam had not sinned.[1] Why? Because "if Adam had not fallen," Wesley argues, "Christ had not died."[2] Thus, the amazing display of divine love at Calvary could not have been known since, "there would have been no occasion for [Christ's] being obedient unto death, even the death of the cross."[3] Moreover, justification by faith, based as it is on this work, would also have no place, nor would the proper motive to neighborly love ("If God so loved us ...") exist any longer.[4]

Second, with the fall of Adam human beings are able to be "more happy in heaven, than otherwise they could have been."[5] Through the pain and suffering left in the wake of the fall, humanity has the opportunity, through the grace of God, to develop all those holy tempers which could not otherwise have come into being such as: "confidence in him [God] in times of trouble and danger, patience, meekness, gentleness, long-suffering, and the whole train of passive virtues."[6] In short, the virtues which make one fit for heaven, so to speak, are hammered out on the anvil of suffering; they can arise in no other way. "And on account of this superior holiness," Wesley declares, "they will then enjoy superior happiness."[7]

IV Some Observations

In many respects, John Wesley's anthropology was quite traditional. His thought resonated with that of Augustine, Luther, and Calvin in highlighting the original goodness of humanity, the universality of human evil after the fall, and the inability of humanity, apart from the grace of God, to remedy this problem. However, despite these broad areas of agreement, it must ultimately be concluded that the anthropological differences which remain between Wesley and the others just cited are in fact considerable. For although Wesley insisted that he upheld the doctrine of original sin — which he clearly did — his defense of the Arminian position on this score as found, for example, in his treatise, *What is an Arminian?* was always suspect in the eyes of Calvinists who claimed Augustine (as did Lutherans) as their spiritual mentor.

To be sure, the doctrine of original sin did not play the same role in Wesley's theology as it did in much of Reformed thought (or in Luther's theology for that matter). Thus, in the former instance, original sin, especially in terms of its present implications, was most often understood against the backdrop of grace, as noted earlier. However in the latter, original sin remained, for the most part,

---

1. Ibid.
2. Ibid., 2:425.
3. Ibid., 2:426. Bracketed material is mine.
4. Ibid., 2:426, 428. See also *On the Fall of Man* 2:411-12.
5. Ibid., 2:425. Outler maintains that this *felix culpa* response of Wesley to the fall of Adam — great good comes out of evil — is sustained by a long tradition which goes back as far as Augustine. Cf. Ibid., note # 9.
6. Ibid., 2:432.
7. Ibid.

unnuanced in its unmitigated, stark horror, and the appropriate anthropological (and spiritual) conclusions were then drawn.

In addition, once Wesley, on the one hand, pointed to the universality of sin and the impotence of humanity to redeem itself, he was quick to focus on the prevenient grace of God which was already in action. The Calvinists, on the other hand, and especially those of Wesley's day, like Walter Shirley and August Toplady, not only underscored the familiar themes of depravity as did Wesley, but they then, in turn, appealed to the doctrine of original sin to support the more "realistic" view that freedom from the power of sin was not likely and that perfection in love was outright illusion — conclusions which Wesley refused to support.[1] How is it then that these two broad theologies which began with a similar notion of total depravity could end up with such significant differences? The answer lies — and it bears repeating — in their divergent conceptions of grace.

---

1. Jackson, *Wesley's Works*, 3:169; 10:379,406,413 (Shirley); and 10:370-74 (Topladly).

CHAPTER SIX

THE DOCTRINE OF SALVATION
"I believe in the forgiveness of sins..." (Continued)

In the preface to the 1746 edition of his sermons, Wesley, among other things, reveals the purpose for publishing these homilies in the first place by employing the image of an arrow in flight. He writes:

> I have thought, I am a creature of a day, passing through life as an arrow through the air. I am a spirit come from God and returning to God, just hovering over the great gulf, till a few moments hence I am no more seen — I drop into an unchangeable eternity! I want to know one thing, the way to heaven — how to land safe on that happy shore.[1]

Observe in this prologue that of all the knowledge which can be obtained by an inquisitive mind — mathematical, scientific, artistic etc., — Wesley much prefers the knowledge which directly pertains to salvation. "I have accordingly set down in the following sermons what I find in the Bible concerning the way to heaven," he writes, "with a view to distinguish this way of God from ... the inventions of men."[2] His task, then, in these pieces is nothing less than to display the "scriptural, experimental religion," which had dominated his interest since 1725 and which was appropriated in more personal depth in 1738. Indeed, the religion of the heart, faith which works by love, is his constant theme and his never-ending interest.

Accordingly, few, if any, scholars can doubt that soteriology is the dominant theme in what has been traditionally referred to as the *Fifty -Three Standard Sermons*. What has not been fully appreciated, however, is that the doctrine of salvation remains a principal theme in the remainder of the sermon corpus. Granted, in many of his later sermons, Wesley branches out and explores such topics as the doctrine of God, the church, and eschatology, to name a few, as this present work has argued. Nevertheless, even here soteriology is still the structure on which many of these considerations are hung. And so when Wesley, again in his preface to the sermons, states "At any price give me the Book of God! ... Here is

---

1. Albert C. Outler, ed., *The Works of John Wesley The Sermons I* 4 Vols. (Nashville: Abingdon Press, 1984), 1:104-105.
2. Ibid., 1:106.

knowledge enough for me,"[1] he can be taken at his word so long as it is realized that he did not renounce his stake in other kinds of knowledge — his reading was much too broad for that — but that he was simply making a vital judgment and revealing to his readers what for him was and remained of first rank; namely, the redemption of souls.[2]

Perhaps the most suitable way to organize the following material is to place it under the two main headings of justification (and regeneration) and entire sanctification and then to include the supporting doctrines of repentance, works, faith etc., in their appropriate areas. In fact, one does not really understand what Wesley meant by the doctrine of justification or entire sanctification unless one first comprehends the role that these "satellite" doctrines play in the reception of each of these two graces. Simply put, Wesley's teaching on justification and entire sanctification must be viewed not only in terms of his own personal history and development, but also, and more importantly, in terms of their specific positioning within the cluster of supporting doctrines as indicated in the distinctive order of salvation which emerged in his summary sermon *The Scripture Way of Salvation*, produced in 1765. Such an approach makes for a more intelligent, probing, and sensitive reading in this area.

I. Justification and Regeneration

Since the subject of prevenient grace in terms of conscience, a measure of restored freedom, knowledge of the general attributes of God, as well as a partial re-inscription of the moral law, was sufficiently treated in the chapter on the Holy Spirit, it is appropriate to begin this present one with a discussion of the fruits of convincing grace or what Wesley in his sermons most often refers to as repentance. Bear in mind, however, that the discussion of convincing grace which follows presupposes the vital and necessary initiative of God in prevenient grace which is free in all and for all[3] — that grace which comes before all

1. Ibid., 1:105.

2. The author of a recent editorial published in *Quarterly Review* has maintained in a tongue-in-cheek fashion that the political writings of John Wesley should be banned because they can be viewed as anti-American and offensive to respectable Methodism. While this might be the case, although I have some questions, it is difficult to understand why the author would allow the reading of Wesley's *Forty-Four Sermons*. If anything, these pieces are among the most potent and radical pieces of reform ever published! They not only call for social amelioration (*Discourses on the Sermon on the Mount, The Use of Money* etc.,), but they contend for that deep and thoroughgoing transformation of the person (*Circumcision of the Heart*) without which all attempts at reforming *others* can so easily and regrettably devolve into envy, bitterness, and class hatred — into all those unholy tempers which Wesley took such great pains to warn against. Clearly, the Oxonian's political thought was informed by his understanding of redemption as expressed in his sermons; the latter, therefore, are not optional at all, as Dunlap seems to suggest, but indeed are the prerequisite for a probing and sensitive reading of the political writings. Cf. Pamela Couture Dunlap, "On the Danger of Reading the Works of John Wesley," *Quarterly Review* Vol 7, No. 1 (Spring 1987): 3-8.

3. Outler, *Sermons*, 3:545. (Free Grace) For material on Wesley's rejection of predestination Cf. 3:546 ff. (Free Grace); 2:418 ff. (On Predestination); 2:376 ff (On the Trinity); 3:403 (The Reward of Righteousness); 3:175 (On Patience); and 3:508 (On God's Vineyard).

human action and which renders men and women in a certain measure free and in every instance responsible.

A. Repentance

At the outset, it should be noted that there are a number of different levels in Wesley's understanding of repentance. First of all, repentance as an expression of convincing grace involves a radical change, a turning, as the etymology of the word itself suggests. Second, in the sermon *The Lord Our Righteousness* repentance is explored in terms of a shift in allegiance, from trust in our own righteousness to that of Christ's. "Till we are delivered from trusting in anything that we do," Wesley points out, "we cannot thoroughly trust in what he [Christ] has done and suffered."[1] Third, and perhaps most importantly, repentance involves considerable self-knowledge which is both therapeutic and humbling as revealed in the following selection from *The Way to the Kingdom*:

> **This is the way: walk ye in it. And first, repent, that is, know yourselves. This is the first repentance, previous to faith, even conviction, or self-knowledge. Awake, then, thou that sleepest. Know thyself to be a sinner, and what manner of sinner thou art. Know that corruption of thy inmost nature, whereby thou art very far gone from original righteousness...[2]**

Note that in the passage just cited Wesley calls this conviction of sin and self-knowledge "the first repentance" which elsewhere he refers to as "legal repentance."[3] As such, it involves a conviction of actual sin, of all voluntary transgressions of a known law of God,[4] and it is wrought in the heart by the Holy Spirit who earnestly reproves, exhorts, and illuminates the sinner. But there is a second kind of repentance which emerges in the sermons as well, and it is called "evangelical repentance." It entails a change of heart from all sin to all holiness and will be treated below.

B. Works Prior to Justification

But first it should be observed that for Wesley, both repentance and "fruits meet for repentance" are in some sense necessary to justification. "God does undoubtedly command us both to repent and to bring forth fruits meet for repentance;" he writes, "which if we willingly neglect we cannot reasonably expect to be justified at all."[5] Again, according to this Oxford don, convinced sinners should labor in works of charity, mercy, and the like; they should employ all the

---

1. Ibid., 1:458. (The Lord Our Righteousness)
2. Ibid., 1:225. (The Way to the Kingdom)
3. John Wesley, *Explanatory Notes Upon the New Testament* (Salem, Ohio: Schmul Publishers), p.15.
4. Outler, *Sermons*, 3:85. (On Perfection) On this head, Wesley notes that "it is the ordinary method of the Spirit of God to convict sinners by the law. It is this which, being set home on the conscience, generally breaketh the rocks in pieces..." Cf. 2:15. (The Original, Nature, Property, and Use of the Law)
5. Ibid., 2:162-63. (The Scripture Way of Salvation)

means of grace at their disposal, like praying, reading the Scriptures, and receiving the Lord's Supper; and they should strive and be earnest in their spiritual walk. Indeed, the incident at the Fetter Lane society, shortly after his own new birth, taught Wesley the mischievousness of undermining the means of grace and works meet for repentance as suggested by the likes of both Bray and Molther in their excessive glorification of faith.[1] For Wesley, however, works prior to justification, though not good strictly speaking, were not "splendid sins" either, simply because the prevenient grace of God, already present, shined through them.

In rejecting quietism, Wesley employed the imperative mood at each stage in the process of salvation — an activity which often led to the charge of "works righteousness" or "legalism" by his detractors. However, his critics not only failed to comprehend the Methodist leader's teaching on the question of works, but, more significantly, they failed to appreciate his doctrine of grace — a doctrine which in highlighting the divine initiative *before* justification was free to call for serious and earnest human *response*. Put another way, Wesley conceived the divine/human relation in the process of salvation in a synergistic fashion, in terms of cooperation: God initiates through His grace (prevenient, convincing, and sanctifying); and men and women respond. "God works; therefore, you *can* work...," he exhorts, "God works; therefore you *must* work."[2] Echoes from Augustine's wise counsel, offered centuries earlier, reverberate here: "he that made us *without ourselves* will not save us *without ourselves*.[3]

Though repentance and its fruits are in some sense necessary to justification, Wesley kept his theology free from all notions of merit and self-justification by arguing that "they are not necessary in the *same sense* with faith nor in the *same degree*."[4] These works are only conditionally necessary, he observes, "if there be time and opportunity for them."[5] Again, repentance and its fruits are "only remotely necessary, necessary in order to faith; whereas faith is *immediately* and *directly* necessary to justification."[6] The difference is important.

C. Faith

On the subject of faith itself, Wesley as a good Anglican had much to write, and his views underwent significant change from the period of 1725 to 1738 and beyond — a fact little noticed by those who erroneously insist that the earlier date was the year of his conversion.[7] For instance, in 1725 young John wrote a

1. Nehemiah Curnock, *The Journal of the Rev. John Wesley, A.M.*, 8 vols. (London: The Epworth Press, 1938), 2:312.
2. Outler, *Sermons*, 3:206. (On Working Out Our Own Salvation)
3. Ibid., 2:490. (The General Spread of the Gospel) For other examples of synergism in Wesley's theology Cf. Outler, *Sermons*, 3:208 (On Working Out Our Own Salvation); 3:136 (On Friendship with the World); and 3:284 (An Israelite Indeed).
4. Ibid., 2:162-63. (The Scripture Way of Salvation)
5. Ibid., 2:163.
6. Ibid.
7. Theodore W. Jennings, "John Wesley *Against* Aldersgate," *Quarterly Review* Vol. 8, No. 3 (Fall 1988): 3-22.

telling letter to his mother in which he defined faith simply as "an assent to a proposition upon rational grounds."[1] And he later added: "Faith must necessarily at length be resolved into reason."[2] Conceived as such, this faith was but a pale shadow of what was to emerge in the sermon *Salvation by Faith* preached by Wesley before the venerable of Oxford a few weeks after his Aldersgate experience. For example, in this homily, a number of different kinds of faith are explored in order to underscore by comparison that which redeems. Accordingly, the faith which saves, which delivers from both the guilt and power of sin, is not that of a "heathen,"[3] nor of a "devil,"[4] nor even that "which the apostles themselves had while Christ was yet upon earth."[5] Instead, it is distinguished by this: "it is not barely a speculative, rational thing, a cold, lifeless assent, a train of ideas in the head; but also a disposition of the heart."[6] Wesley elaborates:

> **Christian faith is then not only an assent to the whole gospel of Christ, but also a full reliance on the blood of Christ, a trust in the merits of his life, death, and resurrection; a recumbency upon him as our atonement and our life, as *given for us*, and *living in us*. It is a sure confidence which a man hath in God, that through the merits of Christ his sins are forgiven, and he reconciled to the favour of God; and in consequence hereof a closing with him ... in one word, our salvation.[7]**

By 1738, therefore, Wesley's conception of faith included two key elements: First, that faith at its most basic level is a rational assent to truth — and this aspect, by the way, never dropped out of his writings — second, that as an instrument of redemption, faith engages not only the mind, but the heart as well and issues in a childlike trust in Jesus Christ, the Savior. The transition, then, from 1725 to 1738 was marked by a shift from *fides* to *fiducia*, from a cold, speculative faith to a lively and hearty trust.

Moreover, in his later years, Wesley explored yet a third sense in which faith could be understood — a sense which was an attempt to meet some of the more pressing questions concerning the doctrine of knowledge (epistemology) of his age. To this end, he composed two sermons both entitled *On Faith.* The first, which was produced in 1788, had Hebrews 11:6 as its text; the other, written two years later, Hebrews 11:1. In these pieces, a more general and philosophical understanding of faith is presented and it emerges as a kind of sense, as an organ which can pierce the veil between the temporal and the eternal, in order to perceive the things of God. Wesley explains:

1. Frank Baker, ed., *The Works of John Wesley,* Vol 25 *Letters* I (New York: Oxford University Press, 1982), p. 175.
2. Ibid., p. 176.
3. Outler, *Sermons,* 1:119. (Salvation by Faith)
4. Ibid.
5. Ibid., 1:120. For a similar set of distinctions Cf. 3:49 (Of the Church); 2:368 (On Eternity); and 3:496 (On Faith).
6. Ibid.
7. Ibid., 1:121.

> But what is *faith*? It is a divine 'evidence, and conviction of things not seen'; of things which are not seen now, whether they are visible or invisible in their own nature. Particularly, it is a divine evidence and conviction of God and of the things of God. This is the most comprehensive definition of faith that ever was or can be given, as including every species of faith, from the lowest to the highest.[1]

Elsewhere, in his later sermon on the same subject, faith again is described as a "divine conviction of the invisible and eternal world."[2] And this "sense" is deemed to be of great value for the strenuous task of living the Christian life, for it places the eternal world continually before the eyes of believers and thereby helps them to prefer the things which are "real, solid, [and] unchangeable" over "a vapour, a shadow, a dream that vanishes away."[3]

Though Wesley's thought embraced all three meanings just enumerated, his focus, not surprisingly, was on the second; namely, the notion that faith entails a subtle, mysterious, and yet potent change in the hearts of believers. More specifically, in terms of the doctrine of salvation, faith has a two-fold task: on the one hand, it is the means by which the believer is justified; on the other hand, it is the gracious vehicle of the new birth. The first work is termed justification; the later, regeneration.

D. Justification Itself

Just what does it mean to be justified according to Wesley? "It is not the being made actually just and righteous," he cautions, "This is *sanctification*.[4] Instead, justification simply means pardon, the forgiveness of sins brought about by the work which Christ did *for us* in his life and death. "It is that act of The Father," he asserts, "whereby, for the sake of the propitiation made by the blood of his Son, he 'showeth forth his righteousness (or mercy) by the forgiveness of sins that are past.'"[5] By this gracious act, then, believers are freed from *the guilt* of sin and are restored to the favor of God, and it therefore forms a vital part, though certainly not the whole, of what Wesley meant by salvation.

Moreover, the basis upon which one is justified is not through self-effort, good intentions, or dedication, nor even through seeing that holiness is the proper goal of religion, as Wesley so clearly saw as a young man of twenty-two. On the contrary, one is justified, declared righteous in the sight of God, only by faith. And though it took Wesley some time to realize fully the significance of this truth — he often confused justification and sanctification, especially when he

---

1. Ibid., 3:492. (On Faith)
2. Ibid., 4:188. (On Faith)
3. Ibid., 2:369. (On Eternity)
4. Ibid., 1:187. (Justification by Faith) Before 1738, while he was in Georgia, Wesley confused the *nature* of justification with that of sanctification. In other words, he made the holy life he so apprised the basis upon which one was justified. That this was a particularly Anglican foible is demonstrated in Wesley's remarks to William Green in 1739. Cf. John Telford, ed., *The Letters of John Wesley, A.M.* 8 vols. (London: The Epworth Press, 1931), 8:178-79.
5. Outler, *Sermons*, 1:189. (Justification by Faith)

was in Georgia[1] — he was unflagging in support of this doctrine, once it was properly understood. In fact, it was through the good graces of *both* the Moravians *and* his own Anglican tradition (Moravian proclamation, Anglican explication), that Wesley finally came to realize that faith is the necessary condition of justification and the *only necessary* condition thereof.[2] It is "the only thing that is immediately, indispensably, absolutely, requisite in order to pardon."[3]

Despite the influence of the Moravians and his own Anglican tradition, Wesley was quite content, at times, to use the formulations typical of the Continental Reformation in his depiction of justification by faith. For instance, with language reminiscent of Luther, Wesley declares in the sermon *Justification by Faith*, produced in 1746, that "faith is ... the *sole condition* of justification."[4] And elsewhere in his homily *On Dissipation*, written many years later in 1784, he asserts that "it is *by faith alone* that he [the believer] is 'created anew in' or through 'Christ Jesus.'"[5] And with respect to the Genevan Reformer, Wesley quipped to John Newton in 1765, priding himself on the continuity of his teaching: "I think on Justification just as I have done any time these seven-and-twenty years, and just as Mr. Calvin does."[6]

The last comment, however, requires some attention. For though Wesley was consistent in his affirmation of justification by faith from 1738 and beyond, it is simply hyperbole to suggest that his own doctrine was the same as that of John Calvin or Martin Luther for that matter. Admittedly, if Wesley's doctrine of justification by faith is isolated from its theological context — in other words, if it is considered apart from the prior movement of prevenient grace, with its resultant synergism and emphasis on works (always performed through grace) — then, yes, remarkable similarity emerges. However, if the Methodist leader's doctrine of justification is seen in terms of the very items just cited, then much less continuity occurs. For Wesley, at least, people are in some sense responsible for whether or not they are justified (although they cannot justify themselves)

1. Wesley writes in his *Farther Appeal*: "I was ordained Deacon in 1725, and Priest in the year following. But it was many years after this before I was convinced of the great truths above recited. During all that time I was utterly ignorant of the nature and condition of justification. Sometimes I confounded it with sanctification; (particularly when I was in Georgia)." Cf. Thomas Jackson, ed., *The Works of John Wesley*, 14 vols. (Grand Rapids, Michigan: Baker Book House, 1978), 8:111.

2. Outler, *Sermons*, 1:196. (Justification by Faith) Bohler filled out Wesley's knowledge of the nature of faith in an indirect way by stressing the fruits that necessarily flow from true faith; namely, dominion over sin and constant peace from a sense of forgiveness. And it was this which Wesley referred to as "new." And though it is not denied that the language of *sola fide* and justification most certainly passed through the lips of John Wesley every time he took Communion and recited from the *Book of Common Prayer*, as Outler indicates, the conversations with Bohler reveal that Wesley had not properly digested the language that had so easily passed through his lips. Cf. W. Reginald Ward and Richard P. Heitzenrater, eds., *The Works of John Wesley* Vol. 18 *Journals and Diaries I* (Nashville: Abingdon Press, 1988), p. 247-48; and Albert Outler, *Theology in the Wesleyan Spirit* (Nashville: Discipleship Resources, 1975), p. 53.

3. Ibid.

4. Ibid. Emphasis is mine.

5. Ibid., 3:119. (On Dissipation) Bracketed material and emphasis are mine.

6. Telford, *Letters*, 4:298.

since the universal and free prevenient grace of God which renders them account-able has already been given. This same concept of prevenient grace is also behind his different evaluation of the role and necessity of works prior to justify-ing faith, and his placing of repentance, for the most part, before justifying faith, not simultaneous with it — ideas that were clearly rejected by the Continental Reformers.[1]

E. The New Birth

From his own spiritual autobiography as displayed in the *Journal*, Wesley knew full well that forgiveness, though important, does not completely meet the needs of the believer. Beyond the remission of sins, there must be a real, defi-nite, and lasting change in those who trust in Christ Jesus. For unless the nature of the believer is transformed, renewed in holiness, as it is in the new birth, one will be unable to live the Christian life in any satisfactory manner. Accordingly, Wesley taught that justification implies only a relative change; the new birth a real one. "God in justifying us does something *for* us; (as noted earlier) in beget-ting us again he does the work *in* us."[2] Again, justification changes the outward relation to God so that sinners are restored to the divine favor; the new birth, on the other hand, changes the inward nature of people so that they are initially made holy. Justification frees one from the *guilt* of sin; the new birth from its *power*.[3] And though as Wesley points out, "In order of time neither of these is before the other...in order of thinking, as it is termed, justification precedes the new birth."[4]

To be sure, the foundation of the new birth, that which makes it necessary, is "the entire corruption of our nature"[5] in original sin as noted in Chapter Five. Not surprisingly, then, regeneration as a gracious act of God, based on the merits of Christ's life and death, restores in some measure the image of God which was polluted by sin. It is that "great change which God works in the soul," Wesley notes, "when he brings it into life."[6] Again, the new birth quickens the spiritu-al senses and is "absolutely necessary in order to holiness."[7] Nevertheless, regeneration, though crucial to a godly life, is not the whole of sanctification, but only a part; it is "the gate of it, the entrance into it."[8] Drawing an analogy between physical and spiritual birth, the Methodist leader explains:

---

1. Kenneth J. Collins, *Wesley On Salvation* (Grand Rapids, Michigan: Francis Asbury Press, 1989), p. 54.

2. Outler, *Sermons*, 1:431-32. (The Great Privilege of Those that are Born of God). Parenthetical material is mine.

3. Ibid., 1:435. Here Wesley affirms the important truth of the Bible that "whosoever is born of God ... doth not commit sin" — a teaching which for whatever reason has seldom been understood even within American Methodism which often has confused this great liberty with the prerogatives of Christian Perfection which is quite another matter.

4. Ibid., 2:187. (The New Birth)

5. Ibid., 2:190.

6. Ibid., 1:193.

7. Ibid., 2:195.

8. Ibid., 2:198.

A child is born of a woman in a moment or at least in a very short time. Afterward he gradually and slowly grows till he attains the stature of a man. In like manner a child is born of God in a short time, if not in a moment. But it is by slow degrees that he afterward grows up to the measure of the full stature of Christ. The same relation therefore which there is between our natural birth and our growth there is also between our new birth and our sanctification.[1]

In terms of the temporal elements, then, Wesley offered a proper balance: the new birth itself is not only instantaneous, but it is also preceded as well as followed by growth in grace. Neither aspect, therefore, should be neglected.[2]

A sermon which further elucidates Wesley's teaching on this head is *The Marks of the New Birth*, written in 1748. In this piece, it is affirmed throughout that the three major theological virtues are suitable evidences of regeneration; namely, a *faith* which is "a sure trust and confidence in God";[3] a *hope* which implies assurance, "the testimony of our own spirit and conscience," as well as that of the Spirit of God;[4] and a *love* which embraces both God and neighbor and is joyfully obedient to the commandments of the Most High.[5]

1. The Emphasis on Regeneration

As noted earlier, since 1725, Wesley's predominant theological interest was holiness or sanctification. However, his new, more sophisticated understandings of both the nature of faith and justification, which were in place by 1738,[6] never adversely affected or diminished this earlier concern. If anything, they augmented it by placing the holy life on the only proper basis possible. And though he energetically preached justification by faith and never doubted its importance after 1738, Wesley's mature theological emphasis seems to lie not so much on forgiveness and a change in the believer's forensic relationship to God, so typical of Luther and Calvin's theology, but on inner transformation and renewal. In fact, so concerned was Wesley with the value of regeneration or initial sanctification that he underscored it in three vital ways.

First, in 1774 Wesley added a note to his earlier Journal statement of January 1738 which had explored the character of a Christian. The note states: "I had even then the faith of a servant, though not that of a *son*,"[7] and it reflects, no doubt, Wesley's seasoned judgment on the matter. And though Jennings believes that this editorial comment undermines the significance that Evangelicals have

---

1. Ibid., 1:198.
2. For additional examples of Wesley's "conjunctive theology" in which he holds together, without contradiction, an instantaneous/gradual tension in relation to sanctification broadly understood Cf. Outler, *Sermons*, 3:204. (On Working Out Our Own Salvation); and 3:507, 3:516. (On God's Vineyard).
3. Ibid., 1:418. (The Marks of the New Birth)
4. Ibid., 1:423.
5. Ibid., 1:427.
6. Collins, *Salvation*, p. 49. ff.
7. W. Reginald Ward and Richard P. Heitzenrater, eds., *The Works of John Wesley* Vol. 18 *Journals and Diaries I* (Nashville: Abingdon Press, 1988), p. 214-15.

traditionally attached to Wesley's Aldersgate experience,[1] it actually supports it. In 1754, for example, in his *Explanatory Notes upon the New Testament*, Wesley defines the faith of a servant in terms of the spirit of bondage and fear that cleaved to the old covenant.[2] Elsewhere he associates the phrase with those who "fear God and worketh righteousness" as in his commentary on Acts 10:35.[3] However, this latter usage makes clear that the faith of a servant was conceived in a very general way by the English leader and included all those believers of *whatever religious tradition* who endeavored to worship God according to the light and grace which they had. Wesley explains:

> But in every nation he that *feareth God and worketh righteousness*... is *accepted of him* — through Christ, though he knows him not.... He is in the favour of God, whether enjoying his written word and ordinances or not.[4]

Continuing this line of thought, since those who fear God and work righteousness are accepted even though they may be ignorant of Christ, the Holy Scriptures, and the sacraments, this demonstrates that such acceptance is not indicative of regeneration or being a real Christian, as is sometimes supposed, but instead is an important implication of Wesley's doctrine of prevenient grace which is both universal and Christologically based.[5] In fact, in this same commentary, but this time on the book of *Romans*, Wesley cautions his readers and affirms that "real Christians have not the spirit of bondage."[6] Indeed, note the difference between the faith of a servant/ faith of a son in the following chart — material culled from Wesley's own homilies.

Servant	*Son*
Fears God (3:497)	Loves God (1:260)
Under the Law (1:258)	Under Grace (1:260)
Sins Unwillingly (1:258)	Free From the Power of Sin (1:261)
Has No Witness (3:498)	"Hath the Witness in Himself" (3:498)
Obeys Out of Fear (4:35)	Obeys Out of Love (4:35)
Includes Jews and All Those Who Work Righteousness (4:49)	Includes Only Those Who Trust In Christ (4:49)

1. Theodore W. Jennings, "John Wesley Against Aldersgate," *Quarterly Review* Vol. 8, No. 3. (Fall 1988), p. 8. This article, on closer examination, merits a name change to "Theodore Jennings against Aldersgate."

2. John Wesley, *Explanatory Notes Upon the New Testament* (Salem, Ohio: Schmul Publishers), p. 646. In this commentary on *Jude*, Wesley also defines a servant in a second sense as one who has the spirit of adoption, but note that this is a definition which is rarely used and is *not* the one which forms the first prong of the distinction the faith of a servant/the faith of a son since only the latter prong is marked by the spirit of adoption. Cf. Wesley, *Notes*, p. 646.

3. Ibid., p. 304.

4. Ibid.

5. See Wesley's sermon *On Conscience* for more details on this aspect of prevenient grace in Outler, *Sermons*, 3:480 ff.

6. Wesley, *Notes*, p. 382.

Also note that it is Wesley himself who identifies the distinction the "faith of a servant/son" with the "faith of a servant/child-of-God" as reflected in the homily *On Faith.*[1] And since the phrase "child of God" is one of Wesley's favorite ways to describe the new birth or regeneration, the above contrasts are more than apt and remarkably revealing. Yes, in January 1738 John Wesley did have the faith of a servant, a faith tinged with fear and which lacked assurance. And in his later years he clearly did not want to discourage — as he once did — those who held this kind of faith, not because it is an especially enviable spiritual state, but because "unless the servants of God halt by the way, they will receive the adoption of sons. They will receive the *faith* of the children of God."[2] Similarly, in the sermon *On the Discoveries of Faith*, the servant of God is exhorted "not to rest till he attain the adoption of sons; till he obeys out of love, which is the privilege of all the children of God,"[3] and as Wesley himself had come to know in an experiential way in May 1738.

A second manner in which Wesley highlighted the new birth was to call attention to the deep and penetrating work that it represents. Thus, the new birth is not merely a superficial or surface change, an amendment of outward life or form, nor is it to be undervalued in the name of Christian Perfection; on the contrary, it is nothing less than, to use his own words, "an inward change from all unholy to all holy tempers ... from an earthly, sensual, devilish mind to the mind that was in Christ Jesus."[4] In 1784, in his sermon *On Charity* Wesley declares:

> ... be our faith ever so strong, it will never save us from hell unless it now save us from all unholy tempers; from pride, passion, impatience; for all arrogance of spirit, all haughtiness and overbearing; from wrath, anger, bitterness; from discontent, murmuring, fretfulness, peevishness.[5]

And as late as 1790, he maintained that "unless [men and women] be so changed ... unless they have new senses, ideas, passions, tempers, they are no Christians!"[6]

In addition, Wesley's estimation of holy tempers, especially the love of God and neighbor, feeds into the third way in which he highlighted the significance of initial sanctification; namely, by associating these dispositions with true religion, real Christianity — an emphasis that contrary to popular belief, never dropped out of his writings, but actually increased over the years. For example, in 1785, in the sermon *The New Creation* "the generality of Christians ... those that are

---

1. Outler, *Sermons*, 3:497.

2. Ibid. For two other references to the distinction faith of a servant/faith of a child Cf. Outler, *Sermons*, 3:130 (On Friendship with the World); and 4:49 (Walking by Sight and Walking by Faith).

3. Ibid., 4:35. (On the Discoveries of Faith) It is interesting to note that Wesley defined "the proper voice of a child of God" utilizing a vocabulary which reflects the Aldersgate account. "The life that I now live in the flesh I live by faith in the Son of God, who loved *me,* and gave himself for *me.*" Cf. Outler, *Sermons*, 4:35-36.

4. Ibid., 3:506. (On God's Vineyard)

5. Ibid., 3:304. (On Charity).

6. Ibid., 4:175. (On Living Without God) Bracketed material is mine.

nominally such" are distinguished from real Christians.[1] In *Of Former Times*, produced two years later, Wesley asserts that Deism, oddly enough, was "the most direct way whereby *nominal* Christians could be prepared, first, for tolerating, and afterwards, for receiving, *real* Christianity."[2] And in an autobiographical note in a late sermon, the elderly Wesley recalls the time when "it pleased God to give me a settled resolution to be not a nominal but a real Christian."[3] Beyond this, in the homily *Walking by Sight, Walking by Faith*, written in 1788, the nature of true religion, real Christianity, is contrasted with many false notions and is displayed in its purity and brilliance. Wesley cautions his readers:

> **Observe well. This is *religion*, and this alone; this alone is true Christian religion. Not this or that opinion, or system of opinions, be they ever so true, ... religion is not *harmlessness*; ... It is not *morality*, excellent as that is ... It is not formality, ... No: religion is no less than living in eternity, and walking in eternity; and hereby walking in the *love* of God and man, in lowliness, meekness, and resignation.[4]**

For his part, Albert Outler has claimed that Wesley's perspective changed over the years and that he greatly modified his earlier distinctions of almost/altogether a Christian, and nominal/real Christianity.[5] In his preface to *The More Excellent Way,* for example, he claims:

> **This is a practical essay in Christian ethics that also illustrates how far the later Wesley had moved away from his earlier exclusivist standards of true faith and salvation. It should be read alongside *The Almost Christian*; the startling contrast between the two reflects a half-century's experience as leader of a revival movement and also a significant change in his mind and heart.[6]**

However, some of the contrasts made in the early sermon *The Almost Christian* are little different from those just cited above. More specifically, in this 1741 sermon, almost Christians are depicted as having a form of godliness (See *The New Creation* 2:501); as having the outside of a real Christian (See *The End of Christ's Coming* 2:483); and as utilizing the means of grace (See *The Unity of the Divine Being* 4:66). What does change in time, however, is the latter part of the equation; that is, what it means to be an "altogether Christian." In *The Almost Christian*, for example, altogether Christians are described as those who love the

---

1. Ibid., 2:501. (The New Creation).
2. Ibid., 3:452. (Of Former Times)
3. Ibid., 3:152. (In What Sense we are to Leave the World)
4. Ibid., 4:57-58. (Walking by Sight, Walking by Faith) For additional references on the theme of "real Christianity" Cf. Outler, *Sermons*, 3:527. (On Riches); 2:482-83. (The End of Christ's Coming); 3:152. (In What Sense we are to Leave the World); 3:99. (Spiritual Worship); 2:501 (The New Creation); 2:543 (On Divine Providence); 3:452-53. (Of Former Times); 4:57-58. (Walking by Sight, Walking by Faith); 4:121-22 (On a Single Eye); 4:66 (The Unity of the Divine Being); and 4:146 (On the Wedding Garment).
5. Ibid., 3:152. Note #40. (In What Sense we are to Leave the World)
6. Ibid., 3:262. (The More Excellent Way)

Lord their God with all their heart, soul, mind, and strength — and their neighbors as themselves.[1] Moreover, they have a faith "which purifies the heart, by the power of God who dwelleth therein, from pride, anger, desire, from all unrighteousness, from all filthiness of flesh and spirit."[2] But the preceding are obviously apt descriptions not of the new birth, what it means to be a real Christian, but of entire sanctification. However, in 1741, Wesley still ran these ideas together, and it would not be until towards the end of the 1740's that he would clearly distinguish the graces of Christian Perfection from those of initial sanctification.[3] So in this sense what Outler argues is, in fact, correct.

Nevertheless, it would be a mistake to contend (and I'm not suggesting that Outler does *this*) that because Wesley clarified his thought and distinguished initial and entire sanctification that he then lowered the threshold for the new birth which in turn eventually became his *standard* for what constitutes real Christianity. In his *On a Single Eye*, for instance, written late in his career, Wesley declares: "How great a thing it is to be a Christian, to be a real, inward, scriptural Christian! Conformed in heart and life to the will of God! Who is sufficient for these things? None, unless he be born of God."[4] Notice here that Wesley not only still uses the language of a "real Christian" in 1789, but that he also correctly identifies it with regeneration and not with entire sanctification as he once did. In other words, almost Christians, those who lack the marks of the new birth, are almost Christians still — in 1741, in 1747, and in 1789 as well.

Given this line of argument, Outler's call for a comparison of *The Almost Christian* and *The More Excellent Way* is in one sense invalid, for he appears to assume that the distinction almost Christian/altogether Christian of the earlier sermon (*The Almost Christian*) corresponds to the distinction of the generality of Christians/the more excellent way as found in the later sermon (*The More Excellent Way*). However, the two *sets* of groups compared in these homilies are *not* the same. To illustrate, in the first sermon, the "almost Christian" is a person who lacks the evidences of both justification and regeneration as set forth in *The Marks of the New Birth*.[5] The "altogether Christian" on the other hand is at the very least justified and regenerated (and possibly entirely sanctified). In light of this, is the phrase the "generality of Christians" as found in the later sermon, *The More Excellent Way* actually equivalent to "the almost Christian" as Outler seems to suggest? Not really. Observe how Wesley defines "the generality of Christians" in this later production:

"From long experience and observation I am inclined to think that whoever finds redemption in the blood of Jesus, whoever is justified, has then the choice of walking in the higher or the lower path."[6]

1. Ibid., 1:137. (The Almost Christian)
2. Ibid., 1:139.
3. Richard P. Heitzenrater, *Mirror and Memory* (Nashville: Kingswood Books, 1989), p. 142.
4. Outler, *Sermons*, 4:122. (On a Single Eye) Emphasis is mine.
5. Ibid., 1:415 ff. (The Marks of the New Birth)
6. Ibid., 3:266. (The More Excellent Way)

In other words, these Christians are already justified and are about to embark either upon the higher path of entire sanctification or not. Simply put, in the sermon *The Almost Christian*, Wesley is comparing almost-Christians (though virtuous) with those who have at the very least been born of God. In his later sermon, he is comparing justified Christians with the entirely sanctified — or with the possibility of entire sanctification. Therefore, those who appeal to a comparison of these pieces in order to show that those who lack the marks of the new birth are indeed real Christians (and again I'm not suggesting that Outler does *this*) have failed to pay significant attention to Wesley's own theological vocabulary. Once again, almost Christians remain almost Christians. The former part of the equation had never really directly changed.[1]

II. Entire Sanctification

Though the new birth is a remarkable and gracious work of God in the soul, it does not constitute the entirety of what Wesley meant by redemption. Indeed, the hearts of those who have been justified by faith are not wholly purified. Consequently, the carnal nature, or original sin, yet plagues believers in the sense that they often feel a contrary principal within — one which is ever-ready to bolt from the Most High. "How prone is our heart still to depart from the living God!" Wesley exclaims. "What a tendency to sin remains in our heart, although we know our past sins are forgiven."[2] Again, experience as well as the universal tradition of the Church shows the believer that "the root [s] of sin, self-will, pride, and idolatry, remain still in his heart."[3] All has not been accomplished in one grand stoke; an additional work is needed.

A. Evangelical Repentance

In order to understand what Wesley meant by evangelical repentance, that repentance which is necessary *after* one is justified, some key distinctions which he made in his doctrine of sin must first be explored. In his sermon *Sin in Believers*, for instance, the Methodist leader asserts:

> The *guilt* is one thing, the *power* another, and the *being* yet another. That believers are delivered from the *guilt* and *power* of sin we allow; that they are delivered from the *being* of it we deny.[4]

Beyond this, in his sermon *The Repentance of Believers*, Wesley readily acknowledges that "he that is born of God doth not commit sin, yet we cannot

---

1. Naturally, if a change is made in terms of what constitutes an altogether Christian, this indirectly affects what it means to be an almost Christian. Nevertheless, the basic characteristics which Wesley employs to describe almost Christians as a class in and of itself never changes. The real changes lie elsewhere. Cf. Outler, *Sermons*, 1:131-37.

2. Outler, *Sermons*, Ibid., 3:53. (Of the Church)

3. Ibid., 4:157. (The Deceitfulness of the Human Heart)

4. Ibid., 1:329. (Sin in Believers)

allow," he insists, "that he does not *feel* it within."[1] In other words, sin "does not *reign*, but it does *remain*."[2] Add to this the distinctions between guilt, power, and being found elsewhere, in several other homilies, and the picture which begins to emerge is that the English Evangelical broadly associated deliverance from the guilt of sin with justification or pardon (*Justification by Faith* 1:189); from the power of sin with the new birth (*Marks of the New* 1:419); and from the being of it with entire sanctification (*Sin in Believers* 1:328).[3]

What are believers to repent of then? Not actual sin, for they are no longer under its dominion, but inbred sin, the carnal nature which yet remains. To be sure, it is the Holy Spirit who by means of the law of God will convict believers of pride, self-will, love of the world, and any other inordinate affection contrary to the love of God and neighbor.[4] The Spirit will expose the desire of the flesh, the desire of the eye, and the pride of life which infect and dull the soul, and he will lead the humbled believer, once again, to the path of repentance.[5]

Moreover, it was Wesley himself, and not the holiness movement, who first championed the notion of a "second" work of grace. Without doubt, the language of "secondness" was very much a part of his own, for the leprosy is not cleansed "till it shall please the Lord to speak to our hearts the second time, 'Be clean.'"[6] And elsewhere he writes, also settling some disputes about the temporal elements involved:

> But if there be no such second change, if there be no instantaneous deliverance after justification, if there be none but a gradual work of God (that there is a gradual work none denies) then we must be content, as well as we can, to remain full of sin till death.[7]

B. Works Prior to Entire Sanctification

For Wesley, the faith through which one is justified and born anew is not a dead faith, devoid of works, but is ever active through the rich sanctifying grace of God. In fact, there is a real sense in his theology that as the grace of God increases (prevenient, convincing, sanctifying) so too does the importance of human response. "To whom much is given, much more will be required."[8] Accordingly, the Methodist leader affirmed on many occasions that "the grand

---

1. Ibid., 1:336-37. (The Repentance of Believers)
2. Ibid.
3. However, this is not to suggest that Wesley was always so exact in his language. At times he wrote more generally, as in his sermon *On Working Out Our Own Salvation*: "By justification we are saved from the guilt of sin ... by sanctification we are saved from the power and root [being] of sin." (Bracketed material is mine) However, since sanctification in this context, no doubt, includes the work of regeneration and entire sanctification, the basic distinctions remain. Cf. Outler, *Sermons*, 3:204.
4. Ibid., 1:337-38. (The Repentance of Believers)
5. Ibid., 1:338.
6. Ibid., 1:346.
7. Ibid.
8. This is my own paraphrase of Luke 12:48.

pest of Christianity" was the teaching of faith without works — a teaching which filled the church with "a wisdom from beneath."[1] "Good works are so far from being insignificant," he warns, "... that supposing them to spring from a right principle, they are the perfection of religion."[2]

Continuing this line of thought, Wesley maintained that the love of God established in the heart by faith naturally leads to works both of piety and of mercy which in the sight of God are truly good since they are preceded by sanctifying grace. By the former, works of piety, he had in mind such things as praying, receiving the Lord's Supper, searching the Scriptures, and fasting; in other words, he had in view the means of grace detailed earlier. By the latter, works of mercy, he underscored the great value of ministering to both the bodies *and* souls of humanity, of "feeding the hungry, clothing the naked, entertaining the stranger, visiting those that are in prison, or sick ... or [awakening] the stupid sinner."[3] But what is even more important for the task at hand is to observe that Wesley considered all these works the normal prelude to that faith which sanctifies entirely. "These are the fruits meet for repentance," he declares, "which are necessary to full sanctification. This is *the way* wherein God hath appointed his children to wait for complete salvation."[4] Just as repentance and its works were in some sense necessary to justification, so too is a second repentance and its works in some sense necessary to entire sanctification. Wesley explains:

> Though it be allowed that both this repentance and its fruits are necessary to full salvation, yet they are not necessary either in the *same sense* with faith or in the *same degree*. Not in the same degree; for these fruits are only necessary *conditionally*, if there be time and opportunity for them....Not in the *same sense*; for this repentance and these fruits are only *remotely* necessary, necessary in order to the continuance of ... faith, as well as the increase of it;[5]

C. Faith

Wesley's discussion on the necessity of faith for entire sanctification mirrors the one on justification. Thus, only faith is both necessary and sufficient to establish the highest spiritual life in the heart of the believer. It is necessary in the sense that entire sanctification cannot occur without it, no matter how numerous or selfless the works of mercy. It is sufficient in the sense that even if only

---

1. Outler, *Sermons*, 2:459. (The Mystery of Iniquity)

2. Ibid., 3:405. (The Reward of Righteousness) John Cennick, who was one of Wesley's lay preachers, and who at Whitefield's suggestion became the first chaplain of Kingswood School, found fault with Wesley's preaching and accused him in February 1741 of preaching up "man's faithfulness" and "righteousness in man." Moreover, the Calvinist Methodists, who coalesced around the Countess of Lady Huntingdon, charged Wesley with legalism and much worse after he published the conference minutes of 1770. Once again, however, these detractors had failed to comprehend Wesley's understanding of grace which was so different from their own. Wesley looked not to Geneva, but to Canterbury. Cf. Curnock, *Journal*, 2:427 and Jackson, *Wesley's Works*, 8:337-38.

3. Ibid., 2:166. (The Scripture Way of Salvation)

4. Ibid. Emphasis is mine.

5. Ibid., 2:167.

faith is present, one may be sanctified.[1] "Exactly as we are justified by faith, so are we sanctified by faith," Wesley declares, "Faith is the condition, and the only condition of sanctification, exactly as it is of justification.[2] However, the marks or traits of this faith which establishes Christian perfection entail a divine evidence or conviction in three areas different from that of justification: first, that God has promised perfect love in the Scriptures; second, that what God has promised He is able to perform, and third that God is both able and willing to sanctify now.[3]

Interestingly enough, in contemporary Methodism, there has been a considerable degree of discussion — some of it quite heated — concerning the third aspect: namely, when entire sanctification occurs. Is it, on the one hand, to be received instantaneously in a crisis event or is it, on the other, to be received gradually as one matures spiritually? Wesley, himself, seems to emphasize different elements in various writings, and this is, no doubt, part of the problem. For example, in one place he argues that entire sanctification is "constantly both preceded and followed by a gradual work,"[4] with the implication that a good deal of time passes before this grace is received. But in his sermon *The Scripture Way of Salvation*, the instantaneous element appears virtually alone: "Look for it then every day, every hour, every moment,"[5] he urges.

However, these two statements just cited are not contradictory so long as it is realized that, for Wesley, the issue of process/instantaneous is a reflection of the larger issue of the relation between faith and works. Gradualism, therefore, highlights the normal spiritual development, the works, and the obedience that are conditionally required if sanctification is to occur — if there be time and opportunity for them. The instantaneous motif, on the other hand, keeps before the believer the unconditional element of faith — that perfection in love may yet occur even if only this ingredient is present. Wesley writes:

And by this token may you surely know whether you seek it by faith or by works. If by works, you want something to be done first, before you are sanctified. You think, 'I must first be or do thus or thus.' Then you are seeking it by works unto this day. If you seek it by faith, you may expect it as you are: and if as you are, then expect it now.[6]

Earlier in describing the change which God brings about in regeneration, Wesley appealed to the image of natural birth to display the instantaneous and gradual aspects of this work. However, in exploring these same aspects but this time in terms of Christian perfection he appeals not to the image of birth, but of death and writes:

1. See my book *Wesley On Salvation* (pages 134 ff.) cited above from which some of this material is taken.
2. Outler, *Sermons*, 2:167. (The Scripture Way of Salvation)
3. Ibid.
4. Jackson, *Works*, 11:442.
5. Outler, *Sermons*, 2:169. (The Scripture Way of Salvation)
6. Ibid.

> From the moment we are justified, there may be a gradual sanctification, a growing in grace, a daily advance in the knowledge and love of god. And if sin cease before death, there must, in the nature of the thing, be an instantaneous change; there must be a last moment wherein it does exist, and a first moment wherein it does not.[1]

Yet another way of viewing this same problem is to consider it against the backdrop of Wesley's apparent distinction between ideal and practice. Thus, for instance, he writes in his *Brief Thoughts On Christian Perfection* that the reception of perfect love is generally just prior to death, "the moment before the soul leaves the body."[2] However, later in this same piece he notes that "I believe it may be ten, twenty, or forty years before."[3] Along these same lines, in the sermon *The Scripture Way of Salvation,* he urges believers to "look for it then every day, every hour, every moment....Certainly you may look for it *now*."[4]

What all of this means, then, is that Christian perfection according to Wesley is a present possibility for all who are born of God and believe, but regrettably, only very few will have the quality of faith required until just prior to the crisis of death. In other words, there is often a lengthy process of spiritual development which prepares one for the reception of this faith, even though, ideally, it can be received in a moment. With these distinctions in mind, it nevertheless appears that the Methodist leader emphasizes the immediate availability of this grace, especially in his sermons.[5]

D. Entire Sanctification Itself

Those outside the Methodist tradition (as well as some within it) are apt to misunderstand John Wesley's doctrine of Christian perfection. Therefore, in order to clear up some of the erroneous interpretations which often emerge, it is necessary, first of all, to indicate what Christian perfection is *not*. It is not, for instance, perfection in knowledge such that believers are freed from all manner of ignorance. How God can be Three in One (the Trinity) or how God became man (the incarnation) are still in some sense mysteries for all believers no matter how holy.[6] Second, it is not freedom from mistake. "The best and wisest of men are frequently mistaken even with regard to facts," Wesley observes.[7] They may misjudge the characters of people, either favorably or unfavorably, or they may

---

1. Jackson, *Works*, 11:329.
2. Ibid., 11:446.
3. Ibid. Also note that Wesley again makes a distinction between ideal and practice as recorded in the Conference Minutes of 1744 where it reads, "Is this ordinarily given till a little before death? It is not, to those who expect it no sooner. But may we expect it sooner? Why not? For, although we grant, (1) That the generality of believers, whom we have hitherto known, were not so sanctified till near death ... yet all this does not prove, that we many not be so today." Cf. *A Plain Account of Christian Perfection* in Jackson, *Works*, 11:387.
4. Outler, *Works*, 2:169. (The Scripture Way of Salvation)
5. Again, some of the preceding material is drawn from my book, *Wesley On Salvation*. Cf. pp. 122-23.
6. Outler, *Sermons*, 2:101. (Christian Perfection)
7. Ibid., 2:102.

misinterpret the Scriptures. Third, Christians are not so far perfect as to be free from such infirmities as "weakness or slowness of understanding, dullness or confusedness of apprehension, incoherency of thought, irregular quickness or heaviness of imagination."[1] And fourth, those perfected in love are still subject to temptation, at times quite severe, as long as they live. "Such perfection," Wesley writes, "belongeth not to this life."[2]

Beyond these four counsels, Wesley rejected a perfection of degrees, a perfection that would not admit of a continual increase and advance as one improves the rich grace of God. Thus, there is no place in this leader's theology for the notion that one has arrived, spiritually speaking. Those whose hearts have been made pure by the blood of Christ must continue to grow. Christian perfection, so understood, is not static but dynamic, not a "perfected perfection" as Outler correctly points out, but a "perfecting perfection."[3] "How much soever any man hath attained, or in how high a degree soever he is perfect," Wesley warns, "he hath still need to grow in grace, and daily to advance in the knowledge and love of God his Savior."[4]

On the other hand, when it comes to describing the nature of Christian Perfection, precisely what it *is*, Wesley proceeds along two major lines. First of all, perfection is conceived in a "negative" sense as freedom from the root and being of sin, even the carnal nature. As such, it is "a deliverance form all evil dispositions implied in that expression, 'I will circumcise thy heart.'"[5] In his sermon *On Perfection* Wesley elaborates:

> **Thus you experience that he whose name is called Jesus does not bear that name in vain; that he does in fact 'save his people from their sins', the root as well as the branches; and this 'salvation from sin', from all sin, is another description of perfection...**[6]

Moreover, commenting on James 1:4, Wesley again pursues this theme in a sermon written in 1784:

> **Ye shall then be *perfect*. The Apostle seems to mean by this expression, *teleioi*, ye shall be wholly delivered from every evil work, from every evil word, from every sinful thought; yea, from every evil desire, passion, temper, from all inbred corruption, from all remains of the carnal mind, from the whole body of sin...**[7]

1. Ibid., 2:103. See also Outler, *Sermons*, 2:482 (The End of Christ's Coming); 2:406 (On the Fall of Man); 3:73 (On Perfection); 3:160 (On Temptation); and 4:165-66 (Heavenly Treasure in Earthen Vessels).
2. Ibid., 2:104.
3. Ibid., 2:98.
4. Ibid., 2:104-05. See also *Wesley On Salvation*, p. 119 ff.
5. Ibid., 4:37. (On the Discoveries of Faith)
6. Ibid., 3:76. (On Perfection)
7. Ibid., 3:179. (On Patience) Observe how Wesley's thought had changed over the years. Earlier, in January 1738, there is evidence to suggest that he confused the prerogatives of Christian Perfection with those of the new birth, for at this time he wrote that he wanted a faith that "whosoever hath it is 'freed from sin'; 'the whole body of sin is destroyed' in him." Compare this statement with the one found in the sermon *On Patience* where it is clearly restricted to Christian Perfection. Cf. Ward and Heitzenrater, *Journals*, 18:216., and Outler *Sermons*, 3:179.

Second, Christian perfection is conceived in a positive sense as simply another name for universal holiness — "inward and outward righteousness — holiness of life arising from holiness of heart."[1] It is having the mind which was in Christ Jesus, "the whole disposition of his mind, all his affections, all his tempers, both toward God and man."[2] It is loving the Lord thy God with all thy heart, soul, and mind, and thy neighbor as thyself. And it is "the planting all good dispositions in their place."[3] Simply put, Christian perfection is love replacing sin, love conquering every vile passion and temper, love resplendent in the restored *imago dei*. Indeed, when the first Methodist conference considered these same issues in 1744, it was agreed that no wrong temper contrary to love remains in the soul; all thoughts, words, and actions are governed by pure love.[4] Moreover, just as the Holy Spirit witnesses to justification so too does he witness to entire sanctification. "None therefore ought to believe that the work is done," Wesley writes, "till there is added the testimony of the spirit, witnessing his entire sanctification *as clearly as* his justification."[5] There is nothing higher than this; nothing more glorious nor more relevant than holy love, a love which worships God and is the engine for service to humanity.

III. Some Observations

It should be apparent by now that the structure of this present chapter is reflective of Wesley's *ordo salutis*. Thus, the discussion of repentance, works, faith, and the witness of the Spirit under the heading of justification is paralleled in the one on entire sanctification. Recall Wesley's conjunctive language cited earlier which sets up the relation: "There is a repentance consequent upon, *as well as* a repentance previous to justification."[6] "*Exactly* as we are justified by faith, so are we sanctified by faith. Faith is the condition, and the only condition of sanctification, *exactly* as it is of justification."[7] And yet again, "None therefore ought to believe that the work is done till there is added the testimony of the spirit, witnessing his entire sanctification *as clearly as* his justification."[8] Parallelism, then, the emphasis on similarity, is one of the first observations which is necessary in order to unravel Wesley's thought on the doctrine of salvation, and this structure is amply displayed in the summary sermon, *The Scripture Way of Salvation*. In the diagram which follows compare each section (A, B, etc.) and point (1, 2, etc.) under the heading of justification with those under entire sanctification and note the similarities.

1. Ibid., 3:75. (On Perfection)
2. Ibid. 3:74.
3. Ibid., 4:37. (On the Discoveries of Faith)
4. Jackson, *Works*, 11:387.
5. Jackson, *Works*, 11:402.
6. Outler, *Sermons*, 2:164. (The Scripture Way of Salvation) Emphasis is mine.
7. Ibid., 2:163.
8. Jackson, *Works*, 11:402.

The *Ordo Salutis* of the *Scripture Way of Salvation*
The end is...salvation; the means, faith (1:156)

Atonement
(Meritorious Cause of Justification) 2:157
Prevenient Grace (2:156) —-> Natural Conscience (2:156),
Convincing Grace (2:157)

Justification
Pardon (2:157), Forgiveness of Sins (2:157)

A. Repentance and Fruits Meet for Repentance
1. Some sense necessary to justification (2:162)

2. Not necessary in the *same sense* with faith, nor in the *same degree* (2:163)
Only necessary conditionally (2:163)
Repentance and its fruits are only *remotely* necessary, necessary in order to faith (2:163)

3. God does undoubtedly command us both to repent and to bring forth fruits meet for repentance; which if we willingly neglect we cannot reasonably expect to be justified at all. (2:162)
Therefore both repentance and fruits meet for repentance are in some sense necessary to justification. (2:162)

B. Faith
4. Divine evidence and conviction (2:161)
Christ loved *me*, and gave himself for *me* (2:161)

5. Faith is immediately and directly necessary to just (2:163)
Faith is immediately and proximately necessary to just (2:163)
Faith is the condition, and the only condition of just (2:162)
This alone is sufficient for justification (2:162)

C. Assurance (Witness of the Spirit)
6. Necessarily implies an *assurance*: (2:161)
That Christ loved *me*, and gave himself for *me* (2:161)

7. None therefore ought to believe that the work is done, till there is added the testimony of the Spirit, witnessing his ... justification. (Jackson, *Works*, 11:402)

Sanctification

Real as well as a relative change (2:158); Sin only suspended (2:159); Entire sanctification, love excluding sin (2:160)

A. Repentance and Fruits Meet for Repentance

1. Repentance ... [is] in some sense necessary to sanctification (2:164)
There is a repentance consequent upon, as well as a repentance previous to, justification (2:164)
The repentance consequent upon justification is widely different from that which is antecedent to it. (2:164)
A conviction wrought by the Holy Ghost of the 'sin' which still 'remains' (2:165)

2. Repentance and its fruits are necessary to full salvation, yet they are not necessary either in the *same sense* with faith or in the *same degree* (2:167)
Only necessary conditionally (2:167)
Repentance and these fruits are only *remotely* necessary, necessary in order to the continuance of faith as well as the increase of it (2:167)

3. These are so necessary [good works] that if a man willingly neglect them, he cannot reasonably expect that he shall ever be sanctified (2:164)
The practice of all good works, works of piety, as well as works of mercy are in some sense necessary to sanctification (2:164)

B. Faith

4. Divine evidence and conviction: (2:167)
First, that God hath promised it in the Holy Scripture (2:167)
Second, what God hath promised he is able to perform (2:167-68)
Thirdly, that he is able and willing to do it now (2:168)
Fourthly, that he doth it (2:168)

5. Faith is immediately and directly necessary to sanct.(2:167)
Faith is ...immediately and proximately necessary to sanctification. (2:167)
Exactly as we are justified by faith, so are we sanctified by faith. (2:163)
Faith is the condition, and the only condition of sanctification, exactly as it is of justification (2:163)
This alone is sufficient for sanctification (2:163)

C. Assurance (Witness of the Spirit)

6. Necessarily implies an *assurance*: (2:161)
The spirit witnesseth ... that he is a child of God (2:161)

7. None therefore ought to believe that the work is done, till there is added the testimony of the Spirit, witnessing his entire sanctification *as clearly as* his justification. (Jackson, 11:402)

In light of this material, it is evident that, on one level, Wesley employs *the same* vocabulary to describe the two quite different processes of salvation from the guilt and power of sin (justification and regeneration) on the one hand and the further work of salvation from the being of sin (entire sanctification) on the other. However, the mere observation of parallelism, with its emphasis upon similarity, is not an appropriate vehicle to convey the notion of movement, the dynamic flavor, implicit in Wesley's goal-oriented (teleological) theology. And this is precisely why it is also important to see *the differences* between these doctrines due to the soteriological distance (growth in grace) between them.[1] For example, Wesley maintains that "the repentance consequent upon justification is widely different from that which is antecedent to it."[2] It is not a conviction of actual sin, but of "the 'sin' which still 'remains.'"[3] Again, the faith which is previous to entire sanctification is in some sense different from that previous to justification in that the latter is a divine evidence and conviction that "Christ loved *me*, and gave himself for *me*,"[4] while the former is a conviction that God "hath promised it [entire sanctification] in the Holy Scripture"[5] and that, among other things, "he is able and willing to do it now."[6] And though it is beyond the scope of this present chapter to explore each one of the six major soteriological differences in detail (if interested, see my earlier book *Wesley on Salvation*), note them as reflected in following chart:

Justification	Entire Sanctification
The Law	
-Similarity —-> Accusation	Accusation
-Difference —-> Actual Sin	Inbred Sin
Repentance	
-Similarity —-> Self-Knowledge	Self-Knowledge
-Difference —-> Legal Repentance	Evangelical Repentance
Works Meet for Repentance	
-Similarity —-> Conditionally Necessary	Conditionally Necessary
-Difference —-> Not Good (Strictly Speaking)	Good (Sanctifying Grace)

1. For a more detailed treatment of this subject Cf. Collins, *Wesley On Salvation*, p. 131 ff.
2. Outler, *Sermons*, 2:164. (The Scripture Way of Salvation)
3. Ibid., 2:165.
4. Ibid., 2:161.
5. Ibid., 2:167. Bracketed material is mine.
6. Ibid., 2:168.

Justification	Entire Sanctification

Faith

-Similarity —-> Unconditionally Necessary	Unconditionally (Exactly As) Necessary
-Difference —-> A Sure Trust That "Christ Died For My Sins"	A Sure Trust That Christ Is "Able to Save From All The Sin Which Remains"

Temporal Dimensions

-Similarity —-> Gradual/ Instantaneous	Gradual/ Instantaneous
-Difference —-> Image of Birth	Image of Death

The Witness of the Spirit

Similarity —-> Direct Witness	Direct Witness (Clearly As)
Difference —-> Sins Forgiven	Sin "Taken Away"

This means, of course, that the similarity and differences of these doctrines, expressed in terms of parallelism and progression respectively, are at the heart of Wesley's basic order of salvation. More to the point, it is the specific *blending* of similarity and difference which gives each doctrine its distinctive hue. And at least by mid-career, this blending is Wesley's chief soteriological fingerprint — a marker without which his thought is hardly understood. The implication for scholarship, therefore, of this dynamic nature of Wesley's theology is that it is not sufficient merely to explore his doctrinal statements or sermons within the context of their historical settings. Although this preliminary task is vital, one must think systematically as well, and determine the theological setting within the *ordo salutis* where each doctrine is found. In other words, once a specific doctrine is located within the Wesleyan order of salvation, it must be expounded with reference to what both precedes and follows it within that theological framework. This approach makes for a more intelligible reading of the entire sermon corpus and reveals that although Wesley was not a systematic theologian in the sense of a Thomas Aquinas or a John Calvin, he was nevertheless highly consistent in his thinking about the process of salvation.[1]

1. Collins, *Salvation*, p. 137.

Excursus

Other Thoughts on Aldersgate:
Has the Conversionist Paradigm Collapsed?

Among contemporary Methodist historians, the marking of the 250th anniversary of John Wesley's Aldersgate experience will perhaps best be remembered not for its joyful commemorations, but for the intense scholarly debate which it has spawned. Theodore Jennings, for instance, not only observed in 1988 that "Aldersgate [was] largely a non-event,"[1] but he also maintained that as Methodism celebrated this anniversary it was only celebrating "its own willful distortion of its own history, its own apostasy from Wesleyan theology."[2] Likewise and more recently, Randy Maddox, editor of *Aldersgate Reconsidered*, decried the sole celebration of Aldersgate and suggested commemorating the formation of the first Methodist society (1739) or even Wesley's death (1791) as suitable, and more theologically appropriate, replacements.[3]

Interestingly, what lies behind such calls for replacement is the assumption that the "standard" theological interpretation of Aldersgate as John Wesley's conversion experience is irretrievably flawed since it is unable to incorporate Wesley's later journal disclaimers (where the Methodist leader modifies some of his entries made in 1738), nor can it reflect adequately the emphases of the mature Wesley.[4] However, the thesis of this present piece is that the methodology used by contemporary historians like Jennings and Maddox, who together seek to deconstruct a rich interpretative tradition, is itself seriously flawed in that it mistakes the *claim* that the conversionist model is unable to take into account the later Wesley for an *argument*. Consequently, this essay will critically examine each of Wesley's journal disclaimers and will, in turn, demonstrate that such evidence does not overturn the conversionist interpretation, as is supposed, but only those distortions and stereotypes which have been mistaken for that interpretation.

1. Theodore Jennings, "John Wesley *Against* Aldersgate," *Quarterly Review* Vol. 8, No. 3 (Fall 1988): 7. Bracketed material is mine; I have changed the present tense to the past.
2. Jennings, 22.
3. Randy L. Maddox, "Celebrating Wesley—When?" *Methodist History* Vol. 24, No. 2 (January 1991): 75. Though Maddox justifies the commemoration of Wesley's death as reinforcing the perspective of the mature Wesley, he hardly demonstrates what theological characteristics of the mature Wesley must be brought into play and, more importantly, what precise difference they would make.
4. See Jennings, "Against Aldersgate," 8-11, and Randy Maddox, ed., *Aldersgate Reconsidered* (Nashville: Kingswood Books, 1990), 15-16. Note that Maddox's description of the "standard" interpretation contains a number of inaccuracies. My own work, for example, is misquoted ("dangerous new wave in Wesley studies"); moreover, Maddox contends, on my behalf, that the standard interpretation has been the position of Methodist scholars ever since Wesley! However, see my piece "Twentieth-Century Interpretations of Aldersgate: Coherence or Confusion?" which is forthcoming in the *Wesleyan Theological Journal* where I clearly state that Frank Baker and Umphrey Lee questioned the accuracy of the conversionist view.

I. The Claim that the Conversionist Model is Faulty

A. The Problem of Definitions

Before the present thesis can be explored, it is necessary to define clearly and succinctly just what constitutes the "standard" or conversionist interpretation of John Wesley's Aldersgate experience. Indeed, one of the difficulties of the work of Jennings and of a volume like *Aldersgate Reconsidered* is the lack of definitional precision in each. Jennings, for instance, quickly moves from a discussion of a conversionist reading of Wesley's journal to what he calls "Aldersgateism" and contends that the latter entails the ability "to date one's conversion and that nothing after this is really important."[1] Moreover, in *Aldersgate Reconsidered*, Roberta Bondi argues — confusing the doctrines of initial and entire sanctification — that the effects of Aldersgate spirituality are destructive,[2] since it indicates that one "ought to be full of simple love for God and neighbor"[3] from the day one becomes a Christian. And David Lowes Watson, for his part, implies that the association of Aldersgate with the new birth has led to a deprecation of the means of grace and to the neglect of the discipline evident in Wesley's General Rules of the United Societies.[4] However, observe that in each of these descriptions, the data are culled not from the arguments of such scholars as Tyerman, Cell, or Rattenbury, who represent the standard interpretation, but from a contemporary ecclesiastical context where all sorts of distortions of a tradition (and stereotypes) can emerge.[5]

In light of this lack of clarity, and also for the sake of hermeneutical responsibility, the conversionist interpretation will be defined not in terms of contemporary church practice or abuse, but in terms of those authors who are the best representatives of this interpretive school — such authors as Henry Moore, Luke Tyerman, Nehemiah Curnock, George Croft Cell, William Cannon, J. Ernest Rattenbury, Martin Schmidt, and V.H.H. Green.[6] When this is done, the conver-

---

1. Jennings, 11, 20.
2. Roberta C. Bondi, "Aldersgate and Patterns of Methodist Spirituality," in *Aldersgate Reconsidered*, ed. Randy L. Maddox (Nashville: Kingswood Books, 1990), 22.
3. Bondi, 21-22.
4. David Lowes Watson, "Aldersgate Street and the General Rules: The Form and the Power of Methodist Discipleship," in *Aldersgate Reconsidered*, Maddox, 36. Though Watson is correct in underscoring the importance of such things as rules and the moral law in the Christian life, he nevertheless overstates his case specially when he contends that "the form *and* the power of early Methodist discipleship lay in its methods." (45-46, emphasis is mine.) It is, however, much more accurate to state that, for Wesley at least, the form indeed lay in the methods, but the power in *the Holy Spirit*. See Wesley's sermons "The Means of Grace" and "The Witness of the Spirit, I" and "The Witness of the Spirit, II" in Albert C. Outler, ed., *The Works of John Wesley*, Vols. 1-4. *The Sermons*. (Nashville: Abingdon Press, 1984.) 1: 376-97 and 1: 267-98.
5. Maddox attempts to offer a more accurate representation of "the standard interpretation." Unfortunately, his use of the phrases "pre-Christian moralist" and "true Christian believer" are left undefined. Cf. Maddox, *Reconsidered*, 13.
6. To be sure, these authors maintain slightly different emphases on this topic; nevertheless, their *general* position clearly resonates with what is defined here as a conversionist view. Cf. Henry Moore, *The Life of the Rev. John Wesley*, Vol. 1. (New York: N. Bangs and J. Emory, for the Methodist Episcopal Church, 1826), 198ff; Luke Tyerman, *The Life and Times of the Rev. John Wes*

sionist model emerges with all of its many nuances intact, and the Aldersgate experience appears as the time when John Wesley encountered a gracious God, exercised justifying faith, was born anew, and when he received a measure of assurance. It is, therefore, in this restricted sense that the phrase will be used throughout this essay.

B. The Four Journal Disclaimers and the Mature Wesley
1. The First Disclaimer
In 1774, Wesley qualified some of his earlier statements which were written in his journal just a few months prior to his Aldersgate experience. Of these four notes, which are often called disclaimers, the first deals with the topic of conversion, and it therefore has received considerable attention. The text, to which it was appended, reads as follows:

> It is now two years and almost four months since I left my native country in order to teach the Georgian Indians the nature of Christianity. But what have I learned myself in the meantime? Why (what I the least of suspected), that I who went to America to convert others, was never myself converted to God.[1]

However, in 1774, Wesley added the editorial comment, "I am not sure of this."[2] But just what does this statement signify? Upon closer examination, the emphasis on uncertainty in the note suggests that neither a) "I was never myself converted to God," nor b) "I was converted to God" can be unequivocally affirmed. In other words, on this level, the question of whether or not Wesley was converted in Georgia remains very much open and not closed as Jennings presumes.[3] Given this ambiguity, it is perhaps best to ascertain the meaning of this note in concert with Wesley's other editorial changes. Beyond this, it should be borne in mind that not only is the word "conversion" one which Wesley seldom used, but also, and more importantly, that he defined it much more broadly than is often done today.[4]

...Continued...

ley, 3 vols.(New York: Burt Franklin), 1:179ff; Nehemiah Curnock, *The Journal of the Rev. John Wesley, A.M.*, 8 vols. (London: The Epworth Press, 1938), 1:33ff; George Croft Cell, *The Rediscovery of John Wesley* (New York: Henry Holt and Company, Inc., 1935), 28, 73, 185, and 361; William Cannon, *The Theology of John Wesley* (Nashville: Abingdon-Cokesbury Press, 1946), 66-80; J. Ernest Rattenbury, *The Conversion of the Wesleys* (London: The Epworth Press, 1938), 25, 42, and 82; Martin Schmidt, *John Wesley: A Theological Biography*, 2 vols. (Nashville: Abingdon Press, 1962), 1:213-311; and V.H.H. Green, *John Wesley* (London: Thomas Nelson Ltd., 1964), 60-63.

1. W. Reginald Ward and Richard P. Heitzenrater, *The Works of John Wesley*, Vol 18., *Journals and Diaries* (Nashville: Abingdon Press, 1988), 214.

2. Ward and Heitzenrater, 214.

3. Jennings, "Against Aldersgate," 8.

4. For an example of Wesley's use of the word conversion see John Telford, ed., *The Letters of John Wesley, A.M.*, 8 vols. (London: The Epworth Press, 1931), 4:40-41. For Wesley's definition of this word see John Wesley, *The Complete English Dictionary*, 3rd. (London: Hawes, 1777). Moreover, though Wesley defined the word conversion differently than is done today, his understanding of the theological complex of justification, regeneration, and a measure of assurance (which contemporaries call conversion) is similar to modern usage and that of this present essay.

2. The Second Disclaimer
a. The Faith of a Servant in Terms of the Spirit of Bondage

The text to which Wesley attached his second note explores the subject of what constitutes a Christian — a subject which, contrary to popular belief, the Methodist evangelist treated often and in considerable depth. In February 1738, for instance, Wesley reasoned:

> Does all this [the having a *rational conviction* of all the truths of Christianity] give me a claim to the holy, heavenly, divine character of *a Christian?* By no means. If the oracles of God are true, if we are still to abide by 'the and the testimony', all these things, though when ennobled by faith in Christ they are holy, and just, and good, yet without it are 'dung and dross', meet only to be purged away by 'the fire that never shall be quenched.'[1]

But, in 1774, in reference to the phrase "yet without it" Wesley explained: "I had even then the faith of a servant, though not that of a son."[2] Remarkably, with the notable exception of Richard Heitzenrater, no one in the current debate about Aldersgate has explored in detail the theological significance of this distinction. In fact, Jennings, who is typical of this tendency, simply concludes after an unmistakably brief discussion:

> Neither before nor after did Wesley find it possible to 'love' the God he so vigorously served. Yet serve he did, whether as servant or as son; and in the end that was all that mattered to him.[3]

However, the distinction between these two kinds of faith was not a matter of indifference to Wesley as demonstrated by its repeated occurrence in his writings. In particular, the Methodist leader defined the phrases "the faith of a servant" and "the faith of a son" in at least two ways: one in terms of the spirit of bondage; the other in terms of the question of assurance. Concerning the former usage, in his sermon *The Spirit of Bondage and of Adoption*, written in 1746, Wesley differentiates the characteristics of the servants of God from those of a child of God. He points out, for example, that servants, those under a spirit of bondage, find that "sin [is] let loose upon the soul."[4] They feel sorrow of heart, remorse, and fear,[5] and they desire to break loose from the chains of sin, but cannot.[6] Indeed, their spiritual condition, Wesley continues, is most aptly described by the Apostle Paul in *Romans*, Chapter Seven.[7] Significantly, not

---

1. Ward and Heitzenrater, *Journals and Diaries*, 18:214-215. Bracketed material is the antecedent of the word "this."
2. Ward and Heitzenrater, 215. Also note that Wesley revealed that he lacked the faith of a son in January 1738 in an additional editorial comment. Cf. Ward and Heitzenrater, *Journals and Diaries*, 18:215.
3. Jennings, "Against Aldersgate," 19.
4. Outler, *Sermons*, 1:257. Bracketed material is mine.
5. Outler, 1:257.
6. Outler, 1:258.
7. Outler, 1:258. Observe that the servants of God are awakened, but they see not a God of love, but One of wrath. It is therefore important not to confuse the issue of awakening with regeneration (and conversion).

only is the distinction servant/son properly associated with that of the spirit of bondage/the spirit of adoption, but it is also one that the *mature* Wesley continued to make as indicated by his comments in 1788: "Exhort him to press on by all possible means, till he passes 'from faith to faith'; from the faith of a *servant* to the faith of a *son*; from the spirit of bondage unto fear, to the spirit of childlike love." [1]

Even more troubling for those contemporary historians who wish to impugn the "standard" interpretation of Aldersgate (as properly defined above) is Wesley's claim, made late in his career, that the servants of God are "still waiting for the kingdom of God."[2] Thus, in his spiritual counsel to Ann Bolton in 1768 the Oxford don remarked: "Certain it is that He loves you. And He has already given you the faith of a servant. You want only the faith of a child."[3] And later, in 1770, Wesley once again assessed Ms. Bolton's spiritual condition: "I am glad you are still waiting for the kingdom of God: although as yet you are rather in the state of a servant than of a child."[4] By implication, then, Wesley's depiction of the faith of a servant here and elsewhere reveals that prior to Aldersgate, by his own mature admission, he himself was still waiting for the kingdom of God.

Furthermore, in line with this interpretation, Wesley's recognition "that there is a medium between a child of God and a child of the devil — namely, a servant of God,"[5] his acknowledgement that there are degrees of faith, and his growing appreciation of the faith of a servant of God[6] must neither be mistaken for an identification of this faith with that of a child of God nor must it serve as the basis for the claim that Wesley lowered the standard of what constitutes a real Christian (the proper Christian faith) in order to include the servants of God.[7] To be sure, though many Methodist historians are well aware that Wesley separated nominal from real Christianity early on, in 1725 to be exact,[8] few have noticed that such a distinction, though slightly modified, frequently surfaced in the Oxford leader's later writings. In 1787, for example, highlighting one of the unexpected consequences of the spread of Deism, Wesley wrote: "this was the most direct way whereby *nominal* Christians could be prepared, first, for tolerat-

---

1. Outler, 4:35-36.
2. Telford, *Letters*, 5:207.
3. Telford, 5:86.
4. Telford, 5:207.
5. Telford, 6:272-73.
6. Telford, 5:207. However, in this letter to Ann Bolton Wesley also exclaims: "it is a blessed thing to be even a servant of God!"
7. Jennings marks the decisive beginning of Wesley's mission and ministry in 1725, the year when he "committed himself to entire holiness of life." But commitment, once again, must not be confused with having the graces and prerogatives of a child of God. Cf. Jennings, "Against Aldersgate," 19. However, there is a sense in which Wesley did, in fact, lower the standard of what constitutes a real Christian. For example, under the early Moravian influence, the Methodist leader had initially confused justification with full assurance (setting the standard much too high), but after this error was noted and corrected, he did not thereby set his standard for the proper Christian faith any lower than the marks of the new birth.
8. Outler, *Sermons*, 3:152.

ing, and, afterwards, for receiving, *real* Christianity."[1] More specifically, observe how the elderly Wesley not only associated real Christians with the new birth, but how he also distinguished these believers from the servants of God — the very thing which conversionist positions often do — in his sermon, *Walking by Sight and Walking by Faith*:

How short is this description of real Christians! And yet how exceeding full! It comprehends, it sums up, the whole experience of those that are truly such, from the time they are born of God till they remove into Abraham's bosom. For who are the 'we' that are here spoken of? All that are true Christian believers. I say 'Christian', not 'Jewish' believers. All that are not only *servants* but *children* of God.[2]

And a year later, in 1789, Wesley's strong identification of real Christianity with regeneration, with the children of God, is again unmistakable. "How great a thing it is to be a Christian, "he declares in his sermon *On a Single Eye*, "to be a real, inward, scriptural Christian! Conformed in heart and life to the will of God! Who is sufficient for these things? None, *unless he be born of God*."[3]

If the preceding analysis is accurate, how then is some apparently contradictory material like that from the sermon *On Faith* to be understood? For in this piece, Wesley confessed:

Indeed nearly fifty years ago, when the preachers commonly called Methodists began to preach that grand scriptural doctrine, salvation by faith, they were not sufficiently apprised of the difference between a servant and a child of God. They did not clearly understand that even one 'who feared God, and worketh righteousness', is accepted of him.[4]

And compare this passage with similar comments made to Melville Horne at about the same time:

When fifty years ago my brother Charles and I, in the simplicity of our hearts, told the good people of England that unless they knew their sins were forgiven, they were under the wrath and curse of God, I marvel, Melville, they did not stone us! The Methodists, I hope, know better now; we preach assurance as we always did, as a common privilege of the children of God; but we do not enforce it, under the pain of damnation, denounced on all who enjoy it not.[5]

That Wesley in 1788 (and much earlier) had a greater appreciation of the faith of those "who feared God and worked righteousness" is clear, and indeed he even pointed out that such people are now accepted of God given the light and grace

1. Outler, 3:452.
2. Outler, 4:49.
3. Outler, 4:121-22. Emphasis is mine. For a technical, detailed, and critical discussion of Outler's argument that the later Wesley moved away from his earlier exclusivist standards of true faith and salvation see my forthcoming article, "The Motif of Real Christianity in the Writings of John Wesley."
4. Outler, 3:497.
5. Robert Southey, *The Life of John Wesley* (New York: W.B. Gilley, 1820), 1:258.

that they have. But this last point of acceptance must not be mistaken for justification or with being a real Christian which is quite a different matter. To illustrate, the only requirement which Wesley established for membership in a Methodist society was a "desire to flee from the wrath to come.[1] And though he obviously did not want to discourage or discount this "fearful faith," as he once did, Wesley did not consider it evidence of either justification or regeneration. Put another way, though the servants of God lack the proper Christian faith — and hence cannot enjoy the privileges of the sons and daughters of God — they yet have a measure of faith which arises from the prevenient and convincing grace which precedes it, and are *for that reason* not to be discouraged. Consequently, Wesley's seasoned and relatively favorable estimation of the faith of a servant probably emerged from his consideration that such a faith, in the normal course of spiritual development, would in time become the faith of a son. In fact, in his sermon *On Faith*, Wesley highlights just such a consideration:

> And, indeed, *unless the servants of God halt by the way*, they will receive the adoption of sons. They will receive the *faith* of the children of God by his *revealing* his only-begotten Son in their hearts.... And whosoever hath this, the Spirit of God witnesseth with his spirit that he is a child of God."[2]

Moreover, Wesley's appreciation of a degree of acceptance and his exhortation to the servants of God to improve the grace of God is likewise revealed in a homily produced in 1788, *On the Discoveries of Faith* in which he counsels:

> Whoever has attained this, the faith of a servant, ... in consequence of which he is *in a degree* (as the Apostle observes), 'accepted with him'... Nevertheless he should be exhorted not to stop there; not to rest till he attains the adoption of sons; till he obeys out of love, which is the privilege of all the *children* of God.[3]

Simply put, the faith of a servant of God is valued not only for the measure of faith that it is, but also for what it will soon become: the qualitatively different faith of a child of God.

b. The Faith of a Servant in Terms of the Question of Assurance

In Wesley Studies today, it is well known, as noted in Chapter Three, that when John Wesley was under the strong influence of the English Moravians, he closely identified justifying faith with full assurance.[4] However, by the summer of 1740, he began to realize that there are both degrees of faith *and* degrees of assurance and that a child of God may exercise justifying faith which is mixed

1. Rupert E. Davies, *The Works of John Wesley*, Vol 9. *The Methodist Societies: History, Nature, and Design* (Nashville: Abingdon Press, 1989), 70.
2. Outler, *Sermons*, 3:497-98. The first emphasis is mine.
3. Outler, 4:35.
4. Richard P. Heitzenrater, "Great Expectations: Aldersgate and the Evidences of Genuine Christianity," in *Aldersgate Reconsidered*, ed. Randy L. Maddox (Nashville: Kingswood Books, 1990), 88-91.

with both doubt and fear.[1] Nevertheless, a second issue, which can be differentiated from the one just cited, concerns the question, once again, of whether Wesley ever lowered the standard of what he termed the proper Christian faith or real Christianity. This time, however, the question will be considered not with respect to the spirit of bondage, and its implications, but with respect to the matter of assurance.

On the one hand, the initial answer to this question must be "yes" since Wesley obviously modified his earlier erroneous views on the association of full assurance with justifying faith as just noted. But, on the other hand, Wesley, for the most part, still identified the assurance that one's sins are forgiven as a vital ingredient of the proper Christian faith. Thus, for example, in response to the question "Is justifying faith a divine assurance that Christ loved me, and gave himself for me?" the Conference Minutes of 1747 recorded: "We believe it is."[2] And in a revealing letter to his brother Charles a month later, John illustrates his doctrine of assurance by pointing out: "(1) that there is such an explicit assurance; (2) that it is the common privilege of *real Christians*; (3) that it is *the proper Christian faith*, which purifieth the heart and overcometh the world."[3] In fact, in 1755, Wesley declared that "a man who is not assured that his sins are forgiven may yet have a kind or degree of faith which distinguishes him not only from a devil, but from an heathen," but he quickly added, clarifying his point, "But still I believe, the *proper Christian faith* which purifies the heart implies such a conviction."[4] And again, in a letter to Richard Tompson on 5 February 1756, Wesley affirms that "every *true Christian* believer has a 'sure trust and confidence in God that through the merits of Christ he is reconciled to God."[5]

Now the usual rebuttal to the antecedent evidence is that it, of course, does not reflect Wesley's mature views on the subject of assurance and, therefore, is to be discounted.[6] Granted, Wesley's later teaching is indeed marked by much more subtlety and sophistication, but what is remarkable about this later material is its basic continuity with the evidence already cited. Accordingly, in 1765 in his sermon *The Scripture Way of Salvation* Wesley acknowledges:

> The Apostle says: 'There is one faith, and one hope of our calling, 'one Christian, saving faith, as 'there is one Lord' in whom we believe, and 'one God and Father of us all.' And it is certain this faith necessarily implies an *assurance* ... that Christ loved me, and gave himself, for *me*.'

1. Heitzenrater, 89.

2. Thomas Jackson, ed., *The Works of John Wesley*, 14 vols. (Grand Rapids, Michigan: Baker Book House, 1978), 8:291.

3. Frank Baker, ed., *The Works of John Wesley*, Vols. 25, 26. *The Letters* (New York: Oxford University Press, 1982), 26:254-55. Emphasis is mine.

4. Baker, 26:575. Emphasis is mine.

5. Telford, 3:162. Emphasis is mine.

6. Maddox, representative of this tendency, criticizes my earlier writings on Aldersgate and claims quite incorrectly that they "focus on Wesley material that is immediately post-Aldersgate (or, at most, "mid-life") Wesley, scarcely mentioning the later Wesley and the qualifying footnotes in the last edition of the *Journal*." Cf. Maddox, *Aldersgate Reconsidered*, 16.

For 'he that believeth ' with the *true, living faith*, 'hath the witness in himself.'[1]

To be sure, it is precisely the aged Wesley who continues to relate, quite strongly, justifying faith with a *measure* of assurance (with an exception which will be detailed below) and hence with the proper Christian faith.[2] For if these relations do not hold, as Jennings seems to suggest, how then are Wesley's observations in 1775, a year *after* the journal disclaimers were written, to be assessed? For at that time, he exclaimed:

> But I know not how *anyone* can be a Christian believer till 'he hath (as St. John speaks) 'the witness in himself'; till 'the Spirit of God witnesses with his spirit 'that he is a child of God' — that is, in effect, till God the Holy Ghost witnesses that God the Father has accepted him through the merits of God the Son...[3]

Again, during the decade of the 1780's, Wesley considered the faith of a son in terms of a spirit of adoption. "There is a medium between a child of God and a child of the devil — namely a servant of God," he writes to Alexander Knox in 1777, "This is *your* state. You are not yet a son, but you are a servant; and you are waiting for the Spirit of adoption..."[4] Beyond this, in 1788, Wesley reasoned that the difference between a servant and a child of God is that "He that believeth, as a child of God, hath the witness in himself.' This the servant hath not."[5] More emphatically, he adds in his sermon *On Faith*, produced in 1788:

> Thus the faith of a child is *properly* and directly a divine conviction whereby every child of God is enabled to testify, 'the life that I now live, I live by faith in the Son of God, who loved me, and gave himself for me.' And whosoever hath this, 'the Spirit of God witnesseth with his spirit that he is a child of God.[6]

Though seldom cited, the significant qualification and caution which Wesley does, after all, add to his association of justification and the assurance that one's sins are forgiven — an assurance occasionally marked by doubt and fear — is aptly expressed in a letter to Dr. Rutherforth in 1768, part of which reads as follows:

> I believe a consciousness of being in the favour of God (which I do not term plerophory, or full assurance, since it is frequently weakened,

---

1. Outler, *Sermons*, 2:161. Emphasis is mine.
2. Wesley displays degrees of assurance in terms of the distinctions between a babe, a young man, and a father in a letter to Joseph Benson in 1771. Note, however, that for Wesley "even babes in Christ are in such a sense perfect, or 'born of God ... as, first, not to commit sin," and so these cannot be mistaken for the servants of God who are under a bondage of sin. Cf. Outler, *Sermons*, 2:105.
3. Outler, *Sermons*, 2:385. Emphasis is mine.
4. Telford, *Letters*, 6:272-73. Compare this with an earlier letter to Richard Tompson in July 1755. Cf. Baker, *Letters*, 26:575.
5. Outler, *Sermons*, 3:498.
6. Outler, 3:498.

nay perhaps interrupted, by returns of doubt or fear) is the common privilege of Christians fearing God and working righteousness.

Yet I do not affirm there are no exceptions to this general rule. Possibly some may be in the favour of God, and yet go mourning all the day long. But I believe this is usually owing either to disorder of Body or ignorance of the gospel promises.[1]

Two issues need to be separated here which are often confused in the contemporary discussion. On the one hand, the elderly Wesley still did not identify nor confuse the faith of a servant, and its measure of acceptance, with the assurance that one's sins are forgiven; since being under "the spirit of bondage," a servant, properly speaking, lacks justifying faith. On the other hand, the Methodist leader recognized that in some exceptional cases those who are justified and regenerated (and hence children of God) may lack an assurance that their sins are forgiven due to either ignorance or bodily disorder.[2] However, in this second instance, since these believers are justified, they are more suitably referred to not as servants, but as the sons and daughters of God. That is, all servants lack assurance and are under a spirit of bondage, but not all who lack assurance are thereby servants, nor are they all under a spirit of bondage. There are, after all, exempt cases. Consequently, Wesley's mature designation of his own faith as that of a servant prior to May 1738 is much more revealing than either Jennings or Maddox has imagined.

3. The Third Disclaimer

Reflecting on his recent missionary work in Georgia, Wesley surveyed his spiritual condition once again in February 1738 and confessed in his journal:

This then have I learned in the ends of the earth, that I am 'fallen short of the glory of God'; that my whole heart is 'altogether corrupt and abominable; ... I am 'a child of wrath', my own righteousness are so far from reconciling me to an offended God, so far from making any atonement for the least of those sins...[3]

Not surprisingly, the statement which Wesley added in errata in 1774 is "I believe not,"[4] and the second disclaimer, already cited, indicates the reason for this third one. In other words, Wesley attached this latter note because he had

---

1. Telford, *Letters*, 5:358. This may reflect Wesley's own condition in 1738. That is, perhaps Wesley experienced justification and regeneration sometime in 1738 prior to Aldersgate, and his assurance on May 24th therefore "completed" the process. Though a conversionist view can argue in this fashion, it would seem that 1738 would have to be the *terminus a quo* simply because before this time Wesley, by his own admittance, confused the nature of justification and sanctification.

2. Though a consciousness of acceptance is the common privilege of the children of God, and though it is a vital ingredient of the proper Christian faith, it is not essential to justifying faith. That is, in certain cases, one may be justified and yet lack assurance. Accordingly, Wesley wrote to Dr. Rutherforth in 1768: "Therefore I have not for many years thought a consciousness of acceptance to be essential to justifying faith." Cf. Telford, *Letters*, 5:359. See also Lycurgus M. Starkey, Jr., *The Work of the Holy Spirit: A Study in Wesleyan Theology* (Nashville: Abingdon Press, 1962), 68-69.

3. Ward and Heitzenrater, *Journals and Diaries*, 18:215

4. Ward and Heitzenrater, 18:215.

since come to realize that there is an intermediate state between a child of God and a child of wrath, namely, a servant of God. This means, then, that while Wesley was in Georgia, he obviously had a measure of faith and a degree of acceptance, but it was not the faith of a child of God, nor was it that of one who had entered the kingdom of God. Instead, it was the faith, once more, of one under the spirit of bondage.

4. The Fourth Disclaimer

A few days after Wesley wrote down and renewed some of his old resolutions in order to foster his spiritual development — a habit he had learned from Jeremy Taylor — he visited his brother, Charles, on 4 March 1738 and wrote in his Journal:

> **I found my brother at Oxford, recovering from his pleurisy; and with him Peter Bohler. By whom (in the hand of the great God) I was on Sunday the 5th clearly convinced of unbelief, of the want of 'that faith whereby alone we are saved.'**[1]

However, in 1774 Wesley appended the phrase "with the full Christian salvation" to the last sentence above so that it now read: "By whom I was on Sunday the 5th clearly convinced of unbelief, of the want of that faith whereby alone we are saved with the *full Christian salvation.*"[2]

For his part, Jennings interprets this additional phrase as indicative of Wesley's later realization that what he had lacked back in March 1738 was not the faith of a child of God, but that which sanctifies entirely![3] However, it is one thing to contend that the early Wesley confused the ideas of initial and entire sanctification; indeed, there is some evidence to suggest that he did,[4] but it is quite another thing to maintain that the English preacher in retrospect attested that what he had lacked in 1738 was Christian perfection. Put another way, one must not confuse Wesley's initial expectation for holiness and full assurance in 1738 with the perspective of the mature Wesley who had since that time separated initial and entire sanctification, and the assurance which pertains to each. That is, Wesley expected full assurance in 1738, not because he was already justified, as Jennings surmises, but because he had suffered under some of the doctrinal misconceptions of the English Moravians.

Now one possible explanation for Jennings' unlikely interpretation might be that when he observed the word "full" in the note, he immediately concluded Christian perfection. However, such a view is problematic for at least two additional reasons: First, if one argues, as Jennings and some Holiness writers do,[5]

---

1. Ward and Heitzenrater, 18:228.
2. Ward and Heitzenrater, 18:228.
3. Jennings, "Against Aldersgate," 10.
4. On February 1, 1738 Wesley recorded in his journal: "I want that faith which none can have without knowing that he hath it....For whosoever hath it is 'freed from sin'; *'the whole body of sin is destroyed'* in him." Cf. Ward and Heitzenrater, *Journals and Diaries*, 18:216. Emphasis is mine.
5. Cf. W. Stephen Gunter, "Aldersgate, the Holiness Movement, and Experiential Religion" in *Aldersgate Reconsidered*. ed. Randy L. Maddox, 121-132.

that what Wesley lacked in March 1738 was the faith which sanctifies entirely, then one must *also* demonstrate in detail at what point prior to this time Wesley was justified by faith and regenerated in heart and life. More importantly, one must establish all of this in terms of Wesley's own theological vocabulary as displayed, for instance, in such important sermons as *The Great Privilege of Those that are Born of God* and *The Marks of the New Birth.* Furthermore, those who contend, like Maddox,[1] that Aldersgate is simply the time of Wesley's assurance, must likewise demonstrate in detail and convincingly when Wesley experienced the new birth prior to this time. Was Wesley born of God and free from the power of sin in 1725, 1733, 1735? If there ever were an impossible hypothesis to confirm, it is this.

Second, the term "full" in the phrase "the full Christian salvation" must be assessed in relation to the distinctions which have emerged from Wesley's other disclaimers. Thus, if Wesley were certain that he was converted in Georgia, and hence waiting for Christian perfection in March 1738, he would not have written in 1774 "I'm not sure of this." In addition, the distinction between the faith of a servant/the faith of a son not only developed over time with the result that Wesley came to a greater appreciation of the former, but he also still identified the faith of a son, in almost all instances, with a measure of assurance (that one's sins are forgiven) and with proper, true, real Christianity. In other words, Wesley's use of the term "full" in this context highlights the assurance which is the privilege of all who are born of God though some, either through ignorance or bodily distress, are not fully aware of this. The term, therefore, is another synonym for "proper", "true," and "real"; it embraces *all* the prerogatives which pertain to the children of God.

II. Conclusion: A Conversionist View with Nuances

Taking into account the insights of the journal disclaimers and the later Wesley, one can now restate the conversionist position in the following theses:

1. Wesley, through the influence of the English Moravians, initially expected to receive holiness and full assurance at Aldersgate.

2. Eventually, Wesley distinguished initial and entire sanctification in terms of freedom from the guilt, power, and being of sin; and assurance in terms of degrees.

3. Wesley developed a greater appreciation for the faith of the servants of God and affirmed that they are accepted in a degree because they fear God and work righteousness.

4. Though accepted for the measure of faith which they have, the servants of God have neither assurance that their sins are forgiven nor freedom from the guilt (justification) and power (regeneration) of sin.

1. Randy L. Maddox, "Aldersgate: A Tradition History," in *Aldersgate Reconsidered,* ed. Randy L. Maddox (Nashville: Kingswood Books, 1990), 145.

5. If the servants of God "do not halt by the way" their faith, in the normal course of spiritual development, should issue in the faith of the children of God.

6. Wesley continued to distinguish nominal from real Christianity throughout his life and almost never identified the faith of a servant with the proper Christian faith or with real Christianity.

Corollary: those who are justified by faith but lack assurance either through ignorance or bodily distress are exceptional cases and are suitably described as children of God.

Therefore:

7. When Aldersgate is stripped of its excesses due to the English Moravian influence what remains is the following:

A. It was the time when John Wesley encountered a gracious God, exercised justifying faith, and received a measure of assurance (occasionally marked by doubt and fear).

B. Since regeneration, according to Wesley, occurs simultaneously with justification, then Aldersgate must also be the occasion of his new birth.

C. Given A. and B., Aldersgate was the time when Wesley became a real, proper Christian according to his own mature criteria.

In summary, it has not been the intention of this present piece to demonstrate fully the cogency of the conversionist model. Much more work, no doubt, needs to be done. However, enough material has been explored to undermine the easy assumption that this interpretive scheme has already been surpassed by a more accurate one. Viewing Aldersgate as a crucial event does not, after all, preclude the incorporation of the wisdom of the later Wesley. If anything, the ongoing discussion among Methodist historians may just well demonstrate the resiliency of the "standard" interpretation.

And, on the other hand, it is not at all clear that the "assurance only" assessment of Aldersgate — which is the preference of those who reject the conversionist view — can satisfactorily address some of the more salient problems in this area, the principal one being when John Wesley experienced justification and regeneration, if not on May 24th? Other problems, of course, include the Oxford don's continued stress on inward religion and his development of the theme of real Christianity throughout his life in terms of both the new birth and assurance as chronicled above. Consequently, Jennings proclamation that Aldersgate is a non-event now appears as both strident and ill founded, and Maddox's call for the de-emphasis of Aldersgate celebrations emerges as both incautious and presumptuous.[1] Indeed, the purported demise of the conversionist interpretation, an event which is now the staple of Methodist journals and professional meetings, reminds one of Mark Twain's wry comment made to the Associated Press in 1897: "The reports of my death are greatly exaggerated."

---

1. For a discussion of the continuing value of Aldersgate as well as a practical guide for its commemoration, Cf. Charles Yrigoyen Jr., "Strangely Warmed," *The Interpreter* (April 1988): 11-13.

CHAPTER SEVEN

PERSONAL AND SOCIAL ETHICS

The Apostles' Creed utilized in this work as a catalyst and as an heuristic, interpretive framework to explore the rich theological content of Wesley's sermons does not contain any language which specifically relates to the important matter of ethics. However, the careful reader will soon note that ethical considerations are, in fact, implicit at several points in this Creed. In addition, since Wesley's sermons, especially many of his later pieces, treat this topic in considerable depth, his personal and social ethics warrant appropriate attention. Indeed, without the following discussion, the effects and goals of Wesley's ministry would be left, for the most part, underdeveloped.

I. The Theological Foundations

A. Grace

One of the difficulties in explicating Wesley's concept of grace, which is a prerequisite for understanding his ethics, is that many Protestants form their notions of this key doctrine at the feet of Calvin and Luther and then make these Reformers the standard. Subsequently, when Wesley's theology is considered, these people are often surprised to learn that the Methodist leader's notion of grace is both similar to and different from that of the continental Reformers. It is similar in the sense that the grace of God is unmerited and represents, at least on one level, divine favor and approval.[1] Thus, God is never in our debt because of anything we have done; all our obedience is already owed, and there is nothing "extra" to offer up that could possibility obligate the Most High. In Wesley's own words, "All the blessings which God hath bestowed upon man are of his mere grace, bounty, or favour: his free, undeserved favour, favour altogether

---

1. Albert C. Outler, ed., *The Works of John Wesley* Vol 3 *The Sermons I* (Nashville: Abingdon Press, 1984), p. 545. (Free Grace) But notice that Calvin, and Luther for that matter, would never have agreed to Wesley's further emphasis that grace is free for all. Such a position would undermine both Calvin's concept of predestination and Luther's notion of the bondage of the will which issues in predestination as well. Cf. McNeill, *Institutes*, 1:920ff., and E. Gordon Rupp and Philip S. Watson, eds. *Luther and Erasmus: Free Will and Salvation* (Philadelphia: The Westminster Press, 1969), p. 223ff.

undeserved..."[1] Salvation is by grace through faith. In this, at least, there is agreement.

But as important as this idea of unmerited divine favor and approval is, it does not constitute the entirety of what Wesley means by the grace of God. In fact, he draws two further important conclusions from the premise of the priority of divine action. As noted in passing in the last chapter, in his sermon *On Working Out Our Own Salvation*, Wesley reasons that if it really is God who works in us, then we can work. The grace of God, therefore, creates the ability to perform what is required; it empowers believers to walk in a godly fashion. But notice that even here this ability does not entail human merit, for it is God, not the believer, who is the principal agent, and yet the believer works. Wesley writes:

> Therefore inasmuch as God works in you, you are now able to work out your own salvation. Since he worketh in you of his own good pleasure, without any merit of yours, both to will and to do, it is possible for you to fulfill all righteousness. It is possible for you to 'love God, because he hath first loved us.'[2]

Grace, so conceived, is the dynamic power, the vigor, of God made available to all who believe. And Wesley cautioned the Methodists to beware of that pessimism and mock humility which "teacheth us to say, in excuse for our willful disobedience, 'Oh, I can do nothing,' and stops there, without once naming the grace of God.'"[3] Divine empowerment not human ability — or inability for that matter — is the chord struck here. We can do all things through Christ who strengthens us.

The second conclusion Wesley draws from the priority of God's action is that if God truly does work in us, then we are obligated to work and to cooperate with the bountiful grace of God. Thus, increasing ability as the result of divine grace and initiative involves its recipients in greater responsibilities. "You must be workers together with him;" Wesley contends, "otherwise he will cease working."[4] The grace of God, in other words, must either be improved by the believer or it will be lost. God is the source of all, to be sure, but God does not do all. Quoting Augustine, Wesley writes: "he that made us without ourselves, will not save us without ourselves."[5] But observe once again that there is no trace of merit here, although there is room for a healthy divine/human cooperation. "Stir up the spark of grace which is now in you," Wesley admonishes, "and he will give you more grace."[6]

From one perspective, when the process of salvation is conceived synergistically, as in Wesley's thought, the burden appears to be on the believer once grace is given. But the Oxonian did not balk at such a prospect. In fact, he constantly exhorted those under his spiritual tutelage to strain, to strive, to work, and to

1. Ibid., 1:117 (Salvation by Faith)
2. Ibid., 3:207. (On Working Out Our Own Salvation)
3. Ibid., p. 208.
4. Ibid.
5. Ibid.
6. Ibid.

labor in light of the preceding, abundant, and powerful grace of God. Such a conception of grace naturally has great consequence for personal and social ethics, since it means not only that the imperative mood is appropriate at every stage of the Christian walk, but also that as grace increases (prevenient, convincing, and sanctifying) so too does responsibility. Simply put, precisely because God has already acted, human *response*, not initiative, is possible. God's prior activity, although presupposed, must never be taken for granted.

B. The Moral Law

When Wesley surveyed the spiritual landscape of eighteenth-century England, he noticed the tendency among many Protestants to undervalue the nature and importance of holy living and of keeping the moral law, and he further observed that this was often done, oddly enough, in the name of real, vital, Christian faith. However, some of these Protestants, whom Wesley often referred to as antinomians, returned the "compliment" in kind and accused him of legalism; that is, they charged him with extolling the moral law, obedience, and human righteousness out of all proportion. John Cennick, for example, who was one of Wesley's lay preachers, criticized the Oxonian's preaching and accused him in February 1741 of preaching up "man's faithfulness"[1] and "righteousness in man."[2] Not content with this, Cennick subsequently claimed that both John and Charles preached "Popery."[3] In a similar fashion, the caustic William Cudworth referred to Wesley's teachings as "the establishment of a new legalism."[4] And Rowland Hill, for his part, maintained in his *Imposture Detected* that John Wesley was basically a legalist who had "renounced the grand Protestant doctrine of justification by faith alone."[5]

In the context of such serious charges, Wesley crafted a theological position over time which highlighted the graciousness of the gospel *and* the importance of faithfulness; the beauty of faith *and* the value of law. In other words, he feared not only the erroneous doctrine of justification by works or by merit, but also the pernicious teaching of antinomianism which makes the moral law void through faith. In fact, one way eighteenth-century antinomians undermined the value of works and the moral law in the Christian life was to contend that the old Mosaic covenant was a covenant of works and the new covenant was one of grace, with the implication, quite naturally, that the latter has utterly displaced the former. But this kind of theological reasoning Wesley clearly and unequivocally disal-

1. Nehemiah Curnock, *The Journal of the Rev. John Wesley, A.M.*, 8 vols. (London: The Epworth Press, 1938), 2:427.

2. Ibid.

3. Earl P. Crow, "John Wesley's Conflict with Antinomianism in Relation to the Moravians and Calvinists." (Ph.D. dissertation, University of Manchester, 1964), p. 154.

4. Donald H. Kirkham, "Pamphlet Opposition to the Rise of Methodism: The Eighteenth Century English Evangelical Revival Under Attack." (Ph.D. dissertation, Duke University, 1973), p. 322. Hervey's *Eleven Letters*, which was a response to Wesley's criticism of the former's *Theron and Aspasio*, was published posthumously by Hervey's brother at the urging of William Cudworth.

5. Thomas Jackson, ed., *The Works of John Wesley*, 14 vols. (Grand Rapids, Michigan: Baker Book House, 1978), 10:449.

lows. In his sermon, *The Lord Our Righteousness*," for example, he points out that both the Mosaic covenant *and* the covenant given by Christ are gracious, and that the covenant of works referred to by the Apostle Paul in a negative manner in his epistle to the Romans concerns not Moses but only Adam in his unfallen state.[1] Neither the Hebrew people nor the church has ever been under a covenant of works. The movement from the Old Testament to the New is, therefore, one from grace to grace.

Yet another way in which Wesley noted the similarity between the covenants (without denying their dissimilarity)[2] was in terms of the relationship between the law and gospel itself. Thus, the moral law, quite simply, is the gospel presented as a demand, and the gospel is the law presented as a promise.[3] In Wesley's own words, "the law (the moral not the ceremonial law) continually makes way for and points us to the gospel; on the other the gospel continually leads us to a more exact fulfilling of the law."[4] To be sure, Wesley attested that Christians are not only free from the ceremonial law but also from the moral law as a means of justification.[5] Nevertheless, since the Methodist leader also defined Christian liberty as freedom *for* law as evidenced by his statement, "This is perfect freedom; thus to keep His law, and to walk in all His commandments blameless,"[6] one can begin to appreciate Lindström, 's claim that it is "the idea of sanctification that dominates his whole theology."[7] What Wesley simply would not brook was an estimation of the gospel which detracted from any measure of obedience to and fulfillment of the moral law in the life of the believer. In his sermon *Upon Our Lord's Sermon on the Mount: Discourse the Fifth* he cautions:

> **It is no other than betraying him with a kiss to talk of his blood and take away his crown; to set light by any part of his law under pretence of advancing his gospel. Nor indeed can anyone escape this charge who preaches faith in any such manner as either directly or indirectly tends to set aside any branch of obedience; who preaches Christ so as to disannul or weaken in any wise the least of the commandments of God.[8]**

---

1. Outler, *Sermons*, 1:202. (The Lord Our Righteousness).

2. What has changed, however, is not the moral law itself, but the believer's relation to it: that is, the law is no longer fulfilled in a literal and external way, but in a new spiritual manner; its height and its depth, not fully appreciated by those under the old covenant, is now realized to a greater degree in all those who believe in Jesus Christ. Cf. Outler, *Sermons*, 2:22 ff.

3. Outler, *Sermons*, 1:554. (Upon Our Lord's Sermon on the Mount Discourse the Fifth).

4. Ibid.

5. On this head Wesley writes: "Allowing then, that every believer has done with the law, as it means the Jewish ceremonial law, or the entire Mosaic dispensation (for these Christ hath taken out of the way); yea, allowing we have done with the moral law, as a means of procuring our justification (for we are justified freely by His grace; through the redemption that is in Jesus'); yet, in another sense, we have not done with this law." Cf. Outler, *Sermons*, 2:17.

6. Ibid., 2:19.

7. Harald Lindström, *Wesley and Sanctification* (Wilmore, Kentucky: Francis Asbury Publishing Co., Inc.), p. 218.

8. Outler, *Sermons*, 1:559. (Upon Our Lord's Sermon on the Mount: Discourse the Fifth)

Modern interpreters of Wesley's thought may discount the moral law; Wesley clearly did not.[1]

So concerned was Wesley with the specter of antinomianism, the teaching which makes the moral law void or of little consequence, that he produced two "tracts for the times" in 1750 to warn against this grave error: *The Law Established Through Faith, Discourse I and II*, and it is highly probable that he had the teaching of such unabashed antinomians as William Cudworth and James Hervey in mind as he wrote these pieces.[2] Interestingly, the structural relationship between these two discourses is perhaps best expressed in terms of a problem and solution model; that is, the problems raised in the first piece, the various ways of making void the law, are then countered in the second by showing how the law may yet be established by Christian faith.

The first and most usual way of making void the law through faith, as Wesley points out in *Discourse I*, is "not to preach the law at all."[3] Here, preaching the gospel is viewed as answering all the ends of the law, and therefore, is deemed the principal, if not the sole, activity of preachers. The problem here, Wesley contends, is one of balance, for to preach Christ properly is "to preach all things that Christ hath spoken: all his promises; all his threatenings and commands; all that is written in his Book."[4] To neglect any aspect of this important ministry is to impoverish the saints. And so in *Discourse II* —as one might expect — Wesley offers a solution to this first problem by admonishing his readers to establish the law by preaching it in its whole extent, in its height, depth, length, and breadth,[5] and by further exhorting them "to explain and enforce every part of it in the same manner as our great Teacher did while upon earth."[6]

A second way of making void the law through faith is to teach that faith supersedes the necessity of holiness. When this is done three things are usually assumed: first, that holiness is less necessary now than before Christ came;[7] second, that a lesser degree of it is necessary,[8] and third, that holiness is less neces-

---

1. Colin Williams, for example, claims that it is dangerous to define sin, as Wesley does, as a voluntary transgression of a known law of God. Therefore, in the place of the moral law as a standard, Williams substitutes a personal relationship with Christ. However, Wesley finds a place for each of these ingredients in his theology: faith understood principally as fiducia *and* the continuing normative value of the moral law. In other words, it is not a matter of either/or, as Williams reckons, but of both/and. Indeed, it is not too much to say that, for Wesley, the phrase "a personal relationship with Christ" considered by itself would be much too amorphous and precisely because of this trait could easily devolve into the kind of antinomianism the English evangelical so rightly deplored. Cf. Colin Williams, *John Wesley's Theology Today* (Nashville: Abingdon Press, 1960), p. 178-79.

2. Outler, *Sermons*, 2:1. (The Original, Nature, Properties, and Use of the Law).

3. Ibid., 2:22. (The Law Established Through Faith, I)

4. Ibid., p. 25.

5. Ibid., p. 35. See also Wesley's letter *To an Evangelical Layman* written most probably to Ebenezer Blackwell on 20 December 1751. Cf. Frank Baker, ed., *The Works of John Wesley*, Vol 26 *Letters II* (New York: Oxford University Press, 1982), p. 482-89.

6. Ibid., 2:34.

7. Ibid., 2:26.

8. Ibid.

sary to believers than to others.[1] What lies behind such mistaken assumptions, as Wesley aptly observes, is a confused notion of Christian liberty where freedom is defined not in terms of freedom *from* the guilt and power of sin, and freedom *to* love God and neighbor, as it should be, but in terms of freedom from the law, works, and consequently, from holiness as well. For though none are justified by works of the law, such works are the inevitable fruit of real, vital faith. Wesley notes:

> ...We are justified without the works of the law as any previous condition of justification. But they are an immediate fruit of that faith whereby we are justified. So that if good works do not follow our faith, even all inward and outward holiness, it is plain our faith is nothing worth; we are yet in our sins.[2]

The third, last, and most common way of making void the law through faith, Wesley states, "is the doing it practically; the making it void in *fact*, though not in *principle*; the living as if faith was designed to excuse us from holiness."[3] When the Christian life is lived in such a manner, it is supposed that less obedience is required under the grace of the gospel than under the law, and that one need not be as scrupulous and as rigorous as before. But these are two conclusions that cannot validly be drawn from the premises of justification by faith and the priority of God's grace. Wesley reasons: "Shall we be less obedient to God from filial love than we were from servile fear? Is love a less powerful motive than fear?"[4] And again he queries: "And have you not learned to say, 'Oh, I am not so scrupulous now,' to which he responds with some measure of exasperation, "I would to God you were!"[5]

So then, obedience to the moral law *is* required in the practical Christian life, not of course as the condition of acceptance, but in order to *continue* in the rich grace of God. Put another way, obedience to the moral law of God does not establish the Christian life, but it is one of the necessary fruits of that *faith* which both justifies and sanctifies. If, for example, faith does not produce obedience to the moral law of God, works of charity and mercy, and holiness, it is clear to Wesley, at least, that such is a dead and not a living faith; it is a faith that is not being acted out in the world of God and neighbor, and is therefore all but useless. Without the normative function of law (*tertius usus*), grace and faith inevitably devolve into pious sentimentality. Indeed, in his piece *A Blow at the Root*, produced in 1762, Wesley rebukes all those antinomians who balk at their task and who look upon commandment keeping as rank legality. He writes:

> You can love him and keep his commandments; and to you his 'commandments are not grievous.' Grievous to them that believe! Far from it. They are the joy of your heart. Show then your love to Christ by

1. Ibid.
2. Ibid., 2:28.
3. Ibid., 2:29. (The Law Established Through Faith, I)
4. Ibid., 2:30-31.
5. Ibid., 2:31.

keeping his commandments, by walking in all his ordinances blameless.[1]

Such an evaluation is also expressed in the threefold use of the law that Wesley displays in his sermon, *The Original, Nature, Properties and Use of the Law.* In this piece, concerning the third or the prescriptive use, Wesley writes, "The third use of the law is to keep us alive. It is the grand means whereby the blessed Spirit prepares the believer for larger communications of the life of God."[2] The law sends one to Christ, to be sure, but Christ also sends one back to the law for guidance and instruction. Both movements are integral to Wesley's assessment of the Christian life, and both are necessary to maintain his emphasis on faith *and* holy living, justification and sanctification.[3]

C. Love

Much of Wesley's theological thought, especially in the area of ethics, is expressed in terms of a means/end structure, what Wesleyan theologians have called a basic teleological orientation. Thus, faith is not intrinsically valuable, as some Protestants have mistakenly supposed, but is extrinsically valuable: it aims at and indeed is the means to something higher than itself, namely, love. In large measure, the purpose of faith, for Wesley, is to establish love in human hearts as revealed, for example, in his sermon *The Law Established through Faith, II*:

In order to this we continually declare ... the faith of the operation of God, still is only the handmaid of love. As glorious and honourable as it is, it is not the end of the commandment. God hath given this honour to love alone. Love is the end of all the commandments of God.[4]

Moreover, this means/end relationship between faith and love is also the vehicle through which Wesley expresses an important value judgment in this area, but this time by means of a temporal distinction. In this line of thought, faith is not eternal in any sense of the word; it had a beginning in human affairs and it

1. Thomas Jackson, ed., *The Works of John Wesley*, 14 vols. (Grand Rapids, Michigan: Baker Book House, 1978), 10:369.

2. Ibid., 2:16. (The Original, Nature, Properties, and Use of the Law) Compare Wesley's third use of the law (*tertius usus*) with that of John Calvin in the latter's *Institutes*. Cf. McNeil, *Institutes*, 1:360 ff.

3. It is interesting to note that in his *Lectures on Galatians* Martin Luther listed only two formal uses for the law: a political and a theological one. The function of the first is to restrain the wicked who care nothing for Christian principles, while the role of the second is to drive the sinner to Christ through its accusatory force. Since Luther considered the theological or the accusatory use of the law as primary this led him to view the relation between law and gospel not so much in terms of continuity, as Wesley saw fit, but in terms of a dialectical tension. Thus, Luther was able to speak of "a time of the law" and a "time of the gospel" which signifies that the process of salvation is characterized by movement. And in one place in his *Lectures on Galatians* he even stated: "Then let the Law withdraw; for it was indeed added for the sake of disclosing and increasing transgressions, but only until the point when the offspring would come. Once He is present, let the law stop..." Cf. Martin Luther, *Luther's Works*, ed., Jaroslav Pelikan, Vol. 26: *Lectures on Galatians* 1535 (Saint Louis: Concordia Publishing House, 1963), p. 308-09, 317.

4. Outler, *Sermons*, 2:38. (The Law Established through Faith, Discourse II)

will have an end as well. Love, on the other hand, as the goal of religion will have no end; it is from everlasting to everlasting. No doubt, having some solafidians in mind, Wesley cautions:

> Let those who magnify faith beyond all proportion, so as to swallow up all things else, and who so totally misapprehend the nature of it as to imagine it stands in the place of love, consider farther that as love will exist after faith, so it did exist long before it.[1]

Beyond this, the supremacy and centrality of the love of God and neighbor is expressed in Wesley's often-quoted maxim "faith working by love," a phrase actually culled from Paul's Letter to the Galatians. "Esteem no faith," Wesley declares, "but that 'which worketh by love';" and "we are not 'saved by faith' unless so far as we are delivered from the power as well as the guilt of sin."[2] And in his sermon *On the Wedding Garment* Wesley makes the connection between faith and holiness, faith and love, explicit:

> In Christ Jesus neither circumcision availeth anything nor uncircumcision', but 'faith which worketh by love.' It first, through the energy of God, worketh love to God and all mankind; and by this love every holy and heavenly temper. In particular, lowliness, meekness, gentleness, temperance, and long-suffering.[3]

More to the point, Wesley adds: "if this faith does not work by love, if it does not produce universal holiness, if it does not bring forth lowliness, meekness, and resignation, it will profit me nothing.[4] Faith will pass away, but love will never pass away.

This preceding discussion of the role of grace, law, and love in Wesley's theology is not beside the point but is necessary in order to understand his ethics, both personal and social. Indeed, neither Wesley's moral reasoning nor his practical activity on behalf of the poor is properly assessed without these ingredients — a claim which will be substantiated in the remainder of this chapter.

II. Personal Ethics

A. Self-Denial

Though love will not ultimately pass away, Wesley was well aware that it could often be frustrated by human sin, by the excessive self-love which festers in unbelief. In light of this, it is not surprising to learn that his basic prescription

1. Ibid., 2:39.
2. Ibid., 1:559-60. (The Lord's Sermon on the Mount, Discourse, V) Cannon affirms that the Wesleyan system of ethics stands in contrast to that of Luther and Calvin. The former is an ethics of realization; the later, of aspiration. Cf. William R. Cannon, *The Theology of John Wesley* (Nashville: Abingdon-Cokesbury Press, 1946), p. 226.
3. Ibid., 4:147. (On the Wedding Garment)
4. Ibid., 3:303. (On Charity) In this same sermon Wesley again touches upon the theme of faith, love, and holiness and maintains: "be our faith ever so strong, it will never save us from hell unless it now saves us from all unholy tempers; from pride, passion, impatience; from all arrogance of spirit, all haughtiness and overbearing; from wrath, anger, bitterness; from discontent, murmuring, fretfulness, peevishness." Cf. 3:304.

for the moral life is one of self-denial. And in a piece by the same name, Wesley maintains, accurate or not, that "no writer in the English tongue ... has described the nature of self-denial in plain and intelligible terms such as lie level with common understandings," a view which constitutes hyperbole, to say the least, according to Outler.[1] At any rate, Wesley argues that earlier treatments of this subject never emerged from a sea of generalities to offer particular, very practical, and clear applications, and such a literary and theological vacuum constitutes the *raison d'etre* for this present homily, *Self-Denial*, which was penned in 1760.

As he crafted this sermon, judging from its contents, the Oxford don, no doubt, had in mind certain Protestant groups which in his estimation discounted the need for rigorous self-denial in the Christian life. Of the predestinarians, for example, Wesley writes, "How few of them even profess to practice it at all! How few of them recommend it themselves, ... as if it were seeking *salvation by works.*[2] And to this indictment he adds: "how readily do antinomians of all kinds, from the smooth Moravian to the boisterous foul-mouthed Ranter, join the cry with their silly unmeaning cant of 'legality,' and 'preaching the law'!"[3] Observe that the language here is both strong and emotive, suggesting that a vital issue is at stake. Indeed, the principal task of this present homily is to argue articulately that self-denial is not merely a theme for Roman Catholicism or Eastern Orthodoxy, but is one for Protestantism as well, that a Protestant can remain faithful to the graciousness of the gospel and yet engage in this spiritual discipline.

Perhaps part of the difference between Wesley and those who rejected self-denial in the name of grace consists in their different understandings of the phrase itself. The antinomians, for instance, may have immediately conjured up images of self-neglect, extreme mortification, and a morbid delight in suffering all of which have had a history in the church.[4] For Wesley, however, the denial of self does not embrace those ascetic practices that are artificially contrived, self-inflicted, and which bear no necessary relation to living the Christian life such as "wearing a haircloth or iron girdles or anything else that would impair our bodily health."[5] Instead, self-denial is, quite simply, "the denying or refus-

---

1. Ibid., 2:236. (Self-Denial) To demonstrate that the theme of self-denial had a rich life in English literature Outler appeals to Richard Baxter's *Treatise of Self-Denyall*, William Penn's *No Cross, No Crown*, as well as to the works of Jeremy Taylor and William Law — writings with which Wesley was clearly familiar.

2. Ibid., 2:241. Cf. Outler's note # 6 where he points out that George Whitefield, by all means a predestinarian, yet valued self-discipline as a means of grace.

3. Ibid.

4. Kenneth J. Collins, *Wesley On Salvation* (Grand Rapids, Michigan: Francis Asbury Press, 1989), p. 96. For example, one of the practices employed by Symeon Stylites was to bind himself in ropes so tightly that they cut through to his bones with the result that the ropes could be removed only by causing extreme pain. This was also the same person who tried to achieve holiness by sitting on the top of a pole for thirty-six years. Cf. Philip Schaff, *History of the Christian Church*, (Grand Rapids: Wm B. Eerdmans Publishing Company, 1910), 3:191 ff.

5. Outler, *Sermons*, 2:245. (Self-Denial) See also Collins, *Salvation*, p. 96., from which some of this material is taken.

ing to follow our own will, from a conviction that the will of God is the only rule of action to us."[1] Thus, only those disciplines which grow out of and foster obedience to the will of God are to be affirmed (so there is a place for prudential rules) but all else is deemed superfluous. It is not discipline for the sake of discipline — which could just be symptomatic of spiritual narcissism — nor suffering for the sake of suffering which matters, but the bearing of those things that cannot be avoided if the will of God is to be accomplished.[2] In fact, so important was this theme of self-denial to Wesley that at one point he called it the "grand doctrine of Christianity."[3]

Closely associated with the discipline of self-denial is that of taking up one's cross. These spiritual exercises are not equivalent in Wesley's mind, although he affirms the one should necessarily lead to the other. Taking up one's cross, for instance, is something higher, more demanding, than simply self-denial, for a cross entails what is actually contrary and displeasing to our nature. In short, the former unavoidably involves suffering; the latter does not. Wesley explains: "So that taking up our cross goes a little farther than denying ourselves; it rises a little higher, and is a more difficult task to flesh and blood, it being more easy to forego pleasure than to endure pain."[4] However, both of these ingredients are integral to discipleship; both are necessary for the imitation of Christ. Moreover, Wesley cautions his readers that when one fails to follow Christ fully, it is always "owing to the want either of self-denial or taking up his cross."[5]

B. Stewardship

Though the notion of self-denial illuminates much of Wesley's moral reasoning, another concept he often appeals to in his homilies is that of stewardship, that all which human beings possess is not their own but properly belongs to God. As creatures, human beings are entrusted by the Creator with the care and development of numerous resources, both material and spiritual — a role which, once again, is informed by a healthy denial of self-will and which is more fully articulated by Wesley in the following:

> And, first, we are to inquire in what respects we are now God's stewards. We are now indebted to him for all we have; but although a debtor is obliged to return what he has received, yet until the time of payment comes he is at liberty to use it as he pleases. It is not so with

---

1. Ibid., 2:242.
2. Collins, *Salvation*, p. 96.
3. Outler, *Sermons*, 2:240. (Self-Denial)
4. Ibid., 2:243. See also Collins, *Salvation*, p. 96.
5. Ibid., 2:245. And at one point in another sermon, *Causes of the Inefficacy of Christianity* Wesley even contends that the person who never fasts is no more on the way to heaven than the one who never prays. Cf. Outler, *Sermons*, 4:94

a steward: he is not at liberty to use what is lodged in his hands as he pleases, but as his master pleases.[1]

Thus, men and women are cautioned to check selfish desire at every opportunity even in terms of their "own" gifts and talents *in order to* accomplish something higher, namely, the will of God. And since freedom (or the lack of it), self-denial, and stewardship are some of the key elements in Wesley's personal moral equation, the following discussion of the proper use of time, money, and dress etc., will be organized under the basic structure which is apparent in *The Good Steward* — a structure which presupposes the initiating grace of God on the one hand and the human response of self denial and accountability on the other.

Almost a year after he had written *The Repentance of Believers*, Wesley produced the homily *The Good Steward* in May 1768. In this piece, he enumerates several gifts and talents for which humanity is responsible. First of all, he points out — perhaps indicating the value he placed on it — that "God has entrusted us with our soul, an immortal spirit made in the image of God together with all the powers and faculties thereof — understanding, imagination, memory, will, and a train of affections."[2] We are, therefore, to employ these talents, Wesley declares, judiciously and "wholly to the glory of him that gave them."[3] And not only is our will to be given up fully to God, but also "all our affections ... as he directs."[4] Beyond this, Wesley intimates that men and women bear a responsibility for the improvement of their intellectual, moral, and spiritual life.

Second, God has entrusted humanity not only with souls but also with bodies, "those exquisitely wrought machines, so 'fearfully and wonderfully made' with all the powers and members thereof."[5] The Christian disciple, then, should cultivate those habits which are suitable to the maintenance of health and should forsake all those, like the use of drams or hard liquor, which injure the body.[6] In

1. Ibid., 2:283. (The Good Steward) Jennings interprets Wesley's concept of stewardship as a denial of the principle of private property and maintains that the Oxford don supposes that "the Methodist movement will produce not only a spread of the gospel throughout the earth but also, and therefore, bring in the communist society." However, in indicating that all human resources are *the Lord's*, Wesley was not denying that men and women, not the State, must, after all, exercise this stewardship. Jennings, once again, is perhaps guilty of reading nineteenth and twentieth century notions and language, no matter how popular, back into the eighteenth century, for he clearly has neglected what Wesley understood by "civil liberty." Cf. Theodore Jennings, "Wesley's Preferential Option for the Poor," *Quarterly Review*, Vol. 9, No. 3 (Fall 1989): 20,22.

2. Outler, *Sermons*, 2:284. (The Good Steward)

3. Ibid., 2:284.

4. Ibid., 2:284-85.

5. Ibid., 2:285.

6. Contrary to popular Methodist belief, Wesley was not a teetotaler. To be sure, the misunderstanding of his position on alcohol is due, in large measure, to a repudiation of an important distinction which Wesley made concerning alcohol; that is, he approved of the use of fermented alcohol such as wine, beer, and ale, but renounced the use of distilled liquor except for medicinal purposes. In fact, Wesley on one occasion referred to wine as "one of the noblest cordials in nature," and in the late 1780's he even began to brew his own ale at home because his palate did not appreciate the re-introduction of hops in the brewing process! Cf. Ivan Burnett Jr., "Methodist Origins: John Wesley and Alcohol." *Methodist History* 13 (July 1975): 4, 11., and Curnock, *Journal*, 5:430.

addition, many of Wesley's judgments in this area are also expressed in his *General Rules of the United Societies* which fall under the general heading of prudential rules and under the title of "doing no harm" in particular.[1] And to the objection, often heard in the Societies and Bands, that these and similar rules like "Do you eat no flesh suppers? No late suppers?"[2] lacked clear Scriptural warrant — in contrast to the instituted means of grace like prayer, reading the Bible, receiving the Lord's Supper etc., — Wesley replied "these are ... prudential helps, grounded on reason and experience, in order to apply the general rules given in Scripture according to particular circumstances."[3]

Third, Wesley observes in this same homily that "God has entrusted us with worldly goods, with food to eat, raiment to put on, and a place where to lay our head."[4] And this concern over how Christians go about satisfying their maintenance needs is also expressed in several other pieces. In his sermon *On Dress,* for example, Wesley warns of the dangers of acquiring costly apparel, for such attire engenders pride, increases vanity, begets anger, inflames lust, is directly opposite to being adorned with good works, and is contrary to having the mind which was in Christ Jesus.[5] And to the objection, once again voiced by the Methodists, that "I can *afford* it,"[6] Wesley sternly replies: "O lay aside forever that idle, nonsensical word! No Christian can *afford* to waste any part of the substance which God has entrusted him with."[7] And this same counsel pertains not only to parents, but to their children as well: "I am pained continually," Wesley writes, "at seeing religious parents suffer their children to run into the same folly of dress as if they had no religion at all."[8]

Another aspect of worldly goods to which Wesley draws attention in his *Good Steward* is the issue of wealth. However, his most detailed comments on money are found not in this piece but in one produced a few years earlier in 1760, namely, *The Use of Money.* In this homily, Wesley underscores the themes of self-denial and stewardship, as expected, but in the first section of this piece, it seems

1. Rupert E. Davies, ed., *The Works of John Wesley* Vol 9 *The Methodist Societies: History, Nature, and Design* (Nashville: Abingdon Press, 1989), p. 70.

2. Jackson, *Works*, 8:324.

3. Ibid., 9:268. Nevertheless, it was Wesley himself who cautioned against too close an identification between prudential norms and Scripture by drawing an important distinction. In contrast to the lasting character of the instituted means, the Oxonian affirmed that the prudential means are temporal, subject to change as common sense and circumstances dictate. In *A Plain Account of the People Called Methodists* he writes: "That with regard to these little prudential helps we are continually changing one thing after another, . . . always open to instruction; willing to be wiser every day than we were before." Cf. Davies, *Societies*, 9:262-63.

4. Outler, *Sermons*, 2:286. (The Good Steward)

5. Ibid., 3:254. (On Dress)

6. Ibid., 3:256.

7. Ibid.

8. Ibid., 3:370. And in another homily, *On Obedience to Pastors*, Wesley reminds the Methodists that he published his advice on this subject more than thirty years ago. "I have repeated it a thousand times since. I have advised you not to be conformable too the world herein." Cf. Outler, *Sermons*, 3:382. For additional material on Wesley's views on raising children Cf. 3:340 (*On Family Religion*); 3:358-59 (*On the Education of Children*); and 3:364 ff. (*On Obedience to Parents*).

as if Wesley rejects his own spiritual prescription by urging the Methodists, interestingly enough, "to gain all you can,"[1] and those who are not well-schooled in the thought of Wesley, who see him as a dour, Puritanical, figure are often surprised to learn this. That Wesley is consistent with his own moral principles is evidenced by his observation drawn from the pages of the New Testament that it is the love of money, not money itself, which is the root of all evil; the fault, in other words, lies not with the object but with the user. Accordingly, the Methodist leader maintains that money is of "unspeakable service to all civilized nations in all the common affairs of life."[2] It is a blessed means to do great good: to bring the Kingdom of God near to the poor, the homeless, and the despised. In the hands of the saints, it is an instrument of "doing all manner of good";[3] it is a means of grace to those in need. Small wonder, then, that he issues this first directive. Nevertheless, such encouragement to freely engage in the pursuit of money is nicely balanced by a few precautions: No persons, Wesley argues may gain at the expense of the health of their own minds and bodies nor those of their neighbors.[4] But barring these precautionary remarks, the Methodists are left free to engage in commerce, to gain all that they can.

The chord of stewardship and self-denial is struck more clearly in Wesley's second admonition to "save all you can."[5] The money gained under the first counsel, through a legitimate use of gifts and talents, is not to be squandered on the self; all needless expense is, therefore, to be cut off. Money should not be used to gratify the desires of the flesh, the desire of the eye, or the pride of life. "Despise delicacy and variety, and be content with what plain nature requires,"[6] Wesley warns. In fact, so insistent was Wesley on this score that he demanded elsewhere that all who wished to remain members of the band societies must forsake the use of snuff and tobacco, not because they were injurious to health — the eighteenth century had little understanding of the toxic nature of these substances since they were often prescribed by Physicians — but because they constituted "needless self-indulgence."[7]

A serious problem emerges, however, if these first two rules are not complimented by a third. If a group of people like the Methodists is both industrious and frugal, the specter of wealth inevitably arises. Indeed, Wesley deems riches one of the most serious threats confronting his people, something that can insidiously transform the love of God and neighbor into a love of the world and self. In order to prevent this, he proposes a third step: having gained and saved all you

1. Ibid., 2:268. (The Use of Money)
2. Ibid.
3. Ibid.
4. Ibid., 2:269-73.
5. Ibid., 2:273.
6. Ibid., 2:274.
7. Jackson, *Works*, 8:274. On this point, irony abounds simply because contemporary prohibitions often focus on the medical problem entailed, and forget that this was principally an issue of self-denial for Wesley. Modern Methodists, for example, often take pride in their abstinence from tobacco products while at the same time some of them live in relative luxury! Such followers clearly miss Wesley's basic principle.

can, now give all you can.[1] Thus, after proper, but not excessive provision, has been made for self and family, followers of Christ are to give as much as they are able.

It should be obvious by now that Wesley's first two rules concerning the use of money are part of a larger whole, and therefore should not be considered in isolation, if distortion of his ethic is not to occur. Clearly, the first two rules are a means to an end; one gains and saves precisely in order to give. By these means people will be able to do the work of God in the world: to feed the hungry, to house the homeless, to clothe the naked — in short to bring about, at least in a small way, the kingdom of God on earth. Moreover, not to take this third step, to indulge in, feed, and thereby aggravate foolish desire is to impoverish the self, spiritually speaking, and to cut off one of the principal channels that God has established to shower His grace upon those in need.

Finally, in the *Good Steward*, Wesley gathers together several talents "which do not properly come under any of these [preceding] heads,"[2] such things as bodily strength, a pleasing person, an agreeable address, grace, learning and the employment of time.[3] The last two items, however, are of special interest since they are indicative of Wesley's character and habits. Indeed, Wesley's unusual practice of reading on horseback as he traveled to his preaching appointments demonstrated his commitment to improving both his knowledge and his use of time. Thus, on the one hand, the Oxford don continually sought to improve his learning, especially in the area of practical divinity, and the breadth and extent of his early reading habits, which continued throughout his career, are chronicled by V.H.H. Green in his *Young Mr. Wesley*.[4] On the other hand, Wesley also sought to be a good steward of his time, (that's why he read on horseback!) a habit learned, in part, from reading Jeremy Taylor's *Holy Living and Holy Dying*. Moreover, anyone who has ever read Ward and Heitzenrater's edition of Wesley's *Journals*, but especially the *Diaries*, will soon realize that John Wesley was a remarkably energetic person who continually "improved the time" and who taught the Methodists both by word and, more importantly, by example.[5]

1. Outler, *Sermons*, 2:277. (The Use of Money)

2. Ibid., 2:286. Bracketed material is mine.

3. Ibid.

4. V.H.H. Green, *The Young Mr. Wesley* (New York: St. Martins' Press, 1961), p. 305-319. Green divides Wesley's early readings under three main headings: classical literature, religion, and general works. Therefore, Wesley's claim of being *Homo unius libri*, made in the preface to his sermons, must be understood not in a descriptive sense but in a prescriptive one. In other words, Wesley did, in fact, read quite widely, but his constant reference, the standard which he used to assess his reading was the Bible.

5. W. Reginald Ward and Richard P. Heitzenrater, eds., *The Works of John Wesley* Vol. 18 *Journals and Diaries I* (Nashville: Abingdon Press, 1988), p. 365 ff. So insistent was Wesley on this topic of improving the time that he stated in his *More Excellent Way* that those who sleep eight or nine hours are not on the way to heaven nor are they denying themselves and taking up their cross daily. Cf. Outler, *Sermons*, 3:267.

C. Teleology

It is becoming increasingly known in Wesley Studies today, largely through the work of Clarence Bence, that Wesley's soteriology demonstrates a clear teleological orientation.[1] What is less known, however, is that this same teleological thrust is indicative of Wesley's ethics as well. Indeed, failure to realize that the basic relationship between Wesley's personal ethics and his social ethics (which will be discussed below) entails a means/end structure constitutes perhaps the most common way of distorting Wesley's moral views. For example, viewed in isolation, Wesley's prescriptions concerning time, money, dress, tobacco, and the reading of plays[2] all appear unduly harsh, and this harshness has surfaced on occasion within the holiness movement in American Methodism. However, if Wesley's moral counsel, especially in the area of personal ethics, is viewed not as an end in itself, but as an appropriate means to a much higher goal, then legalism in the form of rules for the sake of rules and the spiritual immaturity which results from this can be avoided.

Just what is that higher goal to which Wesley's personal moral advice is directed? It is neither self-justification nor moral rigor, but is nothing less than the love of God and neighbor. Hynson, for instance, calls Wesley's ethics "an ethics of love or sanctification."[3] This means, then, that Wesley's personal ethic is not *self*-directed, a means simply to improve one's own spiritual estate, but is *other*-directed. Accordingly, one practices the discipline of self-denial and stewardship precisely in order to serve, in order to be a suitable instrument which can be used by God to shower His blessings on humanity. Needless self-indulgence, therefore, like using tobacco is rejected, the expense of fine dress is quietly put aside, money is saved, sleep is curbed, and all for the suitable end of the love of neighbor. In short, Wesley's personal ethic is best summarized as preparation for service.

III. Social Ethics

A. The Question of Social Religion

In *Upon Our Lord's Sermon on the Mount: Discourse Four* Wesley endeavors to show that Christianity is essentially a social religion, that it prospers and finds its best expression in human communities, in the rough and tumble of life.[4] Remarkably, the chief tension which he has in mind in *Discourse Four* is not between personal and social religion, which is a modern concern, but

1. Clarence L. Bence, "John Wesley's Teleological Hermeneutic" (Ph.D. dissertation, Emory University, 1982), p. 3.
2. Ibid., 3:273 (The More Excellent Way) In this piece Wesley observes with respect to attending the theater that he "could not do it with a clear conscience; at least not in an English theatre." And his reason for avoiding this and other apparently innocent activities, like reading novels and newspapers, was that there were more excellent ways of occupying the time, especially for those who love or fear God. Cf. Outler, *Sermons*, 3:273. (The More Excellent Way)
3. Leon Hynson, *To Reform the Nation* (Grand Rapids, Michigan: Francis Asbury Press, 1984), p 102.
4. Outler, *Sermons*, 1:533. (Upon Our Lord's Sermon on the Mount: Discourse IV)

between solitary and social religion. This means that Christianity precludes, for instance, the practice of running off into the desert or the wilderness as the staple of Christian experience. And, by implication, the hermit's life characteristic of anchoretic monasticism, as exemplified by St. Anthony of Egypt or the unstable Symeon Stylites,[1] appears to be repudiated as well by Wesley in the following judgment:

> Yet such retirement must not swallow up all our time; this would be to destroy, not advance, true religion. For that the religion described by our Lord in the foregoing words cannot subsist without society, without our living and conversing with other men, is manifest from hence, that several of the most essential branches thereof can have no place if we have no intercourse with the world.[2]

It should immediately be added, however, that Wesley does not condemn the "intermixing solitude or retirement with society,"[3] for this practice is often beneficial when employed judiciously. The point is that one does not go to the wilderness to remain there. Moreover, this Anglican cleric is not adverse to some of the spiritual techniques of monasticism such as contemplation, but he is opposed to deeming it the "only way of worshiping God in spirit and in truth."[4] He writes: "Therefore to give ourselves up entirely to this would be to destroy many branches of spiritual worship, all equally acceptable to God, and equally profitable, not hurtful, to the soul."[5]

Wesley so disapproves of solitary religion because it fails to provide its practitioners with the necessary environment for the promotion of such Christian tempers as mildness, gentleness, longsuffering, and peacemaking.[6] These "cannot possibly subsist without society,"[7] he claims, "without our living and conversing with other men."[8] But Wesley goes a step further and declares that "some intercourse even with ungodly and unholy men is absolutely needful in order to the full exertion of every temper which he [Jesus Christ] has described as the way to the kingdom."[9] Christians are not to love the world, to be sure; nevertheless, there is a real sense in which they need the world. "To turn this religion into a solitary one is to destroy it."[10]

1. Cf. Philip Schaff, *History of the Christian Church* (Grand Rapids: Wm. B. Eerdmans Publishing Co., 1910), 3:191 ff.
2. Outler, *Sermons*, 1:534. (Upon Our Lord's Sermon on the Mount: Discourse IV)
3. Ibid.
4. Ibid., 1:544.
5. Ibid.
6. Ibid., 1:534.
7. Ibid., 1:535.
8. Ibid.
9. Ibid., 1:536.
10 Ibid., 1:534. Davies writes that Wesley "knew of no holiness that was not social holiness, but we must not take this to mean that it was a holiness devoted to changing the social order; Wesley's holiness was social in the narrow sense that it related to personal relations with other people, especially those in the fellowship of believers." Cf. Rupert Davies, "Justification, Sanctification, and the Liberation of the Person" in *Sanctification and Liberation*, ed. Theodore Runyon (Nashville: Abingdon Press), p. 80.

The social nature of Christianity is again emphasized by Wesley in his claim that it is impossible to conceal the religion of Jesus Christ. The deep, hidden, and profound work of the heart's renewal in the image and likeness of God cannot remain hidden, for it will inevitably be displayed in the life and works of Christians as they care for a hurting world. "Your holiness makes you as conspicuous as the sun in the midst of heaven,"[1] Wesley writes. And genuine Christian love "cannot be hid any more than light; and least of all when it shines forth in action."[2] To use a familiar Wesleyan phrase, faith works by love; inward religion, so mysterious and personal, is necessarily manifested in outward religion, in public life. Neither aspect can subsist without the other; both ingredients are necessary. "God hath joined them together,"[3] Wesley notes, "let not man put them asunder."[4]

In light of this close connection that Wesley draws between inward and outward religion, two errors are possible: On the one hand, if the interior life is merely stressed, faith will not achieve its proper end: namely, love. What will emerge, however, is a dead faith, the kind of spiritual narcissism that Wesley so rightly deplores in *Discourse IV*. But if, on the other hand, the inward life of the believer, the life of God in the soul, is not seen as the proper foundation for Christian activity in society, then the very heart, reason, and impetus for such activity will be obscured.

B. Love Embracing The Church

Since the basic structural relationship between inward and outward religion can be expressed in terms of a doctrine of revelation where the antecedent work of the believer's renewal, so mysterious and hidden, is manifested quite publicly, it is natural that Wesley tracks the love of God and its rippling effects in two ever-widening circles: towards the church and towards the world. With respect to the first circle, Wesley wrote at least two sermons whose principal point of departure is the character of the relations between believers. In *The Catholic Spirit*," for example, he examines the two grand hindrances that prevent the children of God from loving one another as they should: namely, that they can't all think alike or walk alike."[5] And though the thought and practices of Christians will inevitably differ, then as now, Wesley offers a basis for unity in the very text of this sermon, namely, 2 Kings 10:15, in which Jehu asks Jehonadab: "Is thine heart right, as my heart is with thy heart? ... If it be, give me thy hand." (KJV) The appeal, then, is to the gracious work which God has wrought in the soul. "Is thy faith ... filled with the energy of love?"[6] Wesley writes, "Does the love of God constrain thee to serve him with fear?"[7] It is the common element of love

1. Outler, *Sermons*, 1:539.
2. Ibid.
3. Ibid., 1:543.
4. Ibid.
5. Ibid., 2:82.
6. Ibid., 2:88.
7. Ibid.

which lies behind a diversity of opinions, actions, and ministries. Once again, inward religion is not to be minimized in the name of social religion, for it is what makes social relationships both gracious and fruitful.

However, the obvious irenic tone of *The Catholic Spirit* should not be mistaken for either theological or moral indifference, for Wesley insists that the catholic spirit is not "speculative latitudinarianism."[1] It is not indifferent, therefore, to all opinions such that one teaching is deemed just as good as any other; this in Wesley's judgment is none other than the spawn of hell.[2] But neither is the catholic spirit "practical latitudinarianism."[3] It is not indifferent to modes of worship or thirdly to the choice of a congregation in which one is to live the Christian life. Is the Methodist leader then inconsistent with his earlier principle of catholicity? Not at all, but he is saying two things simultaneously. Believers should be firmly convinced concerning the opinions or the modes of worship they hold, always realizing, though, that other believers will not only differ, but will also be equally convinced of the rightness of their own judgments. Wesley's prescription, therefore, for satisfying relations within the larger church is conviction plus tolerance, and if the latter ingredient is not understood in light of the former, the prospect of a shallow, unprincipled, faith undoubtedly emerges. Wesley advises: "This unsettledness of thought, this being driven to and fro, and tossed about with every wind of doctrine, is a great curse, not a blessing; an irreconcilable enemy, not a friend, to true catholicism."[4] Thus, a mature faith is both tolerant and strongly held; there is no contradiction here.

Although there are many similarities between the sermons *The Catholic Spirit"* and *A Caution Against Bigotry,"* among which is a warning against dogmatism, there is at least one important difference. Whereas the former homily underscores the importance of the interior life in terms of holy love as a prerequisite for common life, the latter highlights the exterior life, the fruits which necessarily flow from a radically transformed heart. This shift in emphasis in *A Caution Against Bigotry* was precipitated, for the most part, by Wesley's apologetical purpose in this work. Several Anglican clergy, for example, expressed disapproval with respect to Wesley's employment of lay preachers during the revival. In this polemic context, Wesley substantiates Methodist polity and practice in a number of ways: through an appeal to Scripture, apostolic practice, and through reason. Nevertheless, the thrust of his argument seems to devolve upon the works that his lay preachers do, and the resultant dissatisfaction of the Angli-

1. Ibid., 2:92.
2. Ibid.
3. Ibid., 2:93.
4. Ibid., 2:92-93.

can clergy.[1] Thus, bigotry is defined with an eye to the latter group as "too strong an attachment to, or fondness for, our own party, opinion, Church, and religion,"[2] such that we forbid those who cast out devils whom Our Lord has not forbidden. Wesley writes:

> **Do you beware of this. Take care, first, that you do not convict yourself of bigotry by your unreadiness to believe that any man does cast out devils who differs from you. And if you are clear thus far, if you acknowledge the fact, then examine yourself ...[3]**

So then in *The Catholic Spirit* different opinions and doctrines are not to spoil the love of God; in *A Caution Against Bigotry* they are not to spoil the work of God.

C. Love Embracing the World
The love of God is also manifested in a second circle: that is, towards the world. Such love can neither be contained nor exhausted in the first circle — nor should it ever be. In the sermon, *The Reformation of Manners*" for example, preached by Wesley in 1763 under the auspices of the society by the same name, he displays his abiding concern for those who were beyond the walls of the church: the poor, the downtrodden, and the forgotten. In this endeavor, he followed in his father Samuel's footsteps who preached for this same society some sixty-five years earlier.[4]

Ostensibly, The Society for the Reformation of Manners was concerned with issues of public vice such as sabbath breaking, drunkenness, gambling, prostitution and the like. This has led at least one scholar to conclude that the substance of this homily "is one of the least evangelical of any of Wesley's sermons after 1738; ... its conclusions are moralistic and hortatory."[5] Nevertheless, a different interpretation can and should be offered in light of the evidence within the sermon itself which strongly suggests that this is an "evangelical" sermon, after all, especially since it flows quite naturally from Wesley's earlier emphasis of the inward renewal in love brought about by the grace of God. In the following quote from this sermon, for instance, notice the development and order pertaining to the circles of salvation. The reform of public life does not stand alone as an instance of moralism, isolated from Wesley's evangelical concerns; instead it is an integral part of a larger, gracious movement. Wesley writes:

> **This is the original design of the church of Christ. It is a body of men compacted together in order, first, to save each his own soul, then to assist each other in working out their salvation, and afterwards, as**

---

1. In the sermon *A Caution Against Bigotry*, Wesley substantiates his use of lay preachers by making the following observation concerning the practice of the early church: "Indeed so far is the practice of the apostolic age from inclining us to think it was *unlawful* for a man to preach before he was ordained, that we have reason to think it was then accounted *necessary*." Cf. Outler, *Sermons*, 2:75. (A Caution Against Bigotry)
2. Ibid., 2:76.
3. Ibid., 2:76-77.
4. Ibid., 2:300. (The Reformation of Manners)
5. Ibid., 2:301.

far as in them lies, to save all men from present and future misery, to overturn the kingdom of Satan.[1]

Moreover, Wesley extols love in this sermon and argues for its indispensability in reforming activities: "And therefore it is highly expedient that all engaged therein have 'the love of God shed abroad in their hearts' that they should all be able to declare, we love him, because he first loved us."[2] The elimination of public vice then is a clear manifestation of the love of God; it is not less than the gospel but is at the very heart of the good news of freedom from all that oppresses the human spirit or detracts from its dignity. And so in this sermon, Wesley boldly exhorts all Christians "to join together in order to oppose the works of darkness, to spread the knowledge of God their Saviour, and to promote his kingdom upon earth,"[3] and it is in these activities as well that the light of the gospel is revealed. Simply put, the reformation of manners is one of the ways the gospel is revealed in a broader arena, in a sinful public context. The dictum here, as elsewhere for Wesley, is that works are preceded by empowering grace, and that grace is ever active in all manner of works, both public and private.

In a real sense, it was both salutary and inevitable that the faith of John Wesley and the Methodists would issue in social reform. The Methodist leader, for example, developed a cotton industry for the unemployed, established a lending-stock company for people in need of money, and created a free medical dispensary for the sick. Beyond this, Wesley founded an orphan house, established the Kingswood Boarding School, and wrote forcefully against slavery.[4] But in all these reforming activities, and they are considerable, it is not apparent that the Oxonian ever, in the words of Meistad, "reflected consciously about the relationships between faith and works on the social level....[for] the theological horizon of his century did not include salvation of the society."[5] And a similar judgment is expressed by Weber who writes:

> Had Wesley completed his theological work by drawing institutions as well as individual persons into the order of salvation, he would have found it necessary to draw on different images with correspondingly different implications for understanding the nature and work of political institutions.[6]

1. Ibid., 2:302. Granted, Wesley does not underscore justification by faith, nor does he name the grace of Christ very often in this sermon; nevertheless, the content of this piece must be understood in line with Wesley's evangelical emphases which, in a sense, are presupposed.

2. Ibid., 2:314.

3. Ibid., 2:301.

4. Tore Meistad, "Wesley's Theology of Salvation and Social Change" 19 November 1990, a paper presented at the Wesley Studies group, The American Academy of Religion, New Orleans, Louisiana. p. 5, 21.

5. Ibid., p. 27. Bracketed material is mine.

6. Theodore R. Weber, "Political Order in *Ordo Salutis*: A Wesleyan Theory of Political Institutions" 19 November 1990 a paper presented at the Wesley Studies group, The American Academy of Religion, New Orleans, Louisiana., p. 6.

And Henry Rack, for his part, in his *Reasonable Enthusiast* maintains that "Wesley was neither the initiator nor the organizer of any major reform, though he often supported philanthropic efforts in various fields..."[1]

What these and other scholars have observed, then, is that Wesley, as a product of his time, was not able to link clearly his *ordo salutis* with the salvation of *institutions*. His theological framework, in other words, was informed largely by a personal conception of redemption — a conception which is no longer viewed very favorably by the twentieth century. Bonino, for instance, a contemporary Methodist liberation theologian, complains that "the inherited theological framework of the ordo salutis is a straitjacket that Wesley was unable to cast off."[2]

But, on the other hand, there are other Methodist scholars, like Dunlap and Jennings, who insist on arguing for compatibility in this area, that Wesley's social and theological thought is unproblematically relevant to the present. Dunlap, for instance, hails Wesley as a "political prophet" and points out, in a tongue-in-cheek fashion, the "danger" of reading his political writings,[3] and Jennings, perhaps reflecting the loss of transcendence in modern culture, declares that economic and political considerations, as expressed in the much-touted phrase "preferential option for the poor,"[4] must become the yardstick by which to measure "the authenticity of Christian existence and of ecclesial life."[5] More importantly, he believes he finds all of this in Wesley! And at one point Jennings even argues that the "preferential option for the poor" *is* the test and norm of personal holiness.[6] In other words, this interpretation begins on the social and political level and then works inward to personal holiness — a modern though decidedly un-Wesleyan approach.

In light of this debate within the Methodist household which involves, on the one hand, a theological/ethical problem, that is, the relation between Wesley's order of salvation and social institutions, and, on the other hand, an historical problem, that is, how relevant is Wesley's eighteenth-century thought to current social problems, the following material drawn largely from the homilies will demonstrate aspects of Wesley's thinking heretofore neglected in the secondary literature and which should help to illuminate these larger problems. Note how-

1. Henry D. Rack, *Reasonable Enthusiast: John Wesley and the Rise of Methodism* (Philadelphia: Trinity Press International, 1989), p. 360.

2. José Miguez Bonino, "Wesley's Doctrine of Sanctification From a Liberationist Perspective" in Runyon, *Sanctification*, p. 55.

3. Pamela Couture Dunlap, "On the Danger of Reading the Works of John Wesley," *Quarterly Review* Vol. 7, No. 1. (Spring 1987): 4.

4. Many scholars agree that liberation theology began in 1968 at the General conference of the Latin American episcopacy in Medellin, Colombia. And it was at this meeting that the phrase "preferential option for the poor" was first coined. Cf. Richard John Neuhaus, *The Catholic Moment* (San Francisco: Harper and Row, Publishers, 1987), p. 174 ff.

5. Theodore W. Jennings, Jr., "Wesley's Preferential Option for the Poor" *Quarterly Review* Vol. 9. No. 3. (Fall 1989): 10.

6. Ibid., p. 26.

ever that the argument offered will be heuristic, not comprehensive; suggestive, not definitive; it will only seek to display a few new ways to think about some very old problems.

In Wesley's "social" and "political" pieces like his *Thoughts on the Present Scarcity of Provisions* and his sermon *National Sins and Miseries* it is, despite protests to the contrary, a largely personal conception of evil which predominates and which constitutes the chief factor in the analysis. Indeed, Wesley's thought, at times, struggles to express in a systematic fashion the corporate evil present in his own society; that is, the materials of his theology are ill-suited to detect the wickedness embedded and concealed in the infrastructures of the social order which cannot readily be traced to personal sin. In the first piece, for example, the Methodist leader blames vice in the form of distilling, excessive taxes (greed), and luxury for the lack of food in the land,[1] and in the latter work, his ultimate prescription for the ills that plague both England and America includes "[fleeing] from sin", "[purifying] your hearts by faith," and "humbling yourselves under the mighty hand of God."[2] — an interpretation that runs the risk of reductionism at its best. Again, in his homily *The Late Work of God in North America*, produced in 1778, riches and the evil dispositions which follow in their wake, such things as pride, luxury, sloth, wantonness, and independency are likewise offered as explanations for the decline of the American people.[3] Wesley elaborates:

> **Immense trade, wealth, and plenty begot and nourished proportionable pride, and luxury, and sloth, and wantonness. Meantime the same trade, wealth, and plenty begot or nourished the spirit of independency. Who would have imagined that this evil disease would lay a foundation for the cure of all the rest? And yet so it was. For this spirit, now come to maturity, and disdaining all restraint, is now swiftly destroying the trade, and wealth, and plenty whereby it was nourished, and thereby makes way for the happy return of humility, temperance, industry, and chastity.[4]**

Continuing this line of thought, though Wesley in the 1780's wrote many homilies which point out the danger of increasing riches (*The Danger of Riches* 1781; *On Dress* 1786; *On Riches* 1788; *The Causes of the Inefficacy of Christianity* 1789; and *The Danger of Increasing Riches*, 1790), these pieces, as products of their time, give little indication that Wesley was ever more than vaguely aware of the kind of critique of wealth that is characteristic of our modern era. In fact, the common theme in each one of these pieces cited above is not a theoretical, probing, assessment of social structures, but that wealth undermines the love of God and neighbor and is therefore destructive of all those holy tempers which immediately flow from such love.

1. Jackson, *Works*, 11:57.
2. Outler, *Sermons*, 3:575-76. (National Sins and Miseries)
3. Ibid., 3:601. (The Late Work of God in North America)
4. Ibid., 3:606.

However, these same pieces on wealth, admittedly, can also be read on a second level and one which offers more promise for the contemporary debate. Thus, in these homilies, Wesley reveals that the accumulation of riches is inimical to caring for our neighbor as an instance of the love of God and it therefore undermines the establishment of the kingdom of God itself. More to the point, in *The Danger of Riches*, the evil of desiring wealth consists in the attempt to find happiness out of God and in things.[1] In *On Riches*, it is a "hindrance ... to the very first fruit of faith, namely, the love of God [and] ... loving our neighbor."[2] In *The Danger of Increasing Riches*, the love of money begets a love of the world in its three manifestations of "'the desire of the flesh', 'the desire of the eyes' and 'the pride of life,'" with the result that the needs of poor are neglected.[3] And at one point in this same homily Wesley even exclaims: "Do not you know that God entrusted you with that money to feed the hungry, to clothe the naked, to help the stranger, the widow, the fatherless ..."[4] The accumulation of money, then, frustrates the good which God desires to shower on the poor; it hinders the work of the Most High among humanity and within the human heart as well. And just why this is a particular problem for "all real Christians" is detailed by Wesley in his *Causes of the Inefficacy of Christianity*, where he states:

> But how astonishing a thing is this! How can we understand it? Does it not seem (and yet this cannot be!) that Christianity, true scriptural Christianity, has a tendency in process of time to undermine and destroy itself? For wherever true Christianity spreads it must cause diligence and frugality, which, in the natural course of things, must beget riches. And riches naturally beget pride, love of the world, and every temper that is destructive of Christianity.[5]

Though Wesley was obviously energetic in ministering to the basic needs of the poor, the amelioration of their physical condition was often explicitly related by him to other valuable kinds of ministry, especially in his sermons. Indeed, it should be observed, though it seldom is, that there is an implicit order within the homilies which contains not a few value judgments in terms of precisely what kind of ministry is of first rank. To illustrate, in his sermon *On Visiting the Sick*, Wesley counsels the Methodists that after the *physical* needs of the sick have been met, the visitors are then to proceed to things of *greater importance*. He elaborates:

> These little labours of love (the provision of sufficient food, raiment, and fuel) will pave your way to things of greater importance. Having shown that you have a regard for their bodies you may proceed to inquire concerning their souls. And here you have a large field before you; you have scope for exercising all the talents which God has

---

1. Ibid., 3:234. (The Danger of Riches).
2. Ibid., 3:521. (On Riches) Bracketed material is mine.
3. Ibid., 4:182. (The Danger of Increasing Riches).
4. Ibid., 4:184.
5. Ibid., 4:96. (Causes of the Inefficacy of Christianity) And notice, once again, that Wesley continues to make the distinction between true Christians and nominal ones very late in his career.

given....See next whether he knows anything of the power [of godliness]; of worshipping God 'in spirit and in truth.'[1]

Two points are noteworthy here: first, for Wesley, a part of what it means to love your neighbor as yourself always involves the exercise of both material gifts and spiritual talents; it entails the employment of all those gifts and graces which will enhance the physical well being of the poor *and* their spiritual character. Thus, Wesley attempted to hold together what our modern age has so often rent asunder. Second, and perhaps more importantly, though the material needs of the neighbor have chronological priority; they clearly do not have valuational priority in Wesley's thought,[2] for their fulfillment prepares the way, to use Wesley's own terminology, for things of greater importance. "While you are eyes to the blind and feet to the lame, a husband to the widow and a father to the fatherless," he writes, "see that you still keep a higher end in view, even the saving of souls from death."[3] And again he notes in this same piece, "labour to make all you say and do subservient to *that* great end."[4]

But perhaps the most lucid expression of the value and necessity of personal, inward transformation (spirituality) for social reform is found in the following selection from the sermon *On Zeal*, a sermon which epitomizes Wesley's thought in this area and which provides insight into his ethical motivation and concern. Notice, for instance, what is at the heart of this ethic and the consequences which flow from it. Wesley declares:

> In a Christian believer *love* sits upon the throne, which is erected in the inmost soul; namely, love of God and man, which fills the whole heart, and reigns without a rival. In a circle near the throne are all *holy tempers*: long-suffering, gentleness, meekness, goodness, fidelity, temperance — and if any other is comprised in 'the mind which was in Christ Jesus' In an exterior circle are all the *works of mercy*, whether to the souls or bodies of men. By these we exercise all holy tempers; by these we continually improve them, so that all these are real *means of grace*, although this is not commonly adverted to. Next to these are those that are usually termed *works of piety*: reading and hearing the Word, public, family, private prayer, receiving the Lord's Supper, fasting or abstinence. Lastly, that his followers may the more effectually provoke one another to love, holy tempers, and good works, our blessed Lord has united them together in one — *the church*, dispersed all over the earth; a little emblem of which, of the church universal, we have in every particular Christian congregation.[5]

1. Ibid., 3:391. The parenthetical material is a part of this sermon as well.
2. Ibid.
3. Ibid., 3:393.
4. Ibid. Wesley's thought in this area, especially the value judgments he makes, is often quietly put aside by contemporary writers like Theodore Jennings who strain to give the material needs of the poor an ultimacy which they cannot bear. Cf. Theodore W. Jennings, Jr. "Wesley's Preferential Option for the Poor *Quarterly Review* Vol. 9, No. 3. (Fall 1989) p. 10 ff. Emphasis is mine.
5. Ibid., 3:313-14. (On Zeal)

In this homily, then, it is as if Wesley has allowed us to peek into the throne room of his entire theological and moral enterprise. And on the throne sits not any political ideology nor works of mercy, however noble or valuable they may be. No, love itself sits on the throne, and next to it are all those holy tempers (holiness) described earlier and which are often discounted in contemporary Christianity. But it is precisely only when these elements are in place, as motivating factors, at the very heart of things, that Wesley is then willing to consider works of mercy, piety and the like (and just why this is so will be detailed below). "No outward works are acceptable to him [God] unless they spring from *holy tempers*,"[1] he cautions. And again, "That all those who are zealous of good works would put them in their proper place! Would not imagine they can supply the want of holy tempers, but take care that they may spring from them!"[2] Therefore all those "dispositions of mind" like meekness, gentleness and long-suffering etc., are not beside the point, a pious extravagance or indulgence, but are "absolutely necessary ... for the enjoyment of present or future holiness."[3] Indeed, they are nothing less than the lodestars of the moral life, the key to Wesley's social ethic.

Moreover, without holy love as its impetus, without a concern for "souls" as its highest ministry, the church runs the risk of self-righteousness, a partisan spirit, and much worse: of fostering perhaps all those unholy tempers which Wesley so often warned against.[4] Again, in his homily *On Zeal*, the Methodist itinerant cautions:

> And, first, if zeal, true Christian zeal, be nothing but the flame of love, then *hatred*, in every kind and degree, then every sort of *bitterness* toward them that oppose us, is so far from deserving the name of zeal that it is directly opposite to it....Secondly; if lowliness be a property of zeal, then pride is inconsistent with it....Thirdly; if meekness be an inseparable property of zeal, what shall we say of those who call their anger by that name? Why, that they mistake the truth totally;...Fourthly; if patience, contentedness, and resignation, are the properties of zeal, then murmuring, fretfulness, discontent, impatience, are wholly inconsistent with it....Fifthly; if the object of zeal be 'that which is good,' then fervour for any *evil thing* is not Christian zeal.[5]

Therefore, a bitter zeal for justice, which views matters of the soul and of human affection as of little consequence is no substitute for the justice which grows out

---

1. Ibid., 3:320. (On Zeal) Bracketed material is mine.
2. Ibid., 3:305. (On Charity)
3. Ibid., 4:223. (On Living Without God) The danger of beginning not with love and holy tempers but with political and economic concerns is that "justice" so conceived will most likely be unreformed, speckled with anger, class animosity, and perhaps even outright hatred of the middle-class or the rich. In other words, its concern for the poor will be expressed in all those unholy tempers against which Wesley inveighed. Once again, love and holiness are the proper starting point. Only then will the poor be properly ministered to and receive the justice they deserve.
4. Ibid., 3:304. (On Charity)
5. Ibid., 3:315-17. (On Zeal)

of a holy, loving, Christlike concern. Jennings, and others, may have begun on the political level; clearly Wesley did not.

D. Some Concluding Observations

Although Wesley was undoubtedly an aggressive reformer, tackling the problems of unemployment, slavery, poverty, ignorance, and war, his thought was, after all, more conducive to the liberal reform characteristic of his pre-Marxist age, for it lacked the kind of radical critique of institutional structures that has become the staple of modern theology. Therefore, those theologians who insist on arguing for compatibility in this area, can do so only by ignoring the historical problem posed in the form of Marxist thought as a watershed in political and economic analysis. Nevertheless, Wesley's broad themes of love, grace, faith, and his example of concern for society and for the individual, can be factored into the modern equation but not, of course, without some measure of translation. Again, twentieth century realities must not be confused with eighteenth-century ones.

Second, although Wesley did not clearly link his order of salvation to the redemption of institutions as some scholars have correctly noted, his ethical and social thought remains highly relevant for our own age especially in its attentiveness to the prerequisites of reform, to all those holy tempers which are vital to spreading the love of God and neighbor in ever-widening circles. Thus, Wesley's teleology, his means/end structure and the importance he placed on the human soul, referred to here and elsewhere, must neither be neglected nor repudiated by an increasingly materialistic church (philosophically speaking) — a church which, ironically enough, in its concern for the poor often mimics the values of Marxism and subtly deems the fulfillment of material needs as an ultimate ministry and not as the penultimate one it actually is and as Wesley himself had realized.

The difficult and prophetic task of contemporary Methodist theologians, then, is to create a truly conjunctive theology which, like Wesley, will be ever attentive to love and holy tempers, and like modern liberation theologians, will be sensitive to *all* which oppresses the human spirit. It will, in other words, be a theology characterized by nothing less than a faith which *works* by *love*.

CHAPTER EIGHT

ESCHATOLOGY
"I believe in ... the resurrection of the body, and the life everlasting."

Few can doubt that John Wesley's main theological interest was the doctrine of salvation: he took part in the Holy Club; he served as a missionary to Georgia; he wrestled with the doctrine of justification by faith; he engaged in field preaching; and he made sure, despite Anglican protests to the contrary, that the Methodists were equipped with a ministerial infrastructure which would sustain the revival sweeping across England. It should come as no surprise, then, to learn that when Wesley entertained the subject of eschatology, that is, the doctrine of last things, his strong soteriological interest was evident throughout.

In his sermons, for instance, the Methodist leader avoids many of the interesting, though highly speculative issues, such as the identification of Gog and Magog and the beast of the Book of Revelation, which have preoccupied popular American religious literature of late. Instead, he much prefers to view eschatology as having great practical import in the sense that it is, for the most part, the continuation of the salvation already begun in this life. In fact, one of Wesley's favorite devices is to consider an aspect of eschatology, like the doctrine of heaven, and then to pose a question to his readers in the form: "how then shall we live?" And this tendency has not escaped Albert Outler who noted that for Wesley, "soteriology and eschatology were actually two sides of the same mystery of God's proffered grace to man."[1]

I. The Question of Eternity

Earlier, in the chapter on the Doctrine of God, the issue of eternity was explored under the distinction of *a parte ante* and *a parte post* as it relates to the divine Being. It will be recalled that the former attribute is exclusive to God, but not the latter. Thus, human beings (and angels) are eternal, not in the sense that they lack a beginning, but in the sense that they will have no end. However, knowing that many of his readers seldom considered the unfathomable, unalter-

1. Albert C. Outler, ed., *The Works of John Wesley   The Sermons* 4 vols. (Nashville: Abingdon Press, 1984), 3:181. (The Important Question)

able nature of eternity, especially as it pertained to salvation, Wesley explores this topic in some detail in his sermon *On Eternity* in which he asks: "What are any temporal things placed in comparison with those that are eternal?"[1] And in partial response to this question, Wesley compares the concept of eternity with several degrees of duration already known as illustrated by the following:

> Suppose there were a ball of sand as large as the globe of earth; suppose a grain of this sand were to be annihilated, reduced to nothing, in a thousand years; yet that whole space of duration wherein this ball would be annihilating, at the rate of one grain in a thousand years, would bear infinitely less proportion to eternity — duration without end — than a single grain of sand would bear to all that mass.[2]

And a similar kind of reasoning is also found in the homilies *The Important Question*[3] and *What is Man?*[4]

To be sure, some will criticize Wesley's understanding of eternity offered here and argue that he is confusing an issue of quality (eternal life) with one of quantity (time without end). However, the Methodist leader's major thrust seems to lie elsewhere, in other, more important, matters. As a result, the appeal to the notion of eternity is not only the context of much of Wesley's eschatology, but it is also the means by which he can stress *present* spiritual realities, giving them added depth and meaning. For instance, in the selection from the sermon which follows, Wesley's appeal to eternity issues in a call for current change, by assessing the relative worth of this life as compared to the next. He observes:

> What then is he — how foolish, how mad, in how unutterable a degree of distraction — who, seeming to have the understanding of a man, deliberately prefers temporal things to eternal? ... prefers the happiness of a year, say a thousand years, to the happiness of eternity.[5]

And again in *The Important Question*, the foolishness of selling one's soul for threescore years of pleasure, of preferring the finite over the infinite, is underscored.[6]

Second, the appeal to the notion of eternity is also the means by which Wesley can entertain some of the more philosophical and seldom-asked questions of life such as: What is the end or purpose of human existence in the first place? And in his piece *What is Man?*, produced in 1788, Wesley replies that we were sent into the world "for one sole end, and for no other — to prepare for eternity. For this alone we live: for this, and no other purpose, is our life either given or

---

1. Ibid., 2:363. (On Eternity)
2. Ibid., 2:364.
3. Ibid., 3:196-97. (The Important Question)
4. Ibid., 3:458-59. (What is Man?)
5. Ibid., 2:367. (On Eternity)
6. Ibid., 3:196. (The Important Question) Wesley's full comments are as follows: "Who can tell the length of eternity!'And how soon will this be the language of him who sold his soul for threescore years' pleasure! How soon will he cry out, 'O eternity, eternity! Who can tell the length of eternity.'"

continued."[1] And a similar judgment is expressed in a much earlier sermon, *The Circumcision of the Heart* which states:

One design ye are to pursue to the end of time — the enjoyment of God in time and in eternity. Desire other things so far as they tend to this .... Whatever ye desire or fear, whatever ye seek or shun, whatever ye think, speak, or do, be it in order to your happiness in God, the sole end as well as source of your being.[2]

Wesley's comment just cited that we were sent into the world to prepare for eternity is expressed in his much-utilized teleological vocabulary. In other words, by means of this language, Wesley — to the offense of many modern sentiments — is not only establishing a means/end relationship (this life is to prepare *for* eternity), but he is also making a value judgment which de-centers finite, temporal, mundane concerns. In fact, in a sermon produced in his mid-career, Wesley compares our earthly existence to that of a "stranger and sojourner [on] his way to the everlasting habitations,"[3] suggesting that our earthly life is fleeting, and that, by implication, to place our trust unduly in it is a subtle, but nonetheless dangerous, form of idolatry. In short, Wesley's consideration of eternity is not really a question of quantity or chronology at all, but one of values.

Admittedly, all of this falls hard on contemporary ears which have been attuned to the voice of Karl Marx who criticized the otherworldly emphasis of religion and who, on one occasion, even referred to religion as the opium of the people — a drug which prevented men and women from seeing their true alienated condition.[4] However, Wesley as an eighteenth century priest, did not suffer from such a distorted view of religion, nor was he, philosophically speaking, a materialist. If anything, events at the end of the twentieth century suggest not only the endurance of religion as a healthy staple of the human diet, but also the failure of those systems and philosophies which have repudiated the spiritual nature of humanity. Indeed, spirituality is such a significant feature of the human condition that Ernst Troeltsch, a nineteenth century figure, defined the human species as *homo theologicus*, and Wesley, for his part, asserted much the same in his own age in his claim that men and women are destined for nothing less than eternity, for nothing less than God.

1. Ibid., 4:25. (What is Man?)
2. Ibid., 1:408. (The Circumcision of the Heart) This semon, produced in 1733, is a good example of Wesley's thinking on the end or goal of religion, what elsewhere he refers to as Christian Perfection. See Outler's introduction to this homily on pp. 398-400.
3. Ibid., 1:692. (Upon Our Lord's Sermon on the Mount, Discourse the Thirteenth) Bracketed material is mine.
4. Karl Marx, "Toward the Critique of Hegel's Philosophy of Law," in *The Essential Marx*, ed. Saul K. Padover (New York: New American Library, 1978), p. 286-87. Once Marx criticized religion along these lines, it seems that theologians thereafter especially tried to demonstrate the political, social, and economic relevance of Christianity. While this was certainly a noble and much-needed emphasis, the deprecation of the afterlife which formed a part of many of these arguments was not. Cf. Kenneth J. Collins, "John Wesley and Liberation Theology: A Closer Look" *The Asbury Theological Journal* Vol. 42 Num. 1 (Spring 1987): 85-90.

II. Death and the Intermediate State

Beyond the division of eternity into past and future, Wesley explores yet another division in terms of a happy or a miserable eternity where either rewards or punishment await. And the entrance to this infinite world, where the consequences of earthly life come to fruition, is none other than death — a reality which, according to Wesley, is best defined as "the separation of the soul from the body."[1] And though the Methodist leader is quite clear with respect to a definition of death, he is less so concerning just when this separation occurs — an event which seems to be known to God alone.[2] However, it is important to realize that Wesley's understanding of death is predicated upon his dualistic understanding of humanity cited earlier. Human beings are composite beings, made up of both body and soul, but at death this union comes to an end.

Continuing this line of thought, Wesley taught the obvious fact that the body dies, but he, as noted in a previous chapter, maintained that the essence of a person, the soul itself, does not die. In his sermon, *What is Man?*, for example, he writes:

I? But what am I? Unquestionably I am something distinct from my body. It seems evident that my body is not necessarily included therein. For when my body dies I shall not die. I shall exist as really as I did before. And I cannot but believe this self-moving, thinking principle, with all its passions and affections, will continue to exist although the body be mouldered into dust.[3]

This means, of course, that death does not put an end to the essence of a human being. The soul "being of a nobler nature," is not affected thereby.[4] Consequently, in his preference for the doctrine of the immortality of the soul — which some, like Oscar Cullmann, argue was originally a Greek idea — Wesley contends that there is a real sense in which human beings do not die. However, for the sake of accuracy, it must also be pointed out that the Oxford don paradoxically maintained that death does not put an end to the body either, but "will only

---

1. Outler, *Sermons*, 4:25. (What is Man?) Keep in mind that Wesley has a dualistic understanding of humanity. A man or woman is composed of both body and soul. At death the body dies, but the soul in some sense remains. Cf. John Wesley, *Explanatory Notes Upon the New Testament* (Salem, Ohio: Schmul Publishers), p. 532.

2. Ibid., 4:25.

3. Ibid., 4:23. Wesley's language of a "self-moving, thinking principle," is reminiscent of the vocabulary of Descartes, for the seventeenth-century Frenchman distinguished the *res cogitans* from the *res extensa*. Cf. Rene Descartes, *Principles of Philosophy*, translated by E. S. Haldane and G.R.T. Ross, in *The Philosophical Works of Descartes* (Cambridge University Press, 1931), Vol 1, pp. 234-40.

4. Outler, *Sermons*, 4:51. (Walking by Sight and Walking by Faith) If the essence of a person does not die, as is maintained in all positions which assert the immortality of the soul, does the person really die, and is death any longer an issue? The Greek origins of this teaching are fairly clear and are recounted in Oscar Cullman's writings. But exactly when this teaching worked its way into Christian theology is less so. Cf. Oscar Cullmann, *Immortality of the Soul or Resurrection of the Dead* (London: Epworth Press, 1958).

alter the manner of [its] existence."[1] What he probably has in mind here is the eventual union of the soul with an imperishable body at the resurrection, and in this specialized sense the body "continues on" as well, though greatly transformed.

But just where does the soul "go" after its separation from the body? In other words, what is the intermediate state of the soul as it exists between the realities of a past life and the one which is to come? In answering this question in his sermon, *On Faith*, written just a little over two years before his own death, Wesley points out the confusion of the words "hades" and "hell" which has occurred in the works of "our English translators."[2] Thus, for example, when the Latin phrase *descendit ad inferos* of the Athanasian Creed was translated into English, it appeared as "descended into hell."[3] However, since such an English phrase could suggest what was for Wesley a very impious notion, that at death Christ proceeded to a place of torment, he made a distinction between the words "hades" and "hell." The former was a general term and simply referred to the "receptacle of separate spirits,"[4] while the latter included only the damned. Not surprisingly, Deschner observes that Wesley omitted any reference to Christ descending into hell in the Methodist Twenty-five Articles.[5] And in his commentary on Acts 2:27, an important passage on this score, Wesley emphatically states: "But it does not appear, that ever our Lord went into hell."[6]

Hades, then, as Wesley uses the term, is a very general one; it is the abode of all the dead; it is the place where separated spirits remain until the judgment. However, since those who die in Christ can no longer be tormented by those who are in rebellion against the Most High, a gulf, a division, is fixed in this realm which separates the good from the evil. Wesley explains:

> And there is a great gulf fixed in Hades between the place of the holy and that of unholy spirits, which it is impossible for either the one or the other to pass over...
> I cannot therefore think that all those who are with the rich man in the unhappy division of Hades will remain there, howling and blaspheming, cursing God and looking upwards, till they are cast into the everlasting fire, prepared for the devil and his angels. And on the other hand, can we reasonably doubt but that those who are now in paradise, in Abraham's bosom, all those holy souls ... will be continually ripening for heaven.[7]

1. Ibid., 2:367. (On Eternity) Bracketed material is mine.
2. Ibid., 4:189. (On Faith)
3. Philip Schaff, ed., *The Creeds of Christendom*, 3 vols. (Grand Rapids, Michigan: Baker Book House, 1983.), 2:69.
4. Outler, *Sermons*, 4:8. (Dives and Lazarus)
5. John Deschner, *Wesley's Christology* (Dallas: Southern Methodist University Press, 1960), pp. 50-51.
6. Wesley, *N.T. Notes*, p. 279.
7. Outler, *Sermons*, 4:190-91. (On Faith) See also Wesley's sermon *Dives and Lazarus* 4:8 ff.

So understood, Hades is both the antechamber of hell and of heaven. Concerning the former, Wesley indicates that as soon as the wicked die, they are conducted to this place of torment by "the devil and his angels,"[1] though he suggests a possible role for wicked human spirits in this affair as well.[2] At any rate, this "unhappy division of Hades" is not "the nethermost hell,"[3] a fate which is reserved for the future judgment. Nevertheless, it is a state beyond all hope of redemption; it is, in short, a God-forsaken condition. In his sermon *On Faith* Wesley cautions:

> **Indeed a gentleman of great learning, the honourable Mr. Campbell, in his account of the middle state published not many years ago, seems to suppose that wicked souls may amend in Hades, and then remove to a happier mansion. He has great hopes that 'the rich man' mentioned by our Lord, in particular, might be purified by that penal fire, till, in process of time, he might be qualified for a better abode. But who can reconcile this with Abraham's assertion that none can pass over the 'great gulf'?[4]**

Being the Church of England man that he was, it is not surprising to learn that, for Wesley, there "cannot be any medium between everlasting joy and everlasting pain."[5] That is, those who are tormented in the antechamber of hell are not thereby purified, but instead remain infected with the dogs of hell: pride, avarice, lust, hatred, and blasphemy. The concept of purgatory, therefore, is put aside as an erroneous teaching which can only detract from the excellency and sufficiency of Christ's death on the cross. "No suffering but that of Christ has any power to expiate sin;" Wesley reasons, "and no fire but that of love can purify the soul, either in time or in eternity."[6]

Furthermore, just as the souls of the wicked do not immediately descend to the nethermost hell, so the souls of the righteous do not instantly enter heaven. They too enter hades, the realm of the dead, but with two important differences: first, they are separated from the wicked; second, they are free from all pain and torment.[7] Indeed, Wesley most often refers to this antechamber of heaven as "paradise" and it is the place to which the penitent thief went at

---

1. Ibid., 3:187. (The Important Question)

2. Ibid., 4:193. (On Faith)

3. Ibid., 4:33. (On the Discoveries of Faith) Although the Oxford English Dictionary indicates that the N T usage of hades refers to the state or the abode of the dead, and is often associated with the Hebrew Sheol, a much earlier usage can be found in Greek mythology where hades refers to the oldest name of the god of the dead, also called Pluto.

4. Ibid., 4:190. (On Faith)

5. Ibid., 2:367. (On Eternity)

6. Ibid., 4:9. (Dives and Lazarus)

7. Ibid., 3:186. (The Important Question) Freedom and rest from the wicked is also a leading idea in Wesley's first published sermon, *The Trouble and Rest of Good Men*. In this piece, however, Wesley put forth a problematic view which he later renounced; that is, that death itself can purify humanity by delivering it, at least in some sense, from its sins. Wesley writes: "For in the moment wherein they shake off the flesh, they are delivered, not only from the troubling of the wicked, not only from pain and sickness, from folly and infirmity, but also from sin." Cf. Outler, *Sermons*, 3:539.

his death, where good souls go to await the general judgment, and into which Christ descended. Moreover, in a letter to George Blackall, written in 1783, Wesley makes it clear that paradise, like the antechamber of hell cited earlier, is not to be confused with the notion of purgatory. "But we believe," he writes, "(as did the ancient Church) that none suffer after death but those who suffer eternally."[1] And Wesley adds in an evangelical manner: "We believe that we are to be here saved from sin and enabled to love God with all our heart."[2]

III. The Judgment

John Wesley was well aware that the Roman Catholic church made a distinction between a particular judgment, which occurs immediately at death, and a general judgment which occurs at the consummation of all things. However, the Methodist leader rejected this teaching largely because he could not find sufficient warrant for two separate judgments in Scripture. In his sermon *The Good Steward*, for instance, he notes:

> 'It is appointed for men once to die, and after this, the judgment.' For in all reason, the word 'once' is here to be applied to judgment as well as death. So that the fair inference to be drawn from this very text is, not that there are two judgments, a particular and a general, but that we are to be judged, as well as to die, once only; not once immediately after death, and again after the general resurrection...[3]

However, even for Wesley, "the moment a soul drops the body, and stands naked before God, it cannot but know what its portion will be to all eternity."[4] Clearly, its place in hades will be indicative of its eternal state; nevertheless, such knowledge does not constitute a judgment *per se*, but is simply an awareness of the awesome and unchangeable verdict which is yet to come.

Just what that verdict will be and the consequences which will flow from it are topics explored in the sermon, *The Great Assize*, written in 1758. In the earliest part of this piece, Wesley considers the circumstances which will precede humanity's standing before the judgment seat of Christ. "And first, 'God will show signs in the earth beneath,'" he writes.[5] There will be earthquakes everywhere, the sea will roar, the powers of heaven will be shaken, and "then shall be heard a universal 'shout'... followed by 'the voice of the archangel' proclaiming the approach of the Son of God and man..."[6] At this point, the dead will rise; the Son of man will have angels gather his elect; and he will then sit upon the throne

1. John Telford, ed., *The Letters of John Wesley, A.M.* 8 vols. (London: The Epworth Press, 1931), 7:168.

2. Ibid.

3. Outler, *Sermons*, 2:292. (The Good Steward)

4. Ibid.

5. Ibid., 1:357. (The Great Assize)

6. Ibid., 1:357-58.

of his glory and separate the sheep from the goats.[1] Note that as Wesley describes these various events which precede the judgment, he seldom departs from the idiom of Scripture.

Details of the judgment itself occupy the next section of this sermon. Thus, the person by whom God will judge the world is none other than his only-begotten Son, while the time of this cataclysmic event is simply referred to as "the day of the Lord."[2] The place, on the other hand, is not specifically accounted for in this homily or in Scripture, but Wesley speculates that "it seems most probable the 'great white throne' will be high exalted above the earth."[3] Again, the persons to be judged are all those "who have sprung from the loins of Adam since the world began."[4] And they will be judged according to their works, what they have done or left undone in this life. However, not only will all the actions of every person then be brought to open view, but "all their words, seeing 'every idle word which men shall speak, they shall give account thereof in the day of judgment."[5] Beyond this, "every inward working of the human soul: every appetite, passion, inclination, [and] affection"[6] will be displayed so that it will then be evident who is righteous and who is unrighteous. Judgment, therefore, is both revelatory and thorough.

In light of the preceding, it must be asked how does Wesley reconcile the notions of justification by faith and a judgment according to works? In his sermon, *On the Wedding Garment*, he explains that these two ideas are not contradictory, for the one pertains to initial justification; the other to final justification. Again, the one refers to present salvation where faith is the only condition; the other to final salvation where works are also in some sense necessary.[7] Wesley explains:

> The righteousness of Christ is, doubtless, necessary for any soul that enters into glory. But so is personal holiness, too, for every child of man. But it is highly needful to be observed that they are necessary in different respects. The former is necessary to *entitle* us to heaven; the latter, to *qualify* us for it. Without the righteousness of Christ we could

---

1. Ibid., 1:358. Wesley's views on the millennium are complex and difficult to understand. In his *N T Notes*, for instance, he remarks: "two distinct thousand years are mentioned throughout this whole passage [Revelation 20]. Each is mentioned thrice; the thousand wherein Satan is bound, ver. 2, 3, 7, the thousand wherein the saints shall reign, ver. 4,5,6.... By observing these two distinct thousand years, many difficulties are avoided. There is room enough for the fulfilling of all the prophecies, and those which before seemed to clash are reconciled: particularly those which speak on the one hand, of a most flourishing state of the Church as yet to come; and on the other, of the fatal security of men in the last days of the world." Cf. John Wesley, *Explanatory Notes Upon the New Testament* (Salem, Ohio: Schmul Publishers), p. 723-24. Bracketed material is mine.

2. Outler, *Sermons*, 1:359.

3. Ibid., 1:361.

4. Ibid.

5. Ibid., 1:362-63.

6. Ibid., 1:363. Bracketed material is mine.

7. Harald Lindström, *Wesley and Sanctification* (Wilmore, Kentucky: Francis Asbury Publishing Co.), p. 208.

have no *claim* to glory; without holiness we could have no *fitness* for it.[1]

According to Lindström, this emphasis of two-fold justification was present, in principle, immediately after 1738, and it was further articulated in the *Minutes* of 1744 and in *A Farther Appeal*.[2]

It should be apparent by now that the essential relationship between initial justification, on the one hand, and final justification, on the other, is best described in terms of the relationship between faith and the fruits of faith; that is, between faith and holiness.[3] And to those Lutherans who rejected this notion of final justification (iustitia duplex), Wesley responded that faith, no matter how valuable, is still only a means, still only a handmaiden to love; but holiness, with all its works and fruits, is the very goal of true religion. Accordingly, the faith which justifies will necessarily issue in all manner of good works such that if these works are lacking, believers may well suspect if they have the proper kind of faith. In fact, to argue otherwise, to maintain that works of charity or mercy and the like are not in some sense necessary in the Christian life (and for the coming judgment) is, according to Wesley, the breeding ground for antinomianism, another way of making void the law through faith.

Lest there be misunderstanding, it should be noted, as Lindström, points out, that Wesley made a distinction between condition and merit as they pertain to final justification. Thus, sanctification or holiness is indeed the condition of redemption at the judgment, but not "as a merit on the strength of which final salvation ... is accorded to man."[4] In short, for Wesley, humanity is always in God's debt; there is never any sense in which God is obligated to redeem His creatures due to what they have done. Both initial and final justification, therefore, are — and remain — by grace.

The third part of the *Great Assize* considers the execution of the sentence pronounced on the good and the evil. Concerning the latter, it is evident as Williams correctly points out, that Wesley believed in a literal hell where the wicked are punished for all eternity.[5] However, Williams, perhaps reflecting modern sentiments, feels compelled to mute this teaching of Wesley's and to claim that the

---

1. Outler, *Sermons*, 4:144. (On the Wedding Garment) This sermon is emblematic of Wesley's soteriology since it displays how he held in tension the idea of justification by faith, which by his own admission he did not understand until 1738, and holiness of heart and life, an emphasis which was present as early as 1725.

2. Lindström, *Sanctification*, p. 208.

3. Ibid., 212-13.

4. Ibid., p. 210. At the conference of 1770, Wesley wrote on the issue of merit in a way that disturbed the Calvinist Methodists as revealed in the following: "As to merit itself, of which we have been so dreadfully afraid: We are rewarded according to our works, yea, because of our works. How does this differ from, 'for the sake of our works?' And how differs this from *secundum merita operum?*" Later on, Wesley admitted that though this was an important and little-understood truth, the language was somewhat unguarded, and he assured his fellow Methodists that he had no intention of asserting justification by works. Cf. Jackson, *Works*, 8:337-38.

5. Colin W. Williams, *John Wesley's Theology Today* (Nashville: Abingdon Press, 1960), p. 199.

Methodist leader actually made small use of the threat of hell.[1] But the sermons suggest otherwise. Granted, Wesley did not intentionally threaten people, nor did he badger them, but the seriousness and earnestness of this eighteenth-century evangelist as he proclaimed the gospel to his neighbors cannot be understood apart from the eternal and unalterable consequences of the judgment. In fact, the subject of hell and damnation play an important role in all of the following sermons: On the *Discoveries of Faith*,[2] *Human Life a Dream*,[3] *On Faith*,[4] *The Important Question*,[5] *Dives and Lazarus*[6] and of course in the brief, but pungent piece, *Of Hell*,[7] to name a few.

In this last sermon, which was written in 1782, Wesley explores the punishment of the wicked under two main headings: *poena damni* (punishment of loss) and *poena sensus* (punishment of sense). The penalty of the former consists in the damned being separated from all the things which they cherished in the previous life, as well as from all those persons whom they loved.[8] But their greatest pain, no doubt, comes from their exclusion from a God of love for all eternity. "Banishment from the presence of the Lord is the very essence of destruction to a spirit that was made for God," Wesley writes, "And if that banishment lasts forever, it is 'everlasting destruction.'"[9]

The punishment of sense, on the other hand, entails the torment of a guilty conscience that continually flails the soul with "self-condemnation, sorrow, shame, remorse, and a sense of the wrath of God."[10] Add to this the assault of such unholy passions as "fear, horror, rage and evil desires,"[11] plus the agony of the unholy tempers of "envy, jealousy, malice, and revenge"[12] let loose upon the soul, and the picture which begins to emerge is one of abject, unending, torment. And elsewhere in his sermon, *On the Discoveries of Faith*, Wesley continues this same theme:

> **They carry with them their own hell, in the worm that never dieth; in a consciousness of guilt, and of the wrath of God, which continually drinks up their spirits; in diabolical, infernal tempers, which are**

1. Ibid.
2. Outler, *Sermons*, 4:33. (On the Discoveries of Faith)
3. Ibid., 4:116. (Human Life a Dream)
4. Ibid., 4:190-91. (On Faith)
5. Ibid., 3:187. (The Important Question)
6. Ibid., 4:8. (Dives and Lazarus)
7. Ibid., 3:36ff. (Of Hell)
8. Ibid., 3:34. (Of Hell)
9. Ibid., p. 35. Wesley also equates exclusion from the presence of God with everlasting destruction in a letter written to William Law in 1756. Cf. Telford, *Letters*, 3:369-70.
10. Ibid., 3:36.
11. Ibid.
12. Ibid. In his *New Testament Theology*, Donald Guthrie, a contemporary evangelical, documents the biblical material which pertains to the subject of hell, but he expresses some uneasiness about this awful *reality* as revealed in his concluding remarks: "The doctrine of eternal punishment is not an attractive doctrine and the desire to substitute for it the view that, at the judgment, the souls of the wicked will cease to exist, is understandable." Cf. Donald Guthrie, *New Testament Theology* (Downers Grove, Illinois: Inter-Varsity Press, 1981), p. 892.

essential misery; and in what they cannot shake off, no, not for an hour, any more than they can shake off their own being.[1]

Beyond this, Wesley maintains that one of the most severe punishments of hell is "the company wherewith everyone is surrounded"[2] and that "all these torments of body and soul are without intermission."[3] Consequently, when these teachings, which are found in several places in the sermon corpus, are considered in light of Wesley's own belief in a literal hell fire,[4] it is difficult, if not impossible, to maintain that the Methodist leader seldom considered or wrote about this admittedly unpleasant topic or that he did not take it very seriously.

On a happier note, it is apparent that Wesley conceived eternal life (and the kingdom of heaven) in a qualitative sense, as a present experience, and not simply as a reality yet to come. Eternal life begins "when it pleases the Father to reveal his Son in our hearts; when we first know Christ being enabled to 'call him Lord by the Holy Ghost.'"[5] To be sure, Wesley was emphatic that the kingdom of heaven must begin in this life, for some very important reasons. In his piece, *A Blow at the Root*, for instance, he maintains: "none shall enjoy the glory of God in heaven, but he that bears the image of God on earth; none that is not saved from sin here can be saved from hell hereafter."[6] In other words, not only does the Oxford leader relate holiness and happiness — which we've come to expect — but also holiness and the kingdom of heaven. In his sermon, *The Way to the Kingdom*, Wesley states:

> This holiness and happiness, joined in one, are sometimes styled in the inspired writings, 'the kingdom of God' (as by our Lord in the text), and sometimes, 'the kingdom of heaven'. It is termed 'the kingdom of God' because it is the immediate fruit of God's reigning in the soul.... It is called the 'kingdom of heaven' because it is (in a degree) heaven opened in the soul.[7]

To deny, therefore, that heaven begins in the here and now is also to deny that holiness of heart and life can be enjoyed by flesh and blood.

It is becoming well known in the field of Wesley studies that John Wesley's understanding of perfection was informed more by the Eastern tradition, by Macarius the Egyptian and Ephraem Syrus in particular, than by any authors from the West. Put another way, Wesley understood perfection not in the sense

---

1. Outler, *Sermons*, 4:33. (On the Discoveries of Faith)

2. Ibid., 3:40. (Of Hell)

3. Ibid.

4. Ibid., 3:37. It is well known that Wesley was interested in the art of holy living and dying, largely through the influence of Jeremy Taylor. What is less known, however, is that Wesley also recorded the fearful deaths of the wicked as examples to be avoided as revealed, for instance, in the following selection from the sermon *The Important Question*: "Some years since, one who turned back as a dog to his vomit was struck down in his mid-career of sin.... The sick man shrieked out with a piercing cry, 'a fiend! a fiend!' and died. Just such an end, unless he die like an ox, may any man expect who loses his own soul." Cf. Outler, *Sermons*, 3:186.

5. Ibid., 3:96. (Spiritual Worship)

6. Jackson, *Works*, 10:364.

7. Outler, *Sermons*, 1:224. (The Way to the Kingdom)

of *perfectus est*, a state which does not admit of growth, but in the sense of *teleosis*, a perfection which is continually growing and prospering.[1] And what makes this point interesting for the present context is that the Oxford don viewed heaven as the place where the saints will continue to grow in grace and knowledge for all eternity. They will, for instance, converse with all the saints who have ever lived, with angels and archangels, and above all with "the eternal Son of God, in whom are hid all the treasures of wisdom and knowledge."[2] And in a manuscript sermon, *The Promise of Understanding*, it is affirmed that knowledge of God's wisdom and goodness will be "an entertainment for heaven."[3] And Wesley enthusiastically adds, "what an entertainment!"[4]

Of heaven as a place of reward, Wesley has a few things to say in his sermons, but not as much as one might initially expect. One of his leading ideas, though, is not only are there different heavens — three are listed in his piece *The New Creation*[5]— but there are different rewards to be received there as well, given according to our inward holiness, our works, and our sufferings.[6] And in his manuscript sermon, *The Wisdom of Winning Souls*, he affirms in a way which highlights the importance of the proclamation of the gospel that the highest of these rewards are promised to "the converters of sinners"[7] — rewards which are to be enjoyed throughout eternity and without intermission.

IV. The Final Consummation

After the judgment, the heavens will pass away and the earth and all its works will be burnt up to prepare for a new creation as promised in the Book of Revelation. However, even in Wesley's time there were many scoffers who questioned how the entire earth could be consumed in this way, and they, therefore, cast doubt on this vital teaching. By way of response, Wesley speculated that perhaps a comet, or "the lightnings which give 'shine to the world,'"[8] or even lava from Aetna, Hecla, or Vesuvius would bring about this momentous end.[9] At any rate, he was certain not of the specific manner of this occurrence, but only of its eventual realization.

Judging from the amount of material on these topics, it appears that the English evangelical was much more interested in the creation of the new than in the destruction of the old — and he tells us as much in his homily *The New Creation*. In it, he reveals, first of all, how both the starry and the lower heavens will be

1. Albert Outler, *John Wesley* (New York: Oxford University Press, 1964), p. 9-10.
2. Outler, *Sermons*, 4:192. (On Faith)
3. Ibid., 4:288. (The Promise of Understanding)
4. Ibid. And the quickness and ease with which one will acquire knowledge in heaven is indicated in Wesley's comment that the understanding will then be free from its present defects. Cf. Outler, *Sermons*, 2:290. (The Good Steward)
5. Ibid., 2:502. (The New Creation)
6. Telford, *Letters*, 8:251.
7. Outler, *Sermons*, 4:311. (The Wisdom of Winning Souls)
8. Ibid., 1:369. (The Great Assize)
9. Ibid.

created anew such that there will no longer be any blazing stars or comets in the former, nor hurricanes or terrifying meteors in the latter.[1] Moreover, the elements which make up the natural world will all be transformed with benign results. Fire, for instance, will loose its capacity to destroy, though not its "vivifying power."[2] The air, in turn, will be unable to support storms and tempests, and the water of the earth, the one-time instrument of God's wrath, will keep its bounds and will no longer issue in floods. In fact, the earth, itself, will be renewed so that there will be neither earthquakes nor burning mountains which destroy, nor thorns, nor briars, nor thistles which frustrate the fruit of the land, nor will any creature "hurt or give pain to any other."[3] But the most glorious of all changes relates not to the elements nor to any inanimate thing, but to the living sons and daughters of God. Wesley writes:

> God shall wipe away all tears from their eyes; and there shall be no more death, neither sorrow nor crying, neither shall there be any more pain: for the former things are done away. As there will be no more death, and no more pain or sickness preparatory thereto; as there will be no more grieving for or parting with friends; so there will be no more sorrow or crying. Nay, but there will be a greater deliverance than all this; for there will be no more sin.[4]

In a real sense, then, Wesley's doctrine of the last things, as just described, suggests the question of theodicy. In other words, the whole problem of natural evil in the form of floods, earthquakes, etc., receives a definite answer only in the coming of a new creation. Here natural evil will finally be a thing of the past, as will sorrow, pain, and death. Thus, grace will triumph where sin once ruled; life will be victorious where death once held sway. The redeemed "shall 'hear a great voice out of heaven," Wesley writes, "saying, Behold, the tabernacle of God is with men, and he will dwell with them..."[5] And he adds, underscoring his point: "Hence will arise an unmixed state of holiness and happiness far superior to that which Adam enjoyed in paradise."[6] Optimism not pessimism, therefore, is the last note struck in this theology.

But there are good and rewarding things in store not only for humanity, but for the animal kingdom as well. Admittedly, what Wesley argues here is somewhat speculative, but it nevertheless deserves consideration since it gives the reader many significant clues concerning the contours of his theological posture, especially in terms of eschatology, our present topic. For example, at one point Wesley asks: "But will *the creature*, will even the brute creation, always remain in this deplorable condition?" To which he emphatically replies: "God forbid that

1. Ibid., 2:503. (The New Creation)
2. Ibid., 2:504.
3. Ibid., 2:509.
4. Ibid., 2:510.
5. Ibid.
6. Ibid. For additional references to the close association between happiness and holiness in Wesley's sermons Cf. 2:600 (The Case of Reason Impartially Considered); 3:37 (Of Hell); 3:100 (Spiritual Worship); 3:194,197 (The Important Question); 4:67 (The Unity of the Divine Being); and 4:121 (On a Single Eye).

we should affirm this"![1] On the contrary, the animals as well will be delivered from the bondage of corruption, from irregular appetites and passions, into glorious liberty, "even a measure, according as they are capable, of 'the liberty of the children of God.'"[2] And though in his sermon, *The General Deliverance*, Wesley denies that God has equal regard for beasts as He does for humanity, he nevertheless conjectures along the following lines:

> **What if it should please him, when he makes us 'equal to angels', to make them what we are now? Creatures capable of God? Capable of knowing, and loving, and enjoying the Author of their being?**[3]

Viewed from another perspective, the implications of this last teaching are of great import. Since the knowledge and love of God are both the privilege and distinguishing characteristic of humanity, as noted in a previous chapter, what then of those who neglect this glorious favor? Some theologies may suggest that those who choose to live in this fashion will eventually descend to the level of beasts; however, Wesley suggests something even more frightful — that wicked men and women, those who stubbornly refuse to love and serve God, will sink even below the level of animals, since the animal kingdom itself will no longer be at so low a rank, but will be invited to enjoy what sinful humanity has willfully rejected: that is, to know, love, and enjoy God forever.[4] How poignant, then, how troubling will the loss of the wicked be! How horrible the realization that all of creation has passed them by to serve a rich and loving God. "Let all who are of a more generous spirit know and maintain their rank in the scale of beings," Wesley admonishes, "Rest not till you enjoy the privilege of humanity — the knowledge and love of God."[5]

V. Some Concluding Observations

As Wesley's theology began with the grace of God, a grace manifested in both creation and redemption, so does it end on this note as well. Clearly, the goodness and favor of God are the threads which are weaved throughout the many doctrines which have been considered. However, such grace is never mistaken for indulgence — as it is in some modern theologies — nor is it ever given for the aggrandizement of the selfish human will. To be sure, grace challenges the unbelief of humanity and the sinful propensity to revel in pride and self-will. It directs

---

1. Ibid., 2:445. (The General Deliverance)
2. Ibid., 2:445.
3. Ibid., 2:448.
4. Ibid., 2:449. Wesley's respect for and kindness towards animals is revealed in his sermon, *On the Education of Children* where he states: They [the parents] will not allow them [their children] to hurt or give pain to anything that has life. They will not permit them to rob birds' nests, much less to kill anything without necessity; not even snakes, which are as innocent as worms, or toads, which, notwithstanding their ugliness, and the ill name they lie under, have been proved over and over to be as harmless as flies. Let them extend in its measure the rule of doing as they would be done by to every animal whatsoever." Cf. Outler, *Sermons*, 3:360. Bracketed material is mine.
5. Ibid., 2:450.

men and women away from themselves and self-interest to the much broader interest of the kingdom of God. Not surprisingly, the grace of God, as understood by John Wesley, is quite paradoxical: it is inviting and yet challenging; enabling and yet demanding; it is not merely the favor of God to be enjoyed, but it is also the power of God to bring about the earnest (and at times painful) and full restoration of the *imago dei*. Again, such grace is inclusive in its reach (all may be saved), yet it may be thwarted by the sinner (all are not saved).

Steering clear of both the Scylla of universalism and the Charybdis of determinism (predestination), Wesley offered his own age the abundant grace of God manifested in the crucified and resurrected Christ as the balm for human ill. To the proclamation of this grace which both empowers people and calls them to responsibility and to labor, Wesley renewed his efforts. To the full realization of this grace, in his life and others, Wesley dedicated his life. To the establishment of the love and worship of a Holy God, in all purity, Wesley ever labored. "Let God be in all your thoughts," he writes in his later years, "and ye will be men indeed. Let him be your God and your all! The desire of your eyes, the joy of your heart, and your portion for ever!"[1]

1. Ibid., 2:450. (The General Deliverance)

BIBLIOGRAPHY
(Selected)

I. Primary Sources: Wesley

Baker, Frank, ed., *The Works of John Wesley*, Vols. 25, 26. The Letters New York: Oxford University Press, 1982.

Burwash, Rev. N. *Wesley's Doctrinal Standards* Salem. Ohio: Convention Book Store, 1967.

Cragg, Gerald R. ed., *The Works of John Wesley*, Vol. 11. *The Appeals to Men of Reason and Religion* New York: Oxford University Press, 1975.

Curnock, Nehemiah *The Journal of the Rev. John Wesley, A.M.*, 8 vols. London: The Epworth Press, 1938.

Davies, Rupert E. *The Works of John Wesley*, Vol 9. *The Methodist Societies: History, Nature, and Design* Nashville: Abingdon Press, 1989.

Jackson, Thomas, ed., *The Works of John Wesley*, 14 vols. Grand Rapids, Michigan: Baker Book House, 1978.

Outler, Albert C., ed., *The Works of John Wesley*, Vols. 1-4. *The Sermons*. Nashville: Abingdon Press, 1984.

Sugden, Edward H., ed., *Wesley's Standard Sermons*, 2 vols. London: The Epworth Press, 1921.

Telford, John, ed., *The Letters of John Wesley, A.M.* 8 vols. London: The Epworth Press, 1931.

Ward, Reginald W. and Heitzenrater, Richard P. eds., *The Works of John Wesley* Vol. 18. *Journals and Diaries I* Nashville: Abingdon Press, 1988.

Wesley, John. *Explanatory Notes Upon the New Testament* Salem, Ohio: Schmul Publishers.

_____. *John Wesley's Sunday Service of the Methodists in North America* Nashville: The United Methodist Publishing House, 1984.

_____. *A Christian Library: Consisting of Extracts from, and Abridgments of, the Choicest Pieces of Practical Divinity Which Have Been Published in the English Tongue.* 50 vols. Bristol: Farley, 1749-1755.

II. Secondary Sources: Wesley

A. Books

Ayling, Stanley. *John Wesley.* Cleveland: Collins, 1979.

Borgen, Ole E. *John Wesley on the Sacraments.* Grand Rapids, Michigan: Francis Asbury Press, 1972.

Burtner, Robert W., and Chiles, Robert E., eds. *John Wesley's Theology: A Collection From His Works.* Nashville: Abingdon Press, 1982.

Cannon, William Ragsdale. *The Theology of John Wesley.* Nashville: Abingdon - Cokesbury Press, 1946.

Cell, George Croft. *The Rediscovery of John Wesley.* New York: Henry Holt and Co., 1934.

Collins, Kenneth J. *Wesley On Salvation.* Grand Rapids, Michigan: Francis Asbury Press, 1989.

Cushman, Robert E. *John Wesley's Experimental Divinity.* Nashville: Kingswood Books, 1989.

Deschner, John. *Wesley's Christology.* Dallas: Southern Methodist University Press, 1960.

Green, V.H.H. *The Young Mr. Wesley.* New York: St. Martin's Press, 1961.

_____, *John Wesley.* London: Nelson, 1964.

Green, William. *John Wesley and William Law.* London: Duncan and Malcolm, 1844.

Hildebrandt, Franz. *Christianity According to the Wesleys*. London: Epworth Press, 1955.

_____. *From Luther to Wesley*. London: Lutterworth, 1951.

Heitzenrater, Richard P. *Mirror and Memory*. Nashville: Kingswood Books, 1989.

Koerber, Charles J. *The Theology of Conversion According to John Wesley*. Rome: Neo-Eboraci, 1967.

Lawson, John. *Notes on Wesley's Forty-Four Sermons*. London: Epworth Press, 1946.

Lee, Umphrey *John Wesley and Modern Religion*. Nashville: Cokesbury Press, 1936.

Lindström, Harald. *Wesley and Sanctification*. Wilmore, Kentucky: Francis Asbury Publishing Co.

Monk, Robert C. *John Wesley: His Puritan Heritage*. New York: Abingdon, 1966.

Moore, Robert L. *John Wesley and Authority : A Psychological Perspective*. Missoula, Montana: Scholars Press, 1979.

Outler, Albert C., ed., *John Wesley*. New York: Oxford University Press, 1964.

Overton, J.H. *John Wesley*. London: Methuen, 1891.

Piette, Maximin. *John Wesley in the Evolution of Protestantism*. London: Sheed and Ward, 1938.

Rattenbury, J. Ernest. *The Conversion of the Wesleys*. London: The Epworth Press, 1938.

Rowe, Kenneth E., ed. *The Place of Wesley in the Christian Tradition*. Metuchen: New Jersey: The Scarecrow Press, 1976.

Sangster, W. E. *The Path to Perfection*. New York: Abingdon, 1943.

Schmidt, Martin. *John Wesley: A Theological Biography*. 3 vols. London: The Epworth Press, 1962.

Simon, J.S. *John Wesley and the Religious Societies.* London: Epworth Press, 1923.

_____. *John Wesley and the Methodist Societies.* London: Epworth Press, 1923.

Snyder, Howard A. *The Radical Wesley and Patterns for Church Renewal.* Downers Grove, Illinois: Inter Varsity Press, 1980.

Southey, Robert. *The Life of Wesley and the Rise and Progress of Methodism.* 2 vols. 3rd ed. London: Longmans, 1846.

Starkey, Lycurgus M. Jr., *The Work of the Holy Spirit: A Study in Wesleyan Theology.* Nashville: Abingdon Press, 1962.

Tyerman, Luke L. *The Life and Times of the Rev. John Wesley, M.A..* 3 vols. New York: Burt Franklin.

Watson, Richard. *The Life of the Rev. John Wesley, A.M.* London: Mason, 1831.

Williams, Colin. *John Wesley's Theology Today.* Nashville: Abingdon Press, 1960.

B. Articles

Arnett, William. "John Wesley and the Bible." *Wesleyan Theological Journal* Vol 3 No. 1 (Spring 1968): p. 3-9.

Baker, Frank. "'Aldersgate' and Wesley's Editors." *London Quarterly and Holborn Review* 191 (1966) 310-319.

_____. "Aldersgate 1738-1963: The Challenge of Aldersgate." *Duke Divinity School Bulletin* 28, 2 (May 1963) 67-80.

_____. "John Wesley's Churchmanship." *London Quarterly and Holborn Review* 185 (1960) 210-215; 269-274.

Bence, Clarence L. "Processive Eschatology: A Wesleyan Alternative." *Wesleyan Theological Journal* 14 (Spring, 1979):XXX

Blankenship, Paul F. "The Significance of John Wesley's Abridgment of the Thirty-Nine Articles as Seen from His Deletions." *Methodist History* 2, 3 (April 1964) 35-47.

Bonino, José Miguez. "Wesley's Doctrine of Sanctification From a Liberationist Perspective" in Runyon, *Sanctification*, 49-63.

Burnett, Ivan Jr. "Methodist Origins: John Wesley and Alcohol." *Methodist History* 13 (July 1975): 3-17.

Collins, Kenneth J. "John Wesley and the Means of Grace." *The Drew Gateway* 56 (Spring 1986): 26-33.

_____. "A Hermeneutical Model for the Wesleyan Ordo Salutis." *Wesleyan Theological Journal* Vol. 19 No. 2 (Fall 1984): 23-37.

_____. "John Wesley and Liberation Theology: A Closer Look." *The Asbury Theological Journal*, Vol. 42, Num. 1 (Spring 1987) pp. 85-90.

Dillman, Charles N. Dillman. "Wesley's Approach to the Law in Discourse V, on the Sermon on the Mount." *Wesleyan Theological Journal* 12 (Spring 1977): 60-65.

Dunlap, Pamela Couture. "On the Danger of Reading the Works of John Wesley." *Quarterly Review* Vol 7, No. 1 (Spring 1987): 3-8.

Hall, Thor. "The Christian's Life: Wesley's Alternative to Luther and Calvin." *The Duke Divinity School Bulletin* 28 (May 1963): 111-26.

Harper, Steve. "Wesley's Sermons as Spiritual Formation Documents." *Methodist History* 26 (April 1988): 131-38.

Hendricks, Elton M. "John Wesley and Natural Theology." *Wesleyan Theological Journal* Vol. 18, No. 2 (Fall 1983): 7-17.

Holland, Bernard G. "The Conversions of John and Charles Wesley and Their Place in Methodist Tradition." *Proceedings of the Wesley Historical Society* 38 (August 1971): 46-53.

Hynson, Leon O. "Christian Love: The Key to Wesley's Ethics." *Methodist History* 14 (October 1975): 44-55.

_____. "Creation and Grace in Wesley's Ethics." *The Drew Gateway* 46 (1975-76): 41-55.

_____. "John Wesley and the Unitas Fratrum: A Theological Analysis." *Methodist History* 18 (October 1979) 26-60.

Jennings, Theodore W. Jennings. "John Wesley *Against* Aldersgate." *Quarterly Review* Vol. 8, No. 3 (Fall 1988): 3-22.

_____. "Wesley's Preferential Option for the Poor." *Quarterly Review* Vol. 9. No. 3. (Fall 1989): 10.

McCarthy, Daryl. "Early Wesleyan Views of Scripture." *Wesleyan Theological Journal* vol. 16, No. 2 (Fall 1981):95-105.

Mullen, Wilbur H. "John Wesley's Method of Biblical Interpretation." *Religion in Life* 47 (Spring 1978): 99-108.

Oswalt, John N. "John Wesley and the Old Testament Concept of the Holy Spirit." *Religion in Life* 48 (Autumn 1979): 283-292.

Outler, Albert C. "Beyond Pietism: Aldersgate in Context." *Motive*, Vol. 23, No. 8 (May, 1963), p. 12-16.

_____. "A Focus on the Holy Spirit: Spirit and Spirituality in John Wesley." *Quarterly Review*, Vol. 8, No. 2 (Summer 1988): 3-18.

_____. "John Wesley: Folk Theologian." *Theology Today* 34 (July 1974): 63-82.

_____. "John Wesley as Theologian-Then and Now." *Methodist History* 12 (July 1974): 63-82.

_____. "The Place of Wesley in the Christian Tradition." in *The Place of Wesley in the Christian Tradition*, pp. 11-38. Edited by Kenneth E. Rowe. Metuchen, New Jersey: The Scarecrow Press, 1976.

_____. "Towards a Re-Appraisal of John Wesley as a Theologian." *The Perkins School of Theology Journal* 14 (Winter 1961): 8-9.

Pillow, Thomas Wright. "John Wesley's Doctrine of the Trinity." *The Cumberland Seminarian* 24 (Spring 1986): 1-10.

Smith, Harmon L. "Wesley's Doctrine of Justification: Beginning and Process." *The Duke Divinity School Bulletin* 28 (May 1963): 88-98.

Smith, Weldon J. "Some Notes on Wesley's Doctrine of Prevenient Grace." *Religion in Life* 34 (Winter 1964), 68-80.

Watson, David Lowes. "Christ Our Righteousness The Center of Wesley's Evangelistic Message" *Perkins Journal* 37 (Spring 1984): 34-47.

Watson, Philip. "Wesley and Luther on Christian Perfection." *The Ecumenical Review* 15 (April 1963): 291-302.

III. Methodism

A. Books

Andrews, Stuart. *Methodism and Society.* London: Longmans, 1970.

Bassett, Paul M., and Greathouse, William M. *Exploring Christian Holiness: Volume 2 The Historical Development,* Kansas City, Missouri: Beacon Hill Press, 1985.

Bonino, Jose Miguez. *Doing Theology in a Revolutionary Situation* Philadelphia: Fortress Press, 1975.

Chiles, Robert E. *Theological Transition in American Methodism: 1790-1935.* Nashville: Abingdon Press, 1965.

Davies, Rupert. *Methodism.* London: Epworth Press, 1963.

Dimond, Sidney. *The Psychology of the Methodist Revival: An Empirical and Descriptive Study.* Oxford University Press, 1926.

Halevy, Elie. *The Birth of Methodism in England.* Trans. and with an introduction by Bernard Semmel. Chicago: University Of Chicago Press, 1971.

Hynson, Leon. *To Reform the Nation.* Grand Rapids, Michigan: Francis Asbury Press, 1984.

North, Eric McCoy. *Early Methodist Philanthropy.* New York: Methodist Book Concern, 1914.

Oden, Thomas C. *Doctrinal Standards in the Wesleyan Tradition.* Grand Rapids, Michigan: Francis Asbury Press, 1988.

Outler, Albert C. *Theology in the Wesleyan Spirit.* Nashville: Discipleship Resources, 1975.

Runyon, Theodore., ed. *Sanctification and Liberation*. Nashville: Abingdon Press, 1981.

Semmel, Bernard. *The Methodist Revolution*. New York: Basic Books, 1973.

Snyder, Howard A. with Runyon, Daniel V. *The Divided Flame*. Grand Rapids, Michigan: Francis Asbury Press, 1986.

Towlson, Clifford W. *Moravian and Methodist*. London: The Epworth Press, 1957.

B. Articles

Arnett, William. "The Role of the Holy Spirit in Entire Sanctification in the Writings of John Wesley." *Wesleyan Theological Journal* Vol. 14, No. 2 (Fall 1979): 15-30.

Burnett, Ivan Jr. "Methodist Origins: John Wesley and Alcohol." *Methodist History* 13 (July 1975): 3-17.

Carter, Charles W. "Man, the Crown of Divine Creation." in *A Contemporary Wesleyan Theology* 2 vols., 1:195-236. Edited by Charles W. Carter. Grand Rapids, Michigan: Francis Asbury Press, 1983.

Dayton, Donald. "The Doctrine of the Baptism of the Holy Spirit: Its Emergence and Significance." *The Wesleyan Theological Journal* Vol. 13 (Spring 1978):114-126.

Heitzenrater, Richard P. "At Full Liberty: Doctrinal Standards in Early American Methodism." *Quarterly Review* Vol. 5, No. 3 (Fall 1985):6-27.

Hynson, Leon. "The Inerrancy Question: A Misplaced Debate." *The Evangelical Journal* 5 (Spring 1987):30-34.

Oden, Thomas C. "Methodist Doctrinal Standards: Reply to Richard Heitzenrater." *Quarterly Review* Vol. 7, No. 1 (Spring 1987):41-42.

Starkey, Lycurgus M. "The Holy Spirit and the Wesleyan Witness." *Religion in Life* 49 (Spring 1980):72-80.

Turner, George Allen. "The Baptism of the Holy Spirit in the Wesleyan Tradition." *The Wesleyan Theological Journal* Vol. 14 No. 1. (Spring 1979):60-76.

IV. Miscellaneous

A. Philosophy

Aristotle. *The Works of Aristotle* trans. W.D. Ross, vol. IX: *Nichomachean Ethics* Oxford: Clarendon Press, 1925.

Beck, Lewis White. ed., *Readings in the History of Philosophy: 18th-Century Philosophy* New York: The Free Press, 1966.

Burnet, J. trans., *Early Greek Philosophy.* London: Black, 1920.

Copleston, Frederick. *A History of Philosophy* Vol 1. *Greece and Rome.* Garden City, New York: Image Books, 1985.

Haldane and Ross, translators. *Meditations* in *The Philosophical Works of Descartes.* Vol. I. Cambridge University Press, 1931.

Jones, W.T. *A History of Western Philosophy: The Classical Mind.* New York: Harcourt, Brace, and World, Inc., 1969.

Jowett, M. A. *The Dialogues of Plato.* 2 vols. New York: Random House, 1937.

Leibniz, Gottfried. *The Philosophical Works of Leibniz.* translated by George Martin Duncan. New Haven: Tuttle, Morehouse and Taylor, 1890.

Marx, Karl. "Toward the Critique of Hegel's Philosophy of Law," in *The Essential Marx*, ed. Saul K. Padover (New York: New American Library, 1978).

Raffel, Burton. trans., *The Essential Horace: Odes, Epodes, Satires and Epistles.* New York: North Point Publishing Co.

Seneca. *Moral Essays.* Cambridge, Massachusetts: Harvard University Press.

Stevenson, Leslie. *Seven Theories of Human Nature.* New York: Oxford University Press, 1987.

B. Religion

Althaus, Paul. *The Theology of Martin Luther* Philadelphia: Fortress Press, 1966.

Baasten, Matthew. *Pride According to Gregory the Great: A Study of the Moralia.* New York: Edwin Mellon Press, 1986.

Bettenson, Henry. ed., *Documents of the Christian Church.* New York: Oxford University Press, 1963.

Brunner, Emil. *The Mediator.* Philadelphia: The Westminster Press.

Colleran, Joseph M. trans., *Cur Deus Homo.* Albany, New York: Magi Books.

Dulles, Avery S.J. *Models of Revelation.* New York: Image Books, 1985.

Durant, Will. *The Story of Civilization* Vol. VI. *The Reformation.* New York: Simon and Schuster, 1957.

Fraenkel, Peter. *Natural Theology: Comprising 'Nature and Grace' by Professor Dr. Emil Brunner and the reply 'No!' by Dr. Karl Barth* London: The Centenary Press, 1946.

McLachlan, A. J. *Socinianism in Seventeenth-Century England.* 1951.

McNeill, John T. *Calvin: Institutes of the Christian Religion,* 2 vols. Philadelphia: The Westminster Press, 1960.

Moorman, John R. H. *A History of the Church in England.* Wilton, Connecticut: Morehouse-Barlow Co., Inc., 1963.

Morris, Leon. *The Apostolic Preaching of the Cross.* Grand Rapids, Michigan: Eerdmans Publishing Co., 1955.

Neuhaus, Richard John. *The Catholic Moment* San Francisco: Harper and Row, Publishers, 1987.

Oswald, Hilton C. ed., *Luther's Works.* vol. 25 *Lectures on Romans.* Saint Louis: Concordia Publishing House, 1972.

Parker, T.H.L. *John Calvin.* Philadelphia: The Westminster Press, 1975.

Pelikan, Jaroslav ed., *Luther's Works* 55 vols., Vol. 26: *Lectures on Galatians 1535* Saint Louis: Concordia Publishing House, 1963.

Rupp, Gordon E., and Watson, Philip S., eds., *Luther and Erasmus: Free Will and Salvation.* Philadelphia: The Westminster Press, 1969.

Russell, Jeffrey Burton. *Lucifer: The Devil in the Middle Ages*. Ithica: Cornell University Press, 1984.

Schaff, Philip ed., *The Creeds of Christendom*, 3 vols. Grand Rapids, Michigan: Baker Book House.

_____. *History of the Christian Church*, 8 vols. Grand Rapids, Michigan: Wm. B. Eerdmans Publishing Company, 1910.

Truesdale, Albert. "Theism" in *A Contemporary Wesleyan Theology*. ed. Charles Carter. Grand Rapids, Michigan: Francis Asbury Press, 1983.

V. Presentations

Tore Meistad, "Wesley's Theology of Salvation and Social Change" 19 November 1990, a paper presented at the Wesley Studies group, The American Academy of Religion, New Orleans, Louisiana.

Theodore R. Weber, "Political Order in *Ordo Salutis*: A Wesleyan Theory of Political Institutions" 19 November 1990 a paper presented at the Wesley Studies group, The American Academy of Religion, New Orleans, Louisiana.

VI. Dissertations

Bence, Clarence L. "John Wesley's Teleological Hermeneutic" (Ph.D. dissertation, Emory University, 1982).

Collins, Kenneth J. "John Wesley's Theology of Law" (Ph.D. dissertation, Drew University, 1984).

Crow, Earl P. "John Wesley's Conflict with Antinomianism in Relation to the Moravians and Calvinists." (Ph.D. dissertation, University of Manchester, 1964).

Kirkham, Donald H. "Pamphlet Opposition to the Rise of Methodism: The Eighteenth Century English Evangelical Revival Under Attack." (Ph.D. dissertation, Duke University, 1973).

Rogers, Charles Allen. "The Concept of Prevenient Grace in the Theology of John Wesley" (Ph.D. dissertation, Duke University, 1967).

Snyder, Howard. "Pietism, Moravianism, and Methodism as Renewal Movements" (Ph.D. dissertation, University of Notre Dame, 1983).

INDEX